Growing Fairly

Growing Fairly

How to Build Opportunity and Equity in Workforce Development

Stephen Goldsmith

Kate Markin Coleman

BROOKINGS INSTITUTION PRESS
Washington, D.C.

Copyright © 2022
THE BROOKINGS INSTITUTION
1775 Massachusetts Avenue, N.W.
Washington, D.C. 20036
www.brookings.edu

The Brookings Institution is a private nonprofit organization devoted to research,
education, and publication on important issues of domestic and foreign policy.
Its principal purpose is to bring the highest quality independent research and
analysis to bear on current and emerging policy problems. Interpretations or
conclusions in Brookings publications should be understood to be solely those
of the authors.

Library of Congress Control Number: 2021949166

ISBN 9780815739487 (pbk)
ISBN 9780815739494 (ebook)

9 8 7 6 5 4 3 2 1

Typeset in Scala Pro

Composition by Elliott Beard

Contents

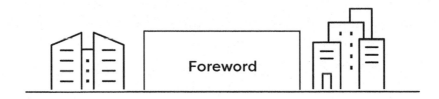

Foreword

Together, we span over forty years of elected and civic leadership in the city of Atlanta—one a former chair of a county commission that includes most of Atlanta's residents, and the other the current mayor of the city. During that time, we have witnessed Atlanta become the tenth largest economy in the country and eighteenth in the world. Atlanta is the headquarters of several Fortune 1000 companies and multinational corporations.

We come together not only as local leaders cheerleading regional successes but as national advocates of more equitable economic opportunity. Even before COVID-19 hit, the Black-white wage gap was worse in 2020 than it was in 2000. The pandemic compounded the problem. COVID-19 has disproportionately affected workers of color, many in service jobs, who suffered the most in terms of both job loss and COVID-related death and illness. Of course, we are not surprised by these results given the numerous social and educational disadvantages faced by lower-income individuals in our region and in our wider society. Black women find themselves even worse off comparatively, as they try to overcome barriers related to race, poverty, and gender.

Our organizations, the city of Atlanta and UNCF, brought together a group of Atlanta educators and skill builders in an effort described in this book to highlight and address these problems. The analysis in that project, indeed, reveals disparities. For example, the data demonstrates that Black workers in Atlanta are concentrated in low-wage roles and have been disproportionately hit by job and wage declines due to COVID-19. These disparities are even more pronounced in the highest paying career areas, including business, finance, information technology, and math-related professions.

However, we write this foreword not as an ode to despair but, rather, as a national call to action to local leaders who can make a true difference by increasing economic mobility for all residents at the same time they address race and gender inequity. In *Growing Fairly: How to Build Opportunity and Equity in Workforce Development*, Stephen Goldsmith and Kate Markin Coleman provide a hopeful and comprehensive set of design principles that, if implemented with fidelity and persistence, will lead to better jobs and greater mobility for more of our residents.

The book emphasizes the critical need for a more effective and comprehensively designed regional workforce approach. We start by stressing the importance of education. We are fortunate. Both of us have advanced degrees. One of us, with a Ph.D., taught college literature before serving as president of Dillard University and has devoted the last sixteen years to moving UNCF to a position where it has exceeded $5 billion in funding for HBCUs and college students everywhere. The other, with a J.D., served as a judge before her election as mayor of one of the country's most influential cities. After seeing men come into court and try to fill out papers without even a ninth-grade education, she implemented a set of major initiatives to assist the separately managed K–12 system, including creating the city's first chief education officer, while establishing partnerships to advance training and apprenticeships. We both acknowledge that educational access includes not just college degrees but helping more individuals achieve the post-secondary necessary training to thrive in the workforce.

Together, we worked with the authors of this book in the Harvard Kennedy School Mayoral Leaders in Education program. The program, when it started, focused on K–12 systems and their ability to achieve college graduation for their students as the ultimate metric of success. We, of course, endorse that goal given its importance to us and to so many other African Americans. But we suggested that the Harvard project partner with us in crafting solutions for another urgent problem—the unnecessarily limited opportunities for young men and women of color who possess skills and have tremendous potential but do not go on to college. We asked for data and policy help in identifying the best set of strategies that regional leaders could employ to improve the outcomes of this marginalized group—to help them add post-secondary skills in a more targeted and intentional fashion that would produce better paying jobs.

These questions led to the Atlanta project profiled in this book. Appropriately, one coauthor of this book was an innovative national nonprofit leader, serving as executive vice president for the national office of the YMCA. Sizeable workforce challenges require mayoral leadership, but the solutions require effective and sustained cross-sector collaboration and a willingness to challenge the status quo. We see the urgent need for behavioral and approach changes in every sector. Employers can reduce disparity by focusing their hiring on skills, not just college credentials. Workforce organizations can use real-time regional data to better match growing mid-skill jobs with workers. Community colleges as well as four-year universities can align their offerings to these local skill-based needs.

The book advocates, as well, for more collective action and less fragmentation. Atlanta has been addressing this issue for some time. We recently merged WorkSource Atlanta—the city's workforce development arm—into Invest Atlanta, the city's economic development unit. The merger will centralize implementation of the One Atlanta: Economic Mobility, Recovery, and Resiliency Plan. Illustrating several of the design principles in *Growing Fairly*, aligning agencies helps job seekers receive training and skill development that employers need and demand—resulting in higher wages, career advancement, a skilled workforce, and increased productivity.

We hope to bring this book and its cause to the attention of local leaders. The campaign for greater economic mobility is not only critical for those struggling to make ends meet. It also improves the region's productivity and its civic infrastructure. Widening economic gaps undermine our sense of community.

The book's charge to look first at the needs of the individual and then at how organizations and systems can respond is the right frame-work. More organizations need to put the individual at the center of their work, and more funders, including philanthropy and govern-ment, need to fund and insist on a comprehensive set of investments for excluded communities. The stakes are too high to waste even a dollar that could be redirected to what works. *Growing Fairly* looks at a related issue of importance in Atlanta as well as most of America's cities—the quality of the neighborhoods where individuals reside. Residents who grow up and live in safe and walkable neighborhoods with positive social contacts do so much better in life. Reducing trauma, enhancing relationships, upgrading transportation, and im-proving safety must be addressed as part of a successful plan to close the wealth gap.

UNCF recently called attention to other solutions incorporated in *Growing Fairly*'s design principles. It advocated for normalizing and destigmatizing nontraditional education paths, such as community colleges, online certification programs, and more. Too many jobs in the United States unnecessarily require a college degree, which penal-izes nontraditional applicants and, disproportionately, those of color. Access to career counseling and more flexibility for those juggling work and family will help, as well.

This leads us back to race and gender. The principles in this book, reinforced by our experiences and those of our organizations, will bring hope and opportunity. But none of this will be sufficient without also addressing obstacles associated with race. Across every level of education, Black Americans, including those with advanced degrees, have not achieved the level of success of their white counterparts.

Stephen Goldsmith is widely known as one of the country's lead-ing and most innovative mayors in the last twenty-five years. We and our staff have benefitted in several different ways working with him as he continues not just to train public officials but to help them see ways to use technology and innovate to improve quality of life for their residents. Kate Markin Coleman brings invaluable insights from her experience helping lead one of the largest nonprofits in the country. In particular, her work focusing the YMCA on the issues of urban communities, reducing the achievement gap, and promoting healthy behaviors reminds us that we can work across geographies, race, and class to produce change.

Our work helped craft the design principles in *Growing Fairly: How to Build Opportunity and Equity in Workforce Development*. We have confidence that, when applied, they can, indeed, increase hope and opportunity.

Mayor Keisha Lance Bottoms, City of Atlanta

Dr. Michael Lomax, Chief Executive Officer
of the United Negro College Fund, Inc.

Acknowledgments

We acknowledge with appreciation the many people who made this book possible.

For many years the Smith Richardson Foundation has played an important role in supporting practical research that guides the work of state and local officials and we thank the foundation for its support of our project. We particularly appreciate the guidance of Mark Steinmeyer, Smith Richardson's senior program officer for domestic public policy, who has for so long provided wise counsel not only to us but to so many others as well.

In this book we synthesize the ideas and activities of those involved in workforce efforts. Over the two years we conducted our research, before and after the first COVID-19 outbreak, we met hundreds of wonderful public servants, in government and nonprofits. We spoke with farsighted business leaders and dedicated academics. And we spoke with scores of individuals who have participated in skill-building programs of all types and who have used what they have learned to build better futures. In many cases we use their voices in the stories we relate. We thank all of the people who generously took the time to share the narratives and ideas that eventually found their way into this book.

We also wish to thank the institutions associated with the publication of this book. First, we thank Bill Finan, director of the Brookings Institution Press, and his staff for their wonderful support. Tony Saich, director of the Ash Center at Harvard's Kennedy School, supports the work we do there with city officials as well as joining with Brookings for this publication. We thank him for both.

Numerous people played critical roles as our book developed. Two individuals in particular were indispensable in our interviews for this book. Bonita Stowell helped us think through and conduct the qualitative research that is the backbone of this book. We feel lucky to have her on our team.

In addition, AEI supported the project and provided the research and interview talents of Caleb Seibert, who, along with Ryan Streeter, director of domestic policy studies, provided invaluable help.

Our thanks to Kate Murphy, faculty assistant at the Ash Center, who provided a broad range of services, including helping us maintain communications with dozens of individuals over a two-year period while we made sure we were accurately chronicling their stories.

Elizabeth Goldsmith spent many hours researching the journals that make up much of the scholarly content for the book.

————————

This book is indeed a synthesis. It uses the words of others to illustrate important points. In gathering these words, we had the support of institutions like Smith Richardson, Ash/HKS, Brookings, and AEI. We benefitted from the talents of individuals who helped us with research and interviews. We are indebted to all of them.

Growing Fairly

1

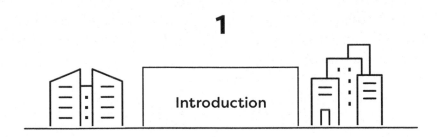

Introduction

Our economy needs to work for more Americans. Current and future workers need realistic pathways to living wage jobs. They need access to the training and education necessary to qualify for better jobs. They need adequate transportation and childcare. In this book, we will meet local leaders who are creating opportunity—for residents seeking their first job and employees seeking their next job. We will see communities that have come together to make a difference and hear from the individuals they helped. The past several decades have witnessed dramatic economic growth, but the benefits of that growth have not been equitably shared. Fair growth requires local action and rethinking how we skill and support working age adults.

While we come to this project with different political philosophies and with work experiences in different sectors, we share a common belief. Economic opportunity lies out of reach for far too many people because of where they live, their race, or their access to quality education.

Stephen, as a mayor of Indianapolis in the 1990s, visited hard working blue-collar employees at the International Harvester foundry, Chrysler foundry, RCA television assembly plant, and General Motors and Ford assembly plants. These facilities historically had provided thousands of reliable jobs with good wages and benefits. RCA, for example, once employed 8,200 workers at its plant, and the GM facility at its height utilized a 5,600-person workforce.

Today, these factories are closed. All their jobs are gone.

Plant closings and other changes in the local economy have been devastating. Indianapolis saw a 20 percent decline in its manufacturing base in the decade ending in 2020 and an 80 percent increase in the number of residents living in poverty.

Kate brings a different perspective to our work. She left the world of fintech in 2001 to join the YMCA of Metro Chicago. Later, she became executive vice president for strategy and advancement for the national YMCA. Kate's experiences at work reflected changes in the city at large. Given the geographic distribution of YMCA branches in Chicago, she literally could visit a Y in a working class all-white community, and on her way to the next branch several blocks away find herself in an entirely Black neighborhood. Segregation in the city was and continues to be stunning. During her fifteen years of YMCA experience, she saw poverty worsen in the city and middle-class workers lose ground—even as the wealth of top earners in the city grew dramatically.

Intracity disparities disclose a harsh reality. A baby born in 2015 in Chicago's mostly white Streeterville neighborhood populated by college-educated families could expect to live to ninety, thirty years more than a baby born the same year in the largely Black Englewood neighborhood. University of Illinois, Chicago maps show that fully half of the city was middle-income in 1970, including large swaths on every side of town. In 2018, just 16 percent of the city's 797 census tracts were considered middle-income, and those areas are confined mostly to the corners of the city and to thin middle-class strips between areas of wealth and poverty.[1]

The story in both cities, and, indeed, across the country, is one of juxtapositions: the upper middle class has expanded even in the face of the overall middle class losses. At the same time Indianapolis lost thousands of manufacturing jobs, it developed a prospering technology sector, with companies such as Salesforce growing significantly alongside an already vigorous healthcare sector. Chicago witnessed the same contrasts as a new tech neighborhood sprouted on the west side of the city's Loop.

This book is about people and potential. It highlights initiatives that have successfully lowered barriers to urban workers' aspirations and their economic mobility. We hope to convince leaders across sectors that collective community action can make a difference. We also aim for a broader audience of those concerned about civic life, hoping to motivate them to come together around a more inclusive narrative that will bridge political divides and produce support for comprehensive solutions.

For more than two years, often in-person pre-COVID-19 and then, subsequently, by video conferencing, we traveled across the country, from San Diego and Los Angeles to New York and Boston, interviewing leaders and staff from high performing organizations. We met with mayors, chiefs of staff, and other leaders from across the country in forums at Harvard's Kennedy School. We interviewed participants involved with dozens of programs, sometimes labeled "workforce" and other times referred to as "education" or "training."

We concentrated primarily on the actions of nonprofits and local and state government but also, albeit to a more limited extent, looked at college and employer-based programs. The review included organizations that help the unemployed and underemployed as well as those fully employed but seeking upward mobility to better jobs. We included programs that focus on education and training and initiatives that support persons struggling to overcome personal, family, or location-based roadblocks. We searched for the key elements that should be incorporated as part of an optimal regional response.

Ours is an expansive definition of "workforce" that includes the larger set of activities designed to improve the skills and opportunities of workers, not just those associated with the federally funded workforce investment boards.

As a joint project of a Republican and a Democrat, this book rejects choosing between conservative views that assume that anyone who works hard will succeed and more progressive views that simply demand more government support. We argue, instead, for a broader shared narrative about potential, one that demonstrates how greater cross-sector collaboration can enhance upward economic mobility for those whose prospects have dimmed.

We are not economists—these chapters do not rely on original empirical research. Nor do we hold ourselves out as the most preeminent workforce experts. We met the experts in our interviews and research, and you will, in turn, meet them in this book. We write from the perspective of local action, as two long-time practitioners who have spent their careers addressing social problems in and with people in dozens of areas across the country.

Both Stephen and Kate have funded, participated in, or overseen programs where a dedicated coach or caseworker helped people find pathways to better lives. As a prosecutor, Stephen was a leader in reforming child support enforcement. He used data to increase collections and initiated fatherhood and jobs programs, as well. He met almost weekly with single mothers receiving Aid to Families with Dependent Children. He heard their aspirational stories but also their realistic pleas for the help they needed in order to work more regularly. Kate crafted national strategy for the Y by visiting local affiliates. She saw how a single staff member's care or participation in a carefully structured program could change a child's trajectory. An advocate for cooperation across organizational boundaries, she also saw the community-wide impact of bringing together multiple organizations with overlapping missions.

We have been fortunate to have thousands of public and nonprofit employees work for us and to fund hundreds of programs with government and philanthropic dollars. Our proximity to individuals serving others and to those they served produced for us insights, context, and empathy.

The chapters that follow reflect the people we met, their lessons, and their successes. Our goal is to identify the various principles of success and then braid them together for regional implementation. The people we met, both those who needed a lift up and those doing the lifting, provide the voices. We provide the vehicle for their stories and connect the threads between their insights and our design principles.[2]

Our Focus: Cities, Individuals, and the Centrality of Work

Not only in Indianapolis and Chicago but across the country in many cities, low-income individuals increasingly live in economically and racially segregated neighborhoods. These deeply impoverished communities lack access to opportunities and suffer the ill effects of historically willful neglect and polluted environments. Residents exposed to the trauma of scarcity and violence start the search for good jobs many laps behind the competition. Workers in many struggling neighborhoods face day-to-day challenges, like inadequate transportation, poor housing, and few childcare options.

A half-century ago, urban design expert Jane Jacobs, in her book *The Death and Life of Great American Cities,* wrote that a "metropolitan economy, if it is working well, is constantly transforming many poor people into middle-class people, many illiterates into skilled people, many greenhorns into competent citizens." Putting aside her questionable labels, that progression has stalled in too many urban areas. Loss of manufacturing jobs is, of course, one reason. But there is also the changing nature of work that puts a premium on content creation and the ability to juggle complex tasks. Many jobs have been displaced by robotics and artificial intelligence. The growth of independent contracting work has often severed the attachment between employers and employees, who once enjoyed the fringe benefits and career ladders their companies offered. Disinvestment, explicit and implicit bias, and unequal access to quality education compound the problem.

The New York City and urban middle class that Jacobs imagined featured integrated and successful public schools, manufacturing jobs, and vibrant neighborhoods. Yet, today, achieving the American Dream, which promises each successive generation will do better , is not remotely achievable for many of our fellow citizens. The urban ladders that supported upward mobility either no longer exist or, at the very least, are missing several of their rungs.

In 2012, a Pew Charitable Trust Economic Mobility Project report showed that not only do Blacks struggle to exceed their parents' income more than whites, they are more "downwardly mobile" as well. Over half of Black children raised in the middle tumble to the bottom or second rung compared to only a third of whites."[3]

Tens of millions of Americans are unemployed or underemployed. While various experts define and categorize these populations differently, all end up with large numbers. One group, called opportunity youth, consists of approximately 6 million young people between the ages of sixteen and twenty-four who are neither enrolled in school nor working. More than 50 million Americans between the ages of twenty-five and forty-four do not have post-secondary degrees and earn less than $35,000 annually.

Harvard Professor David Elwood points out that "while economic success is an essential principle, it does not fully capture people's experiences with poverty and mobility. As important as money are power and autonomy—a sense of control over one's life and a chance to make choices and craft a future. Some refer to this principle as agency."[4]

We believe that work provides people with some sense of power over their lives, depending, of course, on the conditions and pay of that work. In this book, we look for solutions and programs that support work and build worker capabilities, believing those capabilities produce not only economic self-sufficiency but self-esteem, as well. As AEI and Brookings write in their joint project "Work, Skills, Community: "Work is vital for many reasons. It's a way to provide for yourself and your family. It helps grow the economy. For most people, it's more satisfying than almost any other activity, including consumption. And it's character-forming—a first good choice that usually leads to other good choices and essential values like purpose, diligence, responsibility, and self-reliance."[5]

We hosted a discussion group organized by and about the 2019 movie *American Factory*, produced by Barack and Michelle Obama, a documentary that shines a light on the meaning of work by examining the consequences to workers and their families when General Motors closed a major assembly plant in Dayton, Ohio. The factory was subsequently downsized and opened with different working conditions by Fuyao, a Chinese company. One can see vividly in the movie and in the comments by those in our discussion group (which met at the foot of a similarly closed Indianapolis GM factory) the degree to which identity is connected to work. *American Factory* profiles the importance of an adequate income as well as the way workplace conditions can enhance or diminish the self-esteem that derives from employment. These tensions play out on the screen as the workers Bobby and Shawnea, who, unlike many of their colleagues, kept their jobs under the new owner, struggle with the lower pay and reduction of factory floor freedoms:

> Bobby: For a year and a half, [after the plant closed] I didn't have anything. When I started at Fuyao, I was thankful. I was blessed. I was just on my knees, thanking God that I had something. This is the best game in town right now.
>
> Shawnea: At General Motors, I was making $29.00 and some change an hour and at Fuyao, I make $12.84. Back then if my kids wanted a pair of new gym shoes, I could just go get 'em. I can't just do that now. We lost our home. We lost a vehicle.

Watching this documentary with local residents who saw themselves reflected on the screen brought to mind the words of Indianapolis Archbishop Daniel Buechlein, with whom we spoke at a lunch not far from that night's location. Reading from Pope John Paul II's encyclicals, Father Daniel directed us to the encyclical on "Through Work," which underscores its importance to man's humanity because that is how he "achieves fulfilment as a human being and indeed, in a sense, becomes 'more a human being.'" But the encyclical also links industriousness as a virtue with fairness, which requires that man not be degraded through damage to the dignity and subjectivity that are proper to him.[6] Both these themes present themselves in the movie, and the discussions that night underscored the importance of fair economic growth.

This book focuses on programs and policies that create promising pathways for city dwellers who lack jobs or whose upward mobility has stalled, leaving them without a living wage. We examine these pathways in cities and regions across the country. We reject binary, polemic choices. No one-size-fits-all formula works, and the degree and type of support depends greatly on the worker and their circumstances. Although these lessons apply broadly across the country, the book concentrates primarily on cities and their metro areas; in part because it is their leaders who disproportionately participate in our work at the Kennedy School and elsewhere and because their regions often possess the greatest income disparities. Therefore, we start with a quick review of recent developments in the economic ups and downs of workers in America's cities.

Large Cities Attract Growth, Tech, and Inequality

Five metropolitan areas—Boston, San Diego, San Francisco, Seattle, and San Jose—accounted for 90 percent of all U.S. high-tech job growth between 2005 and 2017.[7] These cities—and Los Angeles—are home to the largest median income differences between the bottom and top quintiles in the country. Generally, larger cities produce more wage inequality—a situation that was not the case forty years ago.[8]

Ideas and people flow to tech firms in high performing locales, adding value to those areas. In the United States as a whole, 30 percent of the population has a college degree. In Seattle, that number is 57.4 percent (for those over twenty-five) and just a few points lower in San Francisco and Washington, D.C. In these cities, a person or their significant other can find or switch jobs more easily and has casual access to new ideas.[9] Regional agglomeration economies, according to leading urban expert and Harvard economist Ed Glaeser, occur when industrial clusters of firms and people locate near one another in cities, which, in turn, supports a "strong relationship between density and high wages."[10]

Approximately ten to fifteen years ago, recognizing the benefits produced by attracting qualified college educated talent, many mayors shifted their economic development efforts from chasing jobs to chasing what leading urban theorist Richard Florida called the creative class. Touted as "the great reset" by Florida in *The Rise of the Creative Class*, this strategy identified quality-of-life assets—parks, neighborhoods, amenities, and culture—as the key to retaining or attracting the local talent that would drive a new economy powered by innovation, technology, and sustainability. The imperative to build and maintain attractive cities to entice talent to relocate or stay is insufficient. Cities must develop local talent and invest in neglected neighborhoods if we are to achieve greater equity and enhance upward mobility.

Uneven Growth Produces Even More Uneven Opportunity

Of course, cities differ greatly, and much of the most salient research occurred before the devastation of COVID-19. Yet, as we look out and try to guess the future of work in cities, trends from the recent past provide important guidance. In the first half of the last decade, cities generally gained population. Larger cities, however, began losing residents during the last half of the decade.

A city's center makes a difference. Downtowns tend to be the image of the region, the site of many professional and financial jobs and the locus of tourism, retail, and hospitality clusters that help many into their first jobs. Downtowns often sit adjacent to important education and medical centers. The first fifteen years of the twenty-first century saw large numbers of professionals and others with college degrees return from the suburbs to downtowns, where they found more amenities and improved safety.

Downtowns do not represent entire cities. Even with this resurgence at the core of large regions, many cities registered slowing or declining growth overall. As the country rebounded from the Great Recession in 2008, population once again dispersed toward suburbs and smaller areas. Poverty also increased. For example, in Philadelphia, while the central city fared well between 2000 and 2014, the situation was different for the city as a whole. Twice as many areas of the city suffered income declines versus those that experienced gains.[11]

This shift aggravated the disparity between those born into low-income zip codes and those into wealthier ones. Harvard economist Raj Chetty, whose breakthrough research on cities has changed the way the country discusses opportunity, identified the immensely favorable outcomes for those better positioned by family, education, and living standards in wealthier zip codes where it is easier to take advantage of the new economy. Research by the Urban Institute traces growing wealth disparity and racial wealth gaps not just to differences in income and earnings but also to rates of homeownership and to student loan debt burdens that make it difficult for low-income families to build financial assets.[12] These gaps relate, as well, to historic polices that worked against wealth.

Increasing Segregation Magnifies Inequality

The segregation of cities by race and class vividly reflects differences in opportunity, as well. In 1970, 65 percent of the residents of large metropolitan areas lived in neighborhoods with median incomes close to the median for the entire area. A Stanford Graduate School of Education report shows income segregation growing beginning in the 1980s, with the proportion of people living in middle-income neighborhoods declining to 40 percent in 2012.[13]

Due to the nature of our work in cities over the last two decades, we have seen up close the stark contrasts between affluent neighborhoods with thriving shopping areas and economically challenged neighborhoods with vacant homes, boarded up shops, too few jobs, and too much environmental contamination. Not enough people understand the full scale of these gaps and the consequences to residents living in struggling areas. Those with wealth can distance themselves from the reality of poverty. As Chetty and colleagues summarize, "the spatial variation in intergenerational mobility is strongly correlated with five factors: (1) residential segregation, (2) income inequality, (3) school quality, (4) social capital, and (5) family structure."[14]

This book focuses on programs that help individuals move up the economic ladder regardless of where they might live. But that is not enough. We must acknowledge both how government helped aggravate racial segregation and the role it must play in correcting spatial inequities. HUD policies in Indianapolis and other cities concentrated Black families in certain neighborhoods, which, in turn, contributed to schools segregated by race. FHA policies, until the 1960s, redlined Black neighborhoods. Between 1934 and 1962, whites received 98 percent of the government-backed loans.[15] Banks, in many cases, followed suit. As Stanford's Jennifer Eberhardt in her insightful book *Biased* reminds us, "The instruments of government-sanctioned bias—zoning restrictions, racial covenants, mortgage refusals, and a building boom in suburbs open only to whites—had already taken their toll, forcing Black families to crowd into undesirable areas where amenities were few, the housing stock was often decrepit or cheaply built, and the streets were lined with factories spewing industrial pollution."[16]

However, even the distinction between wealthy and low-income neighborhoods obscures the fact that communities similar in terms of wealth differ in the degree of mobility. Upward mobility can be affected by the strength of social networks and community involvement, by family structures, as measured, for example, by the fraction of single parents, as well as by school quality.[17]

Less Middle

Too many solidly middle-class families have slipped downward—and not just those in industries like manufacturing. Twenty years ago, Stephen toured Golden Rule Insurance, a large Indianapolis employer with substantial back-office functions. He observed floors filled with closely packed desks and workers (mostly women) opening, reading, and processing claims and then filing papers in appropriately colored, marked folders. Office automation destroyed many of these jobs in a manner not dissimilar to the decline of manufacturing jobs. As David Autor notes: "We have shunted non-college workers from middle-skill career occupations that reward specialized and differentiated skills into traditionally low-education occupations that demand primarily generic skills; it has disproportionately depressed middle-wage employment among non-college workers in urban labor markets, thus directly reducing average non-college wages and—to a startling degree—attenuating the urban non-college wage premium that prevailed in earlier decades."[18]

Thus, the women we observed who once performed these back-office jobs mostly moved to lower-skill work. During this same twenty years, more workers achieved college degrees, and they, in turn, increased their return on that investment, driving up their real wages, while those without degrees saw their wages stagnate at best.[19] The labor market tightening that preceded the COVID-19 outbreak increased demand for college-educated workers, but it did not do much to raise the real wages of those pushed down the ladder.[20]

Economists label in various ways what we saw in our work: cities with fewer middle-class people and neighborhoods and not enough workers with mid-tech skills. Autor calls it the hollowing of the middle.[21] Stephen Rose of University of Connecticut, examining the twenty-year period up to 2016, calls it a shrinking middle with some moving to upper middle-class and more slipping down. As troubling, Rose finds that, even before COVID-19, fewer people moved up and out of poverty and more slipped back into it.[22] And Barnard sociologist Angela Sims underscores the challenges faced even by more suburbanized Black middle-class communities as they battle for a sufficient tax base for schools and other essential services.[23]

This book summarizes promising practices, not just for the underemployed and for lower-income workers, but also for lower middle income families who, depending on family size, earn approximately $30,000 to $50,000 a year.

The Growing Middle-Skills Deficit

Major changes in labor availability now and over the next few decades, and the growth of new occupations, will create opportunities. Baby boomers, who as a group are well educated, retired in greater numbers in 2020 than in the prior eight years, from an average annual increase of two million to an increase of three million in 2020.[24] Record low labor force participation also affects the middle skill deficit. The male labor workforce has been declining steadily since the 1980s, recently accelerating as a result of the opioid epidemic. And the effect of COVID-19 greatly reduced the ability of women to work. Plummeting birth rates will compound these and other factors, producing what Korn Ferry predicts will be a deficit of six million workers in ten years.[25]

Digitization will produce new jobs that will require more middle- and high-skill workers, far more than the four-year college pipeline can produce,[26] creating opportunities for those well trained but without four-year degrees. An educational pedigree is not an indispensable requirement in tech.[27] Today, as many as 17 percent of core technical workers in high-tech lack a bachelor's degree. For some jobs, requiring a degree unnecessarily creates misalignment in the labor market, which has important implications for both the economy and individual workers. An insufficient number of middle-skill workers reduces the rate at which employment and output can grow,[28] but it creates opportunity for aspiring workers who can be skilled to meet the demands of current and emerging middle-skill jobs.

Lower-Wage Workers Invoke Different Circumstances

Non-college-degree urban workers are pressed on all sides. Persons of color disproportionately suffered from higher rates of COVID-19 and its effects. Some 54 percent of Hispanic households reported income losses between March and September 2020, along with 47 percent of Black households.[29] Even before the pandemic, urban workers experienced a squeeze as what used to be a wage premium versus their rural colleagues collapsed. At the same time, the cost of urban living increased.

What qualifies as "low wage" varies by place, and low wage can be defined in different ways. The Bureau of Labor Statistics (BLS) considers it as less than "what it would take a full-time worker to earn an income lifting his or her family above the federal poverty threshold."[30] In figure 1-1, Brookings researchers Martha Ross and Nicole Bateman helpfully distinguish among vulnerable and less vulnerable low-income workers; the former should be a higher priority for help.[31]

The chapters that follow feature organizations that work more on the right side of this chart by assisting vulnerable low-wage workers.

Kate often witnessed the challenges confronting vulnerable low-wage workers who were forced to make tradeoffs due to their uncertain employment status. Particularly troubling was the impact these tradeoffs had on their families. In 2011, the Y began scaling several programs to address the achievement gap across its national network. Funded largely by an internal foundation falling into her portfolio, Kate visited early learning, out of school time, and summer learning loss prevention sites around the country. Among the predominately low-wage workers whose children participated in these programs, differences were obvious. Some of the parents and caregivers to whom Kate spoke clearly struggled to get their children to and from classes while working at low-wage jobs that afforded them little if any flexibility. These workers were confronted with difficult choices that their less vulnerable peers were not. For this, they and their children paid a price.

Figure 1-1. **A Note about Economically Vulnerable Workers**

Less vulnerable low-wage workers	More vulnerable low-wage workers
Secondary earners	Sole earners
College students, especially those enrolled full time right out of high school or otherwise are likely to graduate	Parents, especially single parents
Have a postsecondary degree or credential	Have low education levels
Early in their careers	Involuntarily working part time
	Dislocated workers who take a lower-paying job after a layoff
	Have a disability
	Workers who are older, female, Black, or Latino or Hispanic

Source: Martha Ross and Nicole Bateman, "Meet the Low-Wage Workforce," Brookings Institution, November 2019, www.brookings .edu/wp-content/uploads/2019/11/201911_Brookings-Metro_low-wage-workforce_Ross-Bateman.pdf, p. 12.

Cities and a Post-COVID-19 Future

Some say the era of the city is over—hammered by COVID-19 and troubled by issues of racial inequity. We find this view overwrought. Cities will retain the considerable array of physical and soft assets that have for so long attracted residents. Yet, growing concerns, valid or not, about murder rates and instability may deter the professionals who flocked to cities drawn by the amenities and the energy of urban life. While we are loath to predict, we are willing to speculate. Center city population growth may slow or, indeed, abate, and flight from other areas of large cities into prosperous suburbs will continue. Yet cities will likely drive future economic growth, albeit differently than in the past.

One way to strengthen cities is to grow jobs and skill more people to take those jobs. When we began this book, unemployment was at 4 percent, and employers could not fill their open positions. Our focus on improving the workforce development system was born out of this misalignment and our belief that a more equitable approach to skilling would create opportunity for unemployed and underemployed workers. We still believe this, although the challenge has intensified. Two years later, in 2021, unemployment, though abating, is still up and labor market participation is down.

As we emerge from the pandemic with a rebounding economy but without new coordinated efforts, we expect no end to the trends we have seen over the past decade, trends that adversely impact low-wage and nonworking Americans. Even during the COVID-19 resurgence in the summer of 2020, 8 million jobs remained unfilled across the country. Without predicting the exact future of cities, we can, in fact, predict that if more people have more skills and the necessary support to apply them, the result will be enhanced urban opportunity and increased regional wealth and income.

Local Leaders Can Make a Difference

There are practical steps officials can take to increase mobility for workers without a college degree. Many of the challenges affecting those struggling to increase their income are systemic; others are individual. Important distinctions in how to approach and support those in the bottom quintile versus those in the second quintile exist. The future income of children in the lowest (and top) quintiles is sticky, "meaning that the income of children from these quintiles is much more likely to wind up in or near their parents' quintile."[32] Workers and would-be workers stuck in generational and geographic poverty need a broad range of social and work support services while society addresses the systemic barriers that challenge them. Some of the exemplary nonprofit officials we spoke to believe that addressing the ill effects of scarcity on executive function is, in and of itself, an important first step. Others, often academics, focus on the application of data to determine more carefully which low-wage entry jobs are more likely than others to be engines for mobility. While some programs concentrate on getting the hard-to-employ a job, others concentrate on getting them a job that the evidence shows will be more likely to lead to better opportunity.[33]

In the chapters that follow, we examine steps cross-sector local officials can take to improve the lives of those now struggling to make ends meet. We eschew sharp policy differences, looking constructively at improved roles for business while recognizing that government and nonprofits need to address not only neighborhood and racial obstacles but market inefficiencies, as well. Economist Friedrich Hayek observed that market economies operate most efficiently with better information. Imperfect information is a problem that particularly impacts labor markets struggling to price the skills of workers who do not have post-secondary degrees. The highly fragmented approach to workforce initiatives in the United States aggravates these inefficiencies. Imperfections in information create friction not only for workers as they try to make sense of their options but also for employers who would be inclined to hire more inclusively, using skills and not simply degrees. Unfortunately, they lack a common currency by which to make such judgments.

Designing a Labor Market System that Works

The current labor market development system leaves too many individuals unemployed or underemployed. Improvements in our understanding of how and why people learn, coupled with the use of much better real-time data, makes it possible to build a fairer system that creates greater opportunity. The following chapters articulate ten design principles that create a framework for local action and cross-sector collaboration. Together, these principles form the scaffolding upon which to construct a more equitable workforce system, one that will move more people to work and to better jobs.

While important research underlies the actions we profile, we chose examples using a practitioner's lens—ours and that of the people we interviewed. From our investigations, our national network of nonprofit leaders and the insights of local officials brought together at the Harvard Kennedy School, we identified some of the most promising governmental, for-profit, and nonprofit initiatives helping people get a job or move up the economic ladder. We examined available evaluations of the featured programs but also relied on the words of those we met over two years of research. The voices of both those who deliver programs and those who participate paint a picture of what is possible.

Table 1-1 is an abbreviated index of programs you will meet more formally later in the text. The design principles featured in this book fall into three categories: those that apply to the people the system is intended to serve (chapter 2), those that apply to the organizations supporting those individuals (chapters 3 through 6), and those that apply system-wide (chapters 7 through 10).

In chapter 2, we begin our discussion of principles by describing the broad array of people for whom skilling is a pathway to greater mobility. To accommodate the distinctive characteristics of a population diverse in confidence, skills, and background, the system must bring together a broad array of providers whose efforts are tailored to the varying needs of different segments within the population.

We feature the design elements of high performing programs in chapters 3 through 6. Chapter 3 discusses the importance of personalization in organizations that tailor aspects of their approach to meet the unique needs and circumstances of individual participants. Through personalization, these organizations assess fit, determine readiness, and tailor training and resources accordingly.

Skills training and/or education alone is not enough. Individuals face a host of logistical and psychological obstacles that make pro-

gram participation and completion difficult. Effective programs support learners by working with them to remove or mitigate the barriers that stand in their way. Chapter 4 discusses a range of supports, from wraparounds to incentives, highlighting the important role coaches play in helping students access resources and navigate successful completion.

Chapter 5 explores contextualized learning. Because individuals learn in different ways conditioned by their context and informed by the opportunities they seek, exceptional programs often combine technical skill development with career readiness preparation and adult basic education. These learning contexts also integrate business culture, vocabulary, and protocols into classroom material.

Chapter 6 establishes the importance of building bridges or on-ramps to employment into program design. The chapter looks at experiential learning activities, like intern and apprenticeship programs, and sectoral initiatives that clarify career pathways and provide direct access to employers.

Chapters 7 through 10 feature design principles that improve the way the system operates at the regional level. Chapter 7 lays out the critical design principle of using skills as a medium of exchange. We argue that workers who lack a college degree do, in fact, possess in-demand skills. The chapter examines how to create a regional skill-based system and the implications of such a system on major stakeholders, from worker and employer to post-secondary providers of education and training. This chapter also reviews best practices of employers using skills to advance promotion inside their businesses or industry.

Transparency and performance are the focus of chapter 8, which addresses the type of information learners need to advance their journeys. The chapter shows how delivering useable information on required skills and the performance of training and education programs will help consumers of further education or training make informed choices about their options.

Chapter 9 looks at design solutions that address the many "taxes" communities impose on hard-pressed workers and would-be workers. High housing costs, inadequate transportation, lack of affordable/high-quality daycare options, and discrimination based on race or previous incarceration make labor market participation challenging.

No one entity, no one sector, can meet the demands of an effective workforce development system. Fragmentation too often plagues regional efforts. Chapter 10 discusses the need for cross-sector collaboration managed by respected intermediaries and governed by principles that will lead to agreed-upon outcomes. The discussion of cross-sector collaboration focuses on their role in ensuring that all critical parts of the system are reflected in the community's design. The chapter shows how collaborations benefit from the use of shared data to help learners move up the mobility ladder, assist education and training providers be more precise in their offerings, and assist academics and funders in evaluating efficacy.

Chapter 11 examines Houston, Texas, as an example of a community bringing together the design principles discussed in this book. Houston is a work in progress and an example of how one community is attempting to bridge neighborhood, class, and race divides to produce upward economic mobility.

Over the course of two years, we met scores of heroic individuals who inspired and humbled us. We met people working in government and nonprofits who have dedicated themselves to helping others, all with an eye toward doing more wherever possible. We spoke with dozens of people who, when given the opportunity, overcame personal challenges and neighborhood barriers, lifting themselves and their families out of poverty. These chapters bring together lessons from city leaders, program officers, and once-struggling Americans. We weave them into design principles for a more equitable workforce development system, illustrated in figure 1-2. We hope it will inspire local action that allows communities to grow together fairly.

Figure 1-2. **Design Principles**

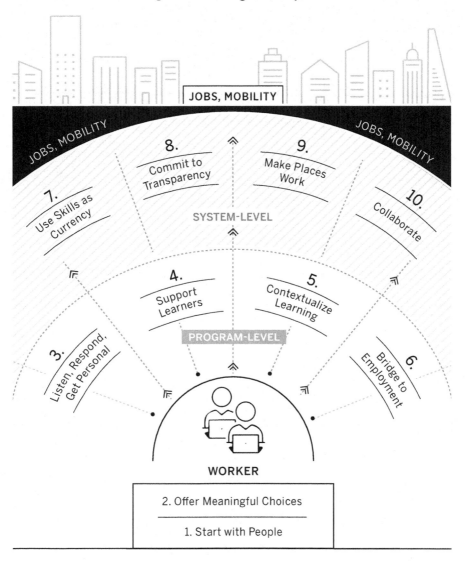

2

Start with People, Offer Meaningful Choices

When we began this book in October 2019, there were more open jobs than unemployed adults seeking work.[1] And while tight labor markets ultimately drive full employment and wage growth, we were troubled by the irony—opportunity out of reach for millions. The human toll manifest in the statistics fueled our motivation to write this book. Even more troubling, twelve months later, there were nearly two job seekers for every open position. Although we are seeing the return of many of the jobs lost to the pandemic, we also expect ongoing structural changes to the economy that, pre-pandemic, had rendered millions of workers and potential workers underprepared. If anything, we believe more strongly that our current economy, which enriches some while leaving many behind, demands a reimagining of the labor-market skilling system. That was our topic in 2019, and it remains our topic today.

In October 2020, there were 160.5 million adults age sixteen to twenty-four in the civilian labor force, meaning they were either employed (149.8 million) or unemployed (11.1 million)—the latter group composed of individuals actively looking for a job within the prior four weeks.[2] Another 100.1 million adult Americans were not in the labor force, among them retirees, students, and individuals caring for children or other family members. Amid the individuals classified as not in the labor force was a substantial cohort, 6.37 million, that would like a job now but who, for a variety of reasons, had not actively sought one in the past four weeks.[3] In this group were people the Bureau of Labor Statistics labels marginally attached and discouraged. Apt but unsettling labels.

Scattered throughout the BLS statistics are low-wage workers, by some estimates 44 percent of working Americans; millions of disconnected young adults age sixteen to twenty-four who are neither working nor in school and who represent 11.2 percent of the young adult population in the United States; and nearly 8 million formerly imprisoned individuals whose lifetime earnings potential pales in comparison to that of their peers.[4] The ranks of the unemployed and underemployed are populated by individuals whose experience of systemic barriers varies, whose exposure to trauma varies, whose access to information about pathways to job mobility varies, and whose attachment to work varies. Consequently, their skilling needs differ considerably.

Understand the Range of Needs and Responses

Over the course of our research, we spoke to hundreds of workers and would-be workers. We encountered Sherman indirectly through Roca, an organization that works with justice-involved youths. We were introduced to Nuha through Jewish Vocational Services (JVS). And we met Johnny through the City University of New York (CUNY), where he had been a student. Sherman, Nuha, and Johnny each entered or are hoping to reenter the world of work through very different doors: Sherman from the criminal justice system and more than one brush with death, Nuha from Sudan and a post-secondary degree, and Johnny from a career in transportation after a dispiriting conversation with his son.

Before he met outreach workers from Roca, Sherman was neither ready, willing, nor able to participate in job training.[5] Nuha still does not work in her chosen field; she is taking English classes that use job readiness as a frame. Johnny had worked for years as a limousine dispatcher. He was employed but felt financially vulnerable, and wanted to model the importance of education for his son. Because Sherman, Nuha, and Johnny's prospects for mobility are shaped by their unique circumstances, their skilling needs are entirely different. We share their stories in this and later chapters to make a point, one that should be obvious but too often is not. A fully functional labor market development system must accommodate the widely varying needs of the people for whom the system exists. Therefore, it must integrate the efforts of multiple actors from different sectors: nonprofit and private skilling intermediaries, employers, educators, state and municipal agencies, and data platforms.

The workforce development systems that operate in most cities and states focus largely on employment, less on mobility. These systems, here defined as the aggregate of government, educator, employer, and nonprofit intermediaries, do not meet the twenty-first-century needs of either individuals or employers.[6] In particular, they fail the ineptly named "hard to employ," who, for reasons of birth, exposure to trauma, lack of access, and structural barriers are poorly served by the current K–12 pipeline.[7]

In an interview with Brookings Institution for an issue of *Social Mobility Memos*, Elizabeth Weigensberg, a senior researcher at Mathematica, notes: "The workforce development field has an unfortunate history of 'creaming'—programs selectively work with individuals most likely to succeed at finding employment, leaving those 'harder-to-serve' individuals struggling to find assistance. Individuals that are often considered 'hard-to-serve' include those who are homeless, disabled, formerly incarcerated, older workers, non-English speakers, low-income, and youth who are disconnected from school and employment."[8]

The current workforce development system also fails adult learners, who find themselves mid-career, vulnerable to the effects of automation and globalization, and with limited pathways for mobility. In her book, *Long Life Learning: Preparing for Jobs that Don't Even Exist Yet*, Michelle R. Weise observes:

We are all going to have to prepare for jobs that don't even exist yet. Enter the concept of life-long learning. Through the lens of human longevity, the future of work becomes inextricably tied to the future of learning. . . . Educators, policymakers, and funders give a lot of lip service to the concept of lifelong learning, but this talk rarely translates into action. In fact, resources and funding are often geared toward the traditional 18- to 24-year-old college-going population and less often to working adults, the growing majority of learners. There is little investment in the systems, architecture, and infrastructure needed to facilitate seamless movements in and out of learning and work.[9]

It is time to redesign both the informal and formal workforce development systems that have evolved over the past several decades. Local leaders must be deliberate in crafting more equitable systems that meet the disparate skilling needs of their residents, from the harder to serve to the incumbent worker. To do so, officials must be willing to reimagine the responsibilities of current players, examine skilling needs in their regions, and reallocate and coordinate resources among organizations in order to address those needs. This brings us to our first two design principles:

- System design starts not with available programs and specific policies but with people, recognizing that individuals' skill-building needs vary widely depending upon their lived experiences.

- The system must offer meaningful choices, support a range of actors from multiple sectors whose programs align, and flex to meet individual needs and reflect local and regional demand for skills.

Start with Brain Science

Phineas Gage and Harvard economist Raj Chetty rarely, if ever, are mentioned in the same sentence. Gage worked for the Rutland and Burlington Railroad Company. Chetty works for Harvard University. Yet both provide context for thinking about the structural hurdles that stand in the way of economic mobility.

Chetty is well known for his description of neighborhood effects and the impact of zip code exposure on children's life prospects.[10] Gage is known for surviving a gruesome accident: While he was clearing rocks to make way for railroad construction, a tamping rod pierced his skull and destroyed the frontal lobe of his brain. According to those who knew him, Gage changed after the accident: He lost his inhibitions. While it would be close to 125 years before the term was formally coined, the damage Gage sustained impacted the areas of his brain responsible for executive functioning.

Variously labeled, executive functioning encompasses multiple skills falling into three categories:

- *Inhibition* (or inhibitory control or self-control), the skills "used to filter distractions, override impulses, resist temptation, maintain focus, pause and reflect before acting, and maintain persistence in the face of worry or despair"

- *Cognitive flexibility* (or mental flexibility or cognitive adaptability), "the ability to . . . switch gears, multitask, adjust plans, reestablish priorities, apply different rules or social skills in different settings, . . . alter strategies based on feedback, and innovate"

- *Working memory*, "the ability to mentally hold and manipulate information over short periods, simultaneously think of multiple things, . . . follow multi-step instructions, and temporarily stop doing something and return to it later without confusion or loss of continuity"[11]

Together, these skills make it possible to "execute routine and complex tasks, solve problems, sustain attention, follow rules, make plans, monitor actions, control impulses, delay gratification, and set and achieve short- and long-term goals . . . they are critical for success in many aspects of life, including school performance, parenting and work."[12] In the absence of well-developed executive functioning, it is difficult to find, execute, and keep a job.

Executive functioning develops over a long period of time, from birth through young adulthood, making children particularly vulnerable to the stresses frequently associated with poverty,[13] scarcity,[14] and exposure to violence.[15] A growing body of research suggests that ongoing exposure to toxic stress can adversely impact the development of executive functioning.[16] This makes it far more challenging "to embark on the difficult process of setting goals, changing . . . behavior, and lifting themselves out of poverty. . . . The prevailing assumption is that if low-income people are given information and/or resources to help them along their way, they should be able to make the necessary behavior changes, ... [but] the evidence suggests otherwise."[17]

In an article for the US Partnership on Mobility from Poverty, Elizabeth Babcock, president and CEO of EMPath and an early and prolific champion of understanding the impact of poverty on executive functioning, puts it this way:

> Acquiring [twenty-first-century] skills poses special challenges for people most in need of family-sustaining jobs because, as scientific research has unequivocally shown, the special stresses of poverty, trauma and discrimination directly compromise such skills. And the traditional education and training programs available to those in poverty are still primarily training them for a job (usually those jobs with the shortest training pathways) and not for the 21st-century navigational skills that would allow them to get and keep jobs with family-sustaining wages. Such skills require coaching and practice, especially for people living under the stresses of poverty."[18]

We raise the subject of executive functioning not to imply that it is the reason people end up in poverty. On the contrary, the stresses associated with living in a state of constant scarcity creates a bandwidth tax that many individuals pay in lack of economic mobility. The cognitive energy required to make ends meet leaves little room for anything else.[19] However, as organizations such as EMPath demonstrated early on, executive functioning can be strengthened through a combination of cognitive behavioral therapy, coaching, goal setting, incentives, and environmental modifications.

We return to the not-so-unlikely pair joined in the sentence beginning this section. Gage "introduced" us to executive functioning; his was a very particularized trauma. Chetty "introduced" us to neighborhood effects, the more generalized trauma of scarcity. Together they provide impetus for thinking more expansively about workforce development.

The remainder of this chapter profiles two organizations: Roca, Inc. and New Moms. Roca works with high-risk, justice-system-involved young adults, and New Moms, as its name suggests, with young mothers. We also highlight MyGoals, a demonstration project testing coaching approaches with recipients of federal Temporary Assistance for Needy Families (TANF) income support.

These three organizations have designed their interventions using current thinking on brain science, and all are on the forefront of an emerging trend in poverty reduction programs and in human services. They do not serve identical populations, although they do overlap. We include Roca, New Moms, and MyGoals here because an equitable system of workforce development must address the needs of all potential workers, including those who may be "harder to serve." For some segments of the population, this requires workforce programs that focus on strengthening executive skills functioning.

Roca, Inc.

Sherman's story is posted on Roca's website. He is being interviewed in a park in Baltimore. Interviewer and interviewee sit on a picnic table. Sherman squints. He is wearing a white T-shirt and a rose-colored sweatshirt with a large Lacoste crocodile. Sherman looks young and not-so-young at the same time. His face is serious, and the squinting creases his forehead. There is no hint of bravado in his voice despite what he has survived, only dignity etched with gravity. "My last two years have been tragic. I been locked up twice; within the second year, I had got shot 12 times, so I took a lot of ups and downs." Sherman, the narrator notes, is one of Roca's success stories; in and out of the justice system, he now has a job and ongoing Roca support. "How many brothers in Baltimore need what you are getting right now?" the interviewer asks. "If I had to put a percent on it, 80 percent of the people here need that," Sherman replies. What a waste of talent; what a loss for the young men; what a loss for the economy; what a loss for the country.

Targeting Those Who Don't Show Up (Yet)

Roca serves a population of young adults who are neither "ready, willing, nor able" to show up for employment. As Anisha Chablani-Medley, chief programming officer and one of the architects of Roca's approach, describes it to us: "Roca is committed to serving young people who are in a really hard place, they're not thinking about change, they're not ready for change. They've experienced extensive trauma and are in survival mode."

Molly Baldwin, Roca's founder and chief executive, puts it even more starkly: "We are focused on the young adults at the center of urban violence. We are trying to help young people stay alive, stay out of jail, and learn to go to work. These young people aren't going to go to a job, aren't going to go to a training program and they aren't going to take part in some really cool social entrepreneurial project." She continues, "A lot of people think if only we could get these young people a job, they'd do better. Well, what's really clear to us is, they can't, they're not ready."

Baldwin raises a critical point for local leaders to consider in the design of a more equitable skilling system. There is a segment of the population for whom vocational training is not a productive option. The challenge for these individuals is to get out of survival mode long enough to focus on self-regulation, flexibility, executive function skills that facilitate their participation in training programs, and, ultimately, in employment. Chablani-Medley adds:

> We designed our programming to align with the theories. We understand how the brain works; we understand what trauma does to the brain. Most of our guys are living in survival brain most of the time, they're hyper vigilant. So, we asked, how do we design and build programming that brings people in, instead of keeping them out? Because most places, you must be totally ready and able to show up to do this stuff. If you mess up once or you act up, you're out. . . . We engage people in a way where they have an opportunity to be in a space where we can create some safety, so that they can get out of survival mode for long enough to start learning

some skills, skills that might actually help them keep a job and start considering that change might be possible.

By design, Roca serves only the highest-risk individuals, those *least* ready to change their behavior. Roca uses a risk assessment tool to determine eligibility. Young men and women deemed to be at the highest risk of incarceration based on their criminal and employment history and their involvement with gangs and drugs constitute Roca's target demographic.

Risk and readiness are closely linked. Roca believes that the individuals they assess as low to moderate risk are ready to change and are not so much in need of their services. Roca refers them to other programs. An intentionally designed system of workforce development accommodates individuals at different stages along the engagement pathway and provides a database of programmatic options to support referrals among programs.

Utilizing Relentless Outreach and Cognitive Behavioral Therapy

Much as we might wish it otherwise, there are no quick fixes in the world of skilling. Roca works with the young adults in its program for as long as four years. After finding the young people who have been referred to them by the criminal or juvenile justice systems and determining their eligibility, youth workers begin the hard work of building trust. Roca characterizes its outreach as "relentless." It takes, on average, eight attempts in Massachusetts and twelve to fourteen in Baltimore to make contact. Once they have succeeded, youth workers are available 24/7. Young adults spend the bulk of their first two years with Roca in programming focused on behavior change. In years three and four, Roca plays a support role, helping participants sustain the changes they have made, staying in regular contact, and stepping in if needed.

Behavior change takes time. It takes persistence. Designing an ecosystem that addresses the needs of harder-to-serve segments of the population means allocating resources to organizations that develop and maintain "transformational" relationships with participants during and after program completion. This helps them sustain the changes necessary for employment. As Roca Baltimore's director of Youth Work and Crisis Intervention James Timpson, better known as "JT," says: "You have to be willing to work with them through the whole process. That's where we're different. We don't give up on [youth] when they make mistakes. Regular consistent contact—no matter what—if we can retain them, we can get outcomes. "

The cognitive behavioral therapy (CBT), central to Roca's model, was developed alongside Massachusetts General Hospital and its Community Psychiatry PRIDE Clinic. Frontline staff work with participants on seven lifesaving (executive function) skills designed to strengthen emotional regulation. The twenty-minute-long skill modules can be delivered anywhere, on the street or in the classroom. They include skills like "labeling your feelings" and "acting in line with your values." Their intent is to teach participants to pause and reflect on what they are thinking and feeling, allowing them to interrupt what might otherwise be an impulsive and possibly inappropriate response to a given situation. Over time and with practice, "young people . . . learn to choose how they want to respond . . . [gaining] control over their lives."[20]

Baldwin explains: "We had to figure out how to transmit emotional regulation skills to young people in a way that's meaningful, that they can remember. It's really, really critical. If it needs to be on a doorstep, OK. If the young person refuses to come to programming, they can call JT . . . between [their] drug deals to work on something. They're building muscle."

They build the "muscle" to show up, to take control, to learn.

To accommodate young adults who may differ in terms of their readiness to participate, Roca offers life skills, education, and employment programs in multiple formats, from drop-in sessions to certificate courses. CBT is woven into all of Roca's programs—which, first and foremost, serve as a platform for young adults to practice their CBT skills. Only secondarily are the classes about content. We do not mean to minimize the importance of classes designed to help participants obtain their GED or prepare a résumé or set up an email address or obtain vocational skills.

Accelerating Behavior Change with Transitional Employment

Roca's philosophy comes alive in discussions of their employment programs. The organization offers transitional employment (TEP), including basic employment skills like showing up on time; prevocational training, which is more sector-specific; workforce readiness programming, covering résumé preparation and the like; and job placement and support. After about six months with Roca, during which participants build increasingly strong and trusting relationships with their youth workers, they discuss participation in additional programming. Some choose the educational track; others move toward employment. Still others continue in relationship-building mode and do not participate in Roca's formal programming. Note the locus of decisionmaking: their goals, their choice. This phase of programming lasts about eighteen months, making up the balance of the two years of intensive involvement participants have with Roca.

Enrolling in TEP, the first stage of Roca's employment programming, is for many an act of courage and an acknowledgement of their willingness to contemplate change and put themselves in a situation where they will inevitably feel uncomfortable. Without the trust-building that comes from their relationship with youth workers, this would not be possible. It speaks to Roca's belief in stage-based programming tied to young people's gradually growing receptivity and capacity for change.

Young adults entering TEP are assigned to a Roca work crew, which is supervised by a Roca staff member. TEP crew members are paid by Roca and work four days a week, with the fifth day reserved for other programming. Crew members are expected to show up, follow orders, complete tasks, and otherwise act appropriately. It is also expected that they will fail. Relapse is built into the program. Participants get high on the job, they swear at their supervisors, they throw weed whackers, they slash tires. They do not show up, and they get fired. But every time someone does not show up or loses control, Roca staff seek them out and debrief. A youth worker asks them what happened and how they might have responded to the situation more appropriately. TEP is designed to reinforce the basic seven executive functioning skills that form the core of Roca's approach to CBT.

It is important to use the words of Director of Roca Baltimore Kurt Palermo, without paraphrase to capture the essence of TEP:

You showed up late. You didn't wear your uniform. You smoked weed at lunch. You told your crew supervisor to go to hell. You whistled at a girl outside the truck. These are actual things that outside of Roca would get a write up, cause you to lose your job, or worse. So, it's critical, while the youth worker and the other staff are building relationships, for the crew supervisor and the employment team to push on them in TEP. Hold them accountable. If you don't hold them accountable, you may as well not even have them there. They need somebody to keep them on task, make sure they're following the rules. It's not about a résumé. It's, can you show up every day, learn the routine of going to work. It's not about learning a particular trade or an advanced employment skill. The first 12 months of TEP is about learning how to show up. Wake up, put your uniform on, go to work, check in, go to the worksite, pick up the trash, mow the lawn, whatever it is. These are fundamental skills that these young people have never had. But underneath it's about emotional regulation and CBT. Can you sustain enough emotional regulation during this very stressful time of employment, all these things are happening in your life, and not blow up your crew supervisor and keep your spot.

Upon completion of the first phase of TEP, young adults are offered three choices. They can work on one of Roca's advanced transitional employment crews, supervised by a Roca team member; they can work for one of the Roca employer partners, still paid through Roca but without a Roca supervisor; or they can seek direct job placement. By this time, many participants will have taken workforce readiness classes to help them prepare a résumé, set up email, and get their identification and other documents in order. After about two years with Roca, most young adults go out on their own, in jobs or to school. Roca maintains the relationship with them, though not as intensely, for an additional two years to support them in sustaining behavior change.

There are no quick fixes, at least not on the path to middle-class wages. We heard this again and again when we spoke to program staff and to community colleges, especially when dealing with individuals who may have limited employment experience or for whom post-secondary education is a family first.

When asked about the applicability of Roca's approach to other populations, staff made the following observation: "Go into the Rite Aid, go into the 7-Eleven, you will see workers behind the register on their phones, swearing at their manager, behaviors that are out of line in the workplace." Why? Because they have not adequately developed the skills to control impulsive behavior. Without these skills, they will continue to be forever behind. "So, what we do is highly applicable to all sorts of training and pre-employment programs."

Herein lies the heart of the design principles that are the subject of this chapter. A fully functioning skilling system must include actors—in the social, public, and private sectors—who address the varying needs of multiple populations. For some individuals, "showing up" is a barrier too high given their readiness to change. For them, relentless outreach and executive skills training shows great promise. Other individuals fall into the category we call aspiring learners; their needs may have more to do with self-confidence or not knowing where to turn for guidance. In whatever stage they enter, the system must accommodate disparities and allocate resources across a spectrum of populations.

New Moms

One of the coauthors of this book, Kate, met New Moms through Social Venture Partners (SVP) Chicago when she coached Jenna Hammond, New Moms's director of development and communications. Hammond had been invited to compete in SVP's annual Fast Pitch challenge. Coaches were paired to work with participating nonprofits to hone a three-minute pitch to a panel of judges and an audience of several hundred people.

Kate visited the New Moms transitional housing facility in the Austin neighborhood of Chicago. Once buzzed through its institutional entrance, she entered a space clearly designed for mothers with young children. With evident pride and a gentle spirit, Hammond took her to see the apartments for young mothers, who constitute a substantial portion of New Moms's clientele. While Kate is no stranger to transitional housing, an important resource provided by YMCAs across the United States and around the world, New Moms's one-bedroom and studio apartments were different. Color block cabinets gave the rooms a child-friendly feel, and unopened boxes of dishes and pots and pans, linens, silverware, and glassware sent a message of respect.

That was in 2018, and this book was nowhere on the horizon. But even then, New Moms captured Kate's attention. First, because New Moms had recently revamped its approach to focus on executive skills functioning using the latest brain science. Second, because the organization partnered with academic centers and leading experts translating theory into practice. And, finally, because the organization was clearly committed to the young mothers in its care.

Meet Tajuor

New Moms did not win Fast Pitch, but they did establish themselves as an organization to watch. Through Hammond, we met New Moms's senior and frontline staff. We also met Tajuor, who participated in both New Moms's family support and its training programs.

When we first speak with Tajuor by phone, it is almost Christmas, and Tajuor is shopping. Somehow, during the early-evening, last-minute fracas she turns her attention to the conversation. The first thing Tajuor says is, "I am the mother of twin boys." And next: "I am currently working as an NA [nurse's assistant or aide], but I am going back to school to get my RN degree."

Tajuor's voice is steady. We ask how she got to New Moms. She responds that she was referred by her Medicaid caseworker, who suggested she reach out to them. Tajuor's voice picks up. She describes being assigned a doula to help her through the last few months of her pregnancy. "My doula was the best," she said. "Her name is Cara and I love her, seriously love her. She helped us through a really tough time. I am so grateful to her."

After she delivered, Tajuor opted to continue her relationship with New Moms and was assigned a family support coach with whom she worked for several years. "It's all based on what you want; what you feel is best for you and your family. Not only do they help you, but they also push you. New Moms makes us do goals every three months. . . . It puts a lot of steps in your life, things to achieve."

And achieve Tajuor did. She graduated high school. She enrolled in and completed New Moms's job training program. She got multiple job offers. She took one that she loves. She set new goals for herself: she wants to save money, get another degree, do more things with her children.

Prior to the first week of New Moms's job training program, eligible mothers attend orientation and participate in interviews to help them decide whether to enroll. Week one of the program includes meetings with staff, engaging with other women in the program, and onboarding. Coaches introduce participants to executive skills (ES), describing what they are and how they impact everyday functioning, and then participants take an executive skills self-assessment.

Weeks two through twelve (all paid) involve working three days a week in Bright Endeavors, New Moms's candle-making social enterprise, and two days a week attending group workshops on everything from parenting to finance. On the production floor, they are assigned to teams based on their self-assessed and observed ES strengths and challenges. During the training phase of the program, the young women receive comprehensive coaching—on the job by production floor coaches, and one-to-one and in groups by life coaches who work with them on their personal and professional goals. Successes and conflicts are addressed in real time, using an ES lens. Job readiness workshops kick in around week six. That's "when you start filling out job applications, working on your résumé, your cover letter, on your elevator pitch," Tajuor tells us.

When we ask Tajuor which of the different components of the job training program had the greatest impact on her, she answers without hesitation, her voice assured: "Executive skills." Tajuor describes what she learned about herself, her strengths and her challenges. She shares how she worked around things that challenged her, like being on time. She talks about how she used executive skills language in job interviews, referring to her professionalism and her organizational, ownership, and teamwork skills. She concludes, "Out of five interviews, I got offers for three. All because of my executive skills. They worked their magic."

As the hour grows late, we imagine Tajuor looking at the time, needing to get home to her children. During the conversation, she has talked about how about her doula and her family support coach pushed her to succeed, how she did not want to let them down, about how good it felt to have somebody on her side, rooting for her. But, bottom line, she concludes: "My kids were my motivation. I had to get my life together. I wanted to be somebody, to set an example that anything is possible. Yeah, I got pregnant, and I didn't finish school but after I had them, I did finish, and I did get a job. So, anything is possible if you set your mind to it."

New Moms's Approach

In 2016, New Moms was invited by the Annie E. Casey (AEC) Foundation to participate in an executive skills coaching pilot designed by Richard Guare and Peg Dawson. The AEC pilot was transformative for New Moms, shifting their mindset and favorably impacting their outcomes. We spoke to multiple members of their frontline and senior staff. To a person, they are evangelical in their belief that executive skills are the base upon which the workforce system of the future must be built. While working on a project with Frontline Focus Institute at the Chicago Jobs Council, Gabrielle Caverl-McNeal, director of workforce development for New Moms created figures 2-1 and 2-2, which capture the staff's views of the workforce system of the future.

New Moms incorporates five key elements, all grounded in behavioral science, into their employment programming. They include environmental modifications, executive skills knowledge, coaching, goal setting, and incentives.

Environmental Modifications

Research from multiple fields has shown that situational factors—that is, factors external to the individual—impact what that individual can or will do. Environmental modifications that remove barriers to action or reduce demands on self-control make it easier for people to

Figure 2-1. **Current Workforce Programs**

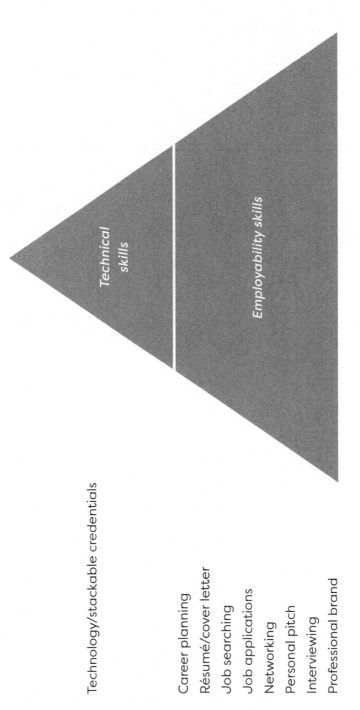

Technology/stackable credentials

Technical skills

Employability skills

Career planning
Résumé/cover letter
Job searching
Job applications
Networking
Personal pitch
Interviewing
Professional brand

Source: Gabrielle Caverl-McNeal and Dana Emanuel, "New Moms: An Executive Skills Approach to Job Training PowerPoint," Chicago Jobs Council, March 11, 2020, https://cjc.net/frontline-focus/workforce-360/.

Figure 2-2. **Future Workforce System**

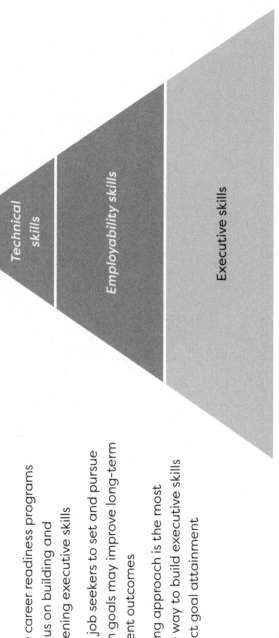

- Technical skills
- Employability skills
- Executive skills

- Effective career readiness programs must focus on building and strengthening executive skills

- Allowing job seekers to set and pursue their own goals may improve long-term emplyment outcomes

- A coaching approach is the most effective way to build executive skills and affect goal attainment

Source: Gabrielle Caverl-McNeal and Dana Emanuel, "New Moms: An Executive Skills Approach to Job Training PowerPoint," Chicago Jobs Council, March 11, 2020, https://cjc.net/frontline-focus/workforce-360/.

complete tasks and achieve goals. For instance, we know that people's actions are influenced by factors like when an intervention is scheduled, or how information is conveyed, or, even, how frequently reminders are sent.[21]

Environmental modification takes many forms. Whether labeled environment modifications or simply called process improvements, program staff from across the organizations we interviewed describe changes they have made to processes as diverse as form filling, scheduling, and seating to make it easier to participate in programming. Indeed, one staffer, when asked what her organization would like to see from local leaders, suggested a "common app" for public benefits.

For New Moms, reducing environmental barriers to success in ways big and small is a near constant exercise. In a tone that suggests it should have been obvious, Melanie Garrett, chief program officer, describes how New Moms streamlined its job training program application process: reducing the questions asked to only those that matter most; reducing the number of visits prospective participants must make to apply; adding a week between program acceptance and onboarding to give participants time to make childcare arrangements; and offering transportation support. With no small amount of exasperation, Garrett notes that many public support processes create unnecessary barriers to participation, almost as if intentionally.

Another staff member shares a simple but powerful example of removing a psychological barrier. "When I first started at New Moms, our participants met in a classroom, with desks reminiscent of high school. If they've been negatively triggered by experiences at school, they're going to walk in and go, oh, Lord, I'm back at school. So, we replaced the desks with conference tables. It changed the tone immediately."

Dana Emanuel, director of learning and innovation, tells us that, in addition to macro level changes to program processes, policies, and infrastructure, "coaches and young moms look for ways they can implement environmental modifications in their own lives."

Which brings us back to Tajuor, who observes that time management is one of her executive skills challenges. She describes her late evening and early morning routine in some detail, and in very telling language. "I use executive skills in my everyday life and in my kids' lives," she says. "Before, I would just get up, just go about the day. Now that I'm working, and the kids are in daycare, I'm putting their clothes out at night. I pack my bag at night. It's like I'm organizing my day for the next day, so I'm not late. It makes my day and my week so much easier." You cannot script this.

Executive Skills Knowledge

Earlier in this chapter, we discussed the role executive functioning plays in individuals' ability to execute tasks, follow rules, control impulses, set goals, and so on. We noted the role adversity sometimes, though not always, plays in ES development, and how it affects individuals' ability to sustain employment. New Moms, like Roca and an emerging group of other workforce development players, operates from the premise that executive functioning can be strengthened, through practice and with coaching, especially in young adulthood.

New Moms groups executive skills into three domains: how we organize (for example, time management, planning/prioritization); how we react (for example, response inhibition, emotional control); and how we get things done (for example, task initiation, sustained attention). Three to five specific skills, including those just named, are identified for each. Everyone in the organization, staff and young moms alike, uses the same nomenclature. Like Tajuor, many participants carry the language with them when they leave the program and enter the world of interviewing and work.

Early in the training program, participants, with their coaches, create individual skills profiles. The profiles identify strengths and challenges. The former includes skills to use to further goals and think through what types of jobs best fit. The latter refers to challenges for which participants need to develop strategies to mitigate behaviors that are unhelpful. Participants know their own profiles, the profiles of other members of their training cohort, and the profiles of staff.

Team members post their skill sets on the walls of the production floor. Like Roca, New Moms uses its training program as a behavior change accelerator. Work teams group participants with complementary skill sets and, when conflict breaks out on the production floor, production coaches use the language of ES to dissect what happened and think through how things might have been better handled.

Coaching and Goal Setting

Goal setting, to quote materials from New Moms, is at the heart of the coaching relationship. With their ES profile in hand, participants work with coaches to set quarterly milestones for themselves, typically in the areas of employment, education, and family well-being. Milestones are backwards mapped, broken into weekly SMART goals and, further, into daily action steps. In weekly one-to-one sessions, participants and coaches set, assess, and track these shorter-term goals and action steps. They analyze whether the goals toward which the young women are working build on their ES strengths. Where they do not, coaches help participants develop strategies to mitigate their ES challenges, arming them with a plan to address obstacles that may arise. Together, coaches and participants celebrate as the women make progress toward their more complex, effortful quarterly milestones. As Garrett describes it, "What am I going to do today, tomorrow or next week that will lead me to the bigger goal?"

New Moms's approach to goal setting builds on what behavioral science tells us about the coaching process and the factors that lead to goal achievement: Participants drive the process, goals are set in a manageable number of domains, small steps encourage forward momentum whereas complex multistep plans discourage it, context matters, and tracking progress is vital. Clearly, it was to Tajuor, who, to this day, continues the practice.

Incentives

In a session for New Moms staff, trainers described New Moms's use of incentives as helping to:

- "Remove barriers to goal achievement and create slack (bus cards).

- Incentivize goal progression to nudge and overcome obstacles or change in context (encouragement, cash).

▪ Reward and celebrate goal achievement success (parties, public acknowledgement)."[22]

Take Risks

Laura Zumdahl, president and CEO of New Moms, is the last person we interview. When we play back the recording of our talk, she seems to speak so rapidly that we check the speed of the Mp4 file of the conversation. But the playback is set to normal speed; rather, it is the animated timbre of Zumdahl's voice that makes it seem as if she is speaking quickly. Zumdahl speaks with a keenness born of synthesis. She and her colleagues are recombining ideas and technologies in new ways. They see possibility, and that is exciting:

> We have to be willing to take risks to get better. We can't be satisfied with the status quo because it's hard to try something new or because we're fearful of it. We have to, as a sector, as an organization, as people, we have to try things and take some risks to really change the game. Because what we've been doing as a society is not working. It's not enough; it's not working. We have got to change that. And that means we have to all be all in all the time and put ourselves out there.

Amen to that.

Roca and New Moms Provide Bold Lessons

Roca and New Moms serve different populations. Roca serves high-risk, justice-system-involved young adults who initially show little to no interest in participating in traditional workforce or education programs. New Moms serves young mothers who, motivated by their children, choose to apply to the program. Nevertheless, both populations have suffered the traumas of poverty and scarcity and their attendant impact on executive functioning. Local leaders would do well to extract lessons from Roca and New Moms when thinking about the necessary attributes of programs designed to build the foundational skills necessary for economic mobility. The two organizations have a number of commonalities.

Understand the Needs of the Populations They Serve

New Moms and Roca have a deep understanding of the populations they serve and have decided to keep their focus narrow, believing, as Zumdahl puts it, that having such a focus:

> Allows us to harness all of our energy as an organization on understanding who that population is, their developmental trajectories, the nuances of the challenges and barriers that they're facing, frankly, the brain science about what's happening in adolescence. It allows us, our whole staff, to be more fluent and educated in that and understand it better. That just doesn't happen when you try and understand the developmental trajectories of all these [different] populations. It allows us to tailor our programs better. It requires a sense of, I think, boundaries and kind of knowing yourself.

Apply Brain and Behavioral Science with a Focus on Executive Functioning

Both organizations recognize that, for some populations, focusing on executive functioning must precede vocational and employment readiness training. "Our job is to get them to the starting line," says Amar Mukunda of Roca Baltimore. He adds:

> Most of our guys when they start off, when it comes to employment, are at the pre-contemplation stage. They are not ready, willing or able to show up every day, be consistent, be professional, communicate well. Our job is to help . . . get [them] to the starting line. When we talk to employers about it . . . it's not about the hard skills that we're teaching them. . . . We are going to take guys who are heavily street-involved and get them to the point where they're able to show up every day, communicate well and be professional.

And once they start with you, we're going to continue to support them, so that any issues that occur, and there definitely will be issues, . . . we can help resolve those and make sure that they don't get out of control.

Use Transitional Employment to Accelerate Behavior Change

Roca and New Moms view transitional employment as a behavioral accelerator as much as anything else. Roca's TEP and New Moms's social enterprise Bright Endeavors create space for young adults to practice work-appropriate behaviors. Both use events that occur on site as stimuli for understanding and rethinking behaviors that are "not helpful," and for celebrating behaviors that are. Additionally, both have requirements for ongoing participation. Roca work crew members can be "fired" (although they are nearly always rehired), and New Moms participants who violate the rules must reapply to the program and, if accepted, start again with a new cohort. In both cases, however, neither Roca nor New Moms youth workers/coaches sever their relationships with the young adults. In fact, both home in on the behavioral issues that resulted in the "termination" to work through and address them.

Eschew Conventional Case Management in Favor of Trusted Coaching Relationships that Privilege Agency

New Moms and Roca emphasize the importance of trusted relationships between coach and participant. For Roca, trust is why participants are willing to try TEP, where they know they will be challenged to address the behaviors that would serve them poorly at work. At New Moms, participants and coaches alike share their ES strengths and challenges, leveling the playing field and allowing skills to frame all conversations, whether about goal setting or conflicts erupting on the production floor. Because Roca's youth workers and New Moms's coaches understand the importance of agency and its favorable impact on goal achievement, they communicate a belief in participants' potential. By contrast, case managers too often position themselves as "experts," whose job is to direct action—not a recipe for success, according to neuropsychology. The structure of goal setting at New Moms and pathway selection at Roca puts choice in the hands of participants.

Accommodate Relapse and Maintain Multiyear Relationships

Behavior change takes time. It is hard work. There are going to be mis-steps and failures. It is not a straight line. Self-regulation, self-efficacy, and motivation "are not built up in traditional case management, or in more didactic training or workshop formats, because they must be repeatedly practiced in order to be built. A large field of academic research on the brain has determined that these skills and mindsets are built up through interaction with others, and that they are built over time; a relatively long-term coaching relationship is the best place to see real growth."[23] Both organizations maintain relationships with participants long after they have completed their programs, checking in periodically and providing support as needed.

Be Open, Challenge Convention, Disseminate

Two other similarities bear mentioning. Both Roca and New Moms apply to themselves the scrutiny they suggest we ask of others. When both organizations were dissatisfied with their outcomes, they found partners; MGH and PRIDE in the case of Roca, and Casey and MRDC in the case of New Moms.

Kate spent the last half of her career in the social sector. During those years, she developed a profound belief in its power to do good. But she also lamented the pace of change and the extent to which the status quo prevails. So often we know what works, or what works better. But too many social-sector intermediaries and local govern-ment agencies labor in relative isolation, doing what they have always done because we do not adequately hold them to account or because we starve them of the resources necessary to free up time to think, learn, and evaluate. It should not be surprising that Roca, New Moms, and EMPath, mentioned earlier in this chapter, willingly share their intellectual property. Roca and EMPath have created formal organizational entities to do so.

MyGoals

As noted at the beginning of this chapter, a fully functioning workforce development system begins with an understanding of the range of skilling needs within its catchment area and supports a variety of actors to address those needs. This requirement must extend to programs run by state and municipal government. After all, New Moms and Roca, as successful as they may be, together serve a fraction of the population for whom executive skill-building may provide an important first step toward economic mobility. A report introducing My-Goals, a demonstration project using executive skills coaching and incentives to improve "self-sufficiency outcomes" such as employment, earnings, mobility, and personal well-being, begins as follows:

> Success in the world of work depends on more than having the capacity to perform technical tasks required for jobs that employers need to fill. Success is also influenced by the strength of one's "executive function" or "executive skills." . . . A growing body of research in neuroscience and cognitive behavioral psychology finds that the stress and chaos of poverty can impair one's executive skills and thereby may impede a person's success in navigating the labor market, acquiring occupational credentials, performing well at a job, and advancing at work.[24]

Recipients of federal housing assistance who either receive housing choice vouchers or live in public housing in Baltimore or Houston have been recruited to participate in this project's pilot. Only those who are unemployed or minimally employed are accepted into the study. MyGoals was designed by MRDC with Richard Guare, who also designed the Annie E. Casey pilot in which New Moms participated. Not surprisingly, MyGoals echoes what we have seen in this chapter and in many of the successful organizations profiled elsewhere in this book.

"MyGoals combines a highly structured coaching model with a

set of financial incentives to support participants in making step-by-step progress toward economic mobility over a three-year period."[25] Participants develop long-term goals in four domains: employment, education and training, finances, and personal and family well-being. While the emphasis is on employment, the pilot recognizes the importance of each of the other domains to employment success. Long-term goals are broken into intermediate milestones, SMART goals, and near-term action steps. Goal setting is participant driven, with coaches providing nondirective guidance.

Executive skills are introduced in the first step of the MyGoals coaching process, at which time participants assess their own skills. They use their understanding of their ES strengths and challenges in the goal-setting process to determine whether their employment goals are a good fit and, conversely, to anticipate where their ES challenges might interfere with goal and task attainment so they can develop strategies to work around them. Financial incentives are tied to participation and include a "getting started" bonus and an ongoing monthly stipend based on engagement. Other elements of the program include market data to help participants with career decisions, financial management training, and referrals to other organizations in the community as needed.

MyGoals was launched in 2017 and continues through 2022, so results are not yet available. Nevertheless, we view programs like MyGoals as necessary. If we are to address economic mobility at scale, we must learn how to translate and disseminate what works in smaller, innovative organizations to other, larger organizations and agencies whose aggregate reach is broad. What forms that translation and dissemination take is increasingly the subject of experimentation and study.

3

Listen, Respond, Get Personal

Frustrated by the lack of effective programs to help mothers on welfare find jobs in Indianapolis, we were excited many years ago to hear Peter Cove and Lee Bowes at a conference explain their successes assisting struggling New York City residents. Considered controversial at the time, their company America Works operated using a pay for performance (PfP) model, in which it would get compensated by the city only if the person needing a job found one and kept it for six months.

Impressed, we invited America Works to Indianapolis. The PfP model appealed to us in a general way, but we noticed something even more consequential in our visits to their offices in Indianapolis and New York. Because America Works received pay for performance, and not pay for rendering any one service, like job counseling, the agency personalized its offerings to the individual needs of its clients. Bowes and Cove's team knew the budget and could spend it in any reasonable way to help a mom overcome problems that stood in her way.

Case workers at other organizations with city and state contracts often complain that their clients need services outside the scope of their government contracts, services they cannot arrange. Essentially, there is a government program for every conceivable issue, but combining and personalizing them ranges from impossible to impractical due to the legal, bureaucratic, and administrative costs involved in securing flexibility.

An effective, equitable workforce development system must, as argued in the previous chapter, address the diverse needs of unemployed and underemployed workers. For some people, that might entail a focus on executive skills functioning so they can meet basic job requirements, such as showing up on time. For others, it may involve employer-sponsored upskilling so they can move into a new role. Populations vary in their skilling needs and vary in their beliefs and circumstances. Understanding what people value and what stands in the way of their acting is critical if we are to increase participation and attachment to skilling programs.

In workforce development, as in industry, tension inevitably exists between standardization and personalization. The former enhances efficiency and scalability; the latter customer acquisition and retention. Successful companies find a balance. In this chapter, we discuss the third of our ten design principles—listen-respond-get personal, or personalization for short(ish)—and its application to the challenges of encouraging greater participation, persistence, and success in skilling programs.

This exploration kicks off with a review of attitudes of working-age Americans to understand how individuals' mindsets impact whether they take the first step necessary for success. We explore how these beliefs shape the needs of prospective learners—needs that a program must address to foster attachment and ensure retention. The chapter closes with examples of organizations that excel at personalizing different stages of participants' journeys.

A Snapshot of the American Worker, or Prospective Worker

What must someone believe to consider further education or training in the first place? What would cause someone who is considering further education or training to act and enroll in a course or training program? What must organizations do to appeal to aspiring learners and to remove the barriers that make participation difficult? The insights drawn from multiple surveys[1] conducted over the years by Strada Education Network help us answer these questions.

Taking the First Step: From Inaction to Consideration

Slightly more than half of nonretired (working and nonworking) adults age eighteen and older have a dim view of their economic prospects (figure 3-1). Seven in ten Americans feel something is holding them back when it comes to getting a good job or advancing their career. Their reasons, shown in figure 3-2, are a sad reflection of both systemic and individual issues felt most acutely by African Americans and Latinxs, young adults and men in particular.

Historically at least, most Americans have believed that more education or training would improve their ability to get a job or to advance at work. Individuals without college degrees, however, are more skeptical than their degreed counterparts. One in four say it would make no difference at all (figure 3-3).

If we want more individuals to consider further education and training, we must listen and respond to their concerns about its value,

Figure 3-1. **Beliefs about Job Prospects**

Half of Americans don't believe a good job is within their reach of that they can advance their careers

Finding a good job is difficult/my opportunities to advance at work are limited.

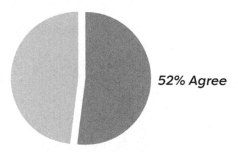

52% Agree

Source: Strada Center, Public Viewpoint Surveys, October 14–29, 2020.

Figure 3-2. **Beliefs about Barriers to Advancement**

Many Americans feel powerless over their ability to get a good job or advance in their career

Thinking about why you may feel your opportunities to advance at work or find a good job may be limited, please rate each of the following for how well they describe your situation

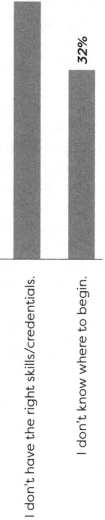
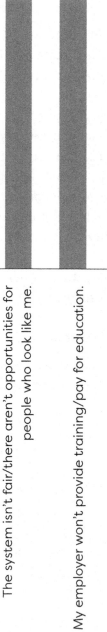

The system isn't fair/there aren't opportunities for people who look like me.	46%
My employer won't provide training/pay for education.	46%
I don't have the right skills/credentials.	44%
I don't know where to begin.	32%

Responses aggregated and include well/very well.

Source: Strada Center, Public Viewpoint Surveys, October 14–29, 2020.

Figure 3-3. **Beliefs about the Value of Education**

Many Americans believe education would give them some advantage, but Americans without college degrees are more skeptical of its value

How would more education or training impact your ability to get a good job and advance at work? More education and training would provide a:

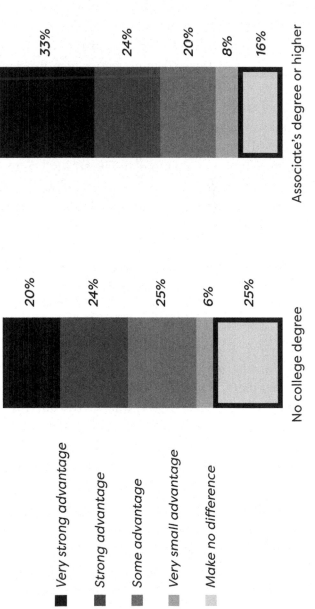

- Very strong advantage
- Strong advantage
- Some advantage
- Very small advantage
- Make no difference

No college degree: 20%, 24%, 25%, 6%, 25%

Associate's degree or higher: 33%, 24%, 20%, 8%, 16%

Source: Strada Center, Public Viewpoint Surveys, October 14–29, 2020.

especially in light of the economic fallout from the pandemic. Just over a third of individuals without a college degree believe one would be worth the cost—compared to 70 percent of their peers who already hold a degree. Over the course of 2020, Americans without college degrees grew increasingly pessimistic about the value of additional education, as the number doubting that it would help them secure a stable job nearly tripled, from 12 to 35 percent.

We asked Dave Clayton, senior vice president of consumer insights, who led Strada's research about this crisis of confidence. His response was sobering: "It is the most concerning thing I have seen in our surveys because it is so widespread. Whether they are current college students, disrupted workers or adults without degrees interested in enrolling, less than one in five strongly agree that education will be worth the cost. At this point, people need to believe there will be immediate career opportunities for them as a result of their education program."

If we want more individuals to consider additional training or education, we must make the case as to the value it confers in terms of job acquisition and advancement.

Understanding What Aspiring Learners Want

Within the working-age population is a segment Strada calls "aspiring learners." These are individuals age twenty-five to forty-four, without a postsecondary degree, who are considering or planning to enroll in further education or training. To move them from consideration to action, we must understand what they want from further education—and what they see standing in the way of enrolling in a program that would meet their needs. For providers and regional workforce collaborations, this understanding provides guidance on how to engage aspiring learners, accommodate their individual circumstances, and help them navigate their choices.

Coming out of high school, most aspiring learners were very interested in more education but delayed it, often because they lacked role models, did not know where to begin, or could not afford it. Their life circumstances and other responsibilities got in the way. Today, especially post-COVID, they need to be convinced that further education will provide a better life and ease their immediate financial needs. While the jump in the importance of taking care of immediate needs may be transitory, it is likely that aspiring learners will continue to give priority to financial considerations (figure 3-4).

What Stands in the Way

Aspiring learners are concerned that they will not be able to balance school and work, afford to pay the cost of education, and/or have the ability to succeed. City officials and service providers need to better understand the critical role self-efficacy plays in an aspiring learner's decisionmaking about more education or training. When a person doubts herself or questions her ability to complete a program or be successful, she will not take the necessary steps. This is evident both in Strada's survey work and in their interviews with aspiring learners.

We listened to interviews with learners conducted by Holly Custard, deputy director of institute partnerships and outreach for Strada Education Network between January 2019 and March 2020. In their words, we hear their doubts—about themselves and about the costs of pursuing further education and training.

We begin with a woman we call Lorena. Lorena dropped out of high school in the eleventh grade and got into trouble. She became pregnant, sold drugs, and found herself in New York City's infamous Riker's Island before ending up in a New York state prison, away from her son. While in prison, she got her GED with honors and, when released, took a job as a receptionist. Lorena's big break came after several years, when she had the following conversation, which led her to community college and a four-year degree on weekends. She now works in criminal justice.

> My boss, he came out one day and pulled me in his office and said, "Where do you see yourself in five years?" . . . He said, "If you're going to move forward, you need to be reading; you need to be doing something." . . . Eventually, I connected to the right person, and he encouraged me to go to a community college. . . . So, I

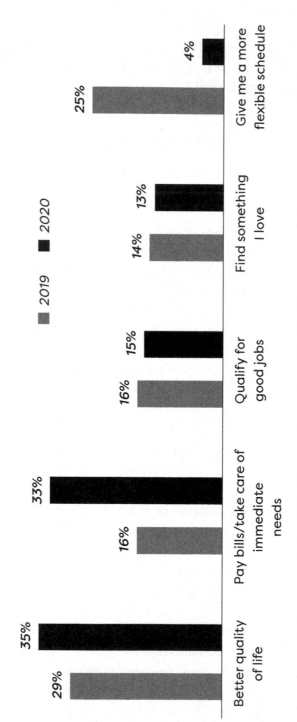

Figure 3-4. **What Individuals without Advanced Degrees Want from Education**

In 2020, adults without degrees are more focused on paying bills and taking care of immediate needs

Thinking about the potential benefits of the additional education you are considering, please rate each of the following benefits based on how important each is to you personally (% most important)

■ 2019 ■ 2020

	Better quality of life	Pay bills/take care of immediate needs	Qualify for good jobs	Find something I love	Give me a more flexible schedule
2019	29%	16%	16%	14%	25%
2020	35%	33%	15%	13%	4%

Online survey with Heart+Mind Strategies August–September 2019. Base: Americans ages 25–44 with no post-secondary degree or credential who are considering enrolling in education, n=1,007.

Source: Strada Center, Public Viewpoint Surveys, August 19–September 3, 2020.

didn't really think I could—that I could read, and study. It turned out, I was great at running classes and doing stuff, but I still can't believe I really have those talents.

Not unexpectedly, many aspiring learners find themselves stymied by financial concerns, including the cost of tuition and other expenses, like transportation or the wages lost while taking classes. We hear these concerns in the words of Crystal, a high school graduate between the ages of twenty-five and thirty-four from the western part of the country, who evaluated her choices in the following way:

Some elements of my future plan to attain education that are important to me are location, cost and length of the course. I would rather do training online because transportation seems to be a common problem in my life. I also would opt for a course that is cheaper or something that I could get a grant to pay for. I am looking for the quickest results, so a shorter course would get more serious consideration from me.

What Would Trigger a Step?

What would cause someone to take the next step? Americans want programs that will help them produce income for day-to-day living. Relevance is the gold standard: How does training or education translate to a higher-quality life? Pragmatism factors into decisionmaking, as well. People want choices, flexibility, and streamlined and stackable options (figure 3-5).[2] They need information about tuition support, financial aid, scholarships, loans, and other income-sustaining options.

Indeed, practical considerations drive many Americans to place less value on whether a program leads to a degree, per se, than whether it helps them get a better job to support their family. Adults eighteen years or older prefer skill training to degrees, as can be seen in figure 3-6. Fielded between April and August 2020, the majority of respondents considering further education or training within the next six months were looking at either skills training or nondegree credential options (certificates, certifications, or licensing).

We wanted to see these various factors through the eyes of a learner,

Figure 3-5. **What would Cause Someone to Take the Next Step**

Americans' preferences for degree or nondegree opportunities are most commonly being driven by relevance

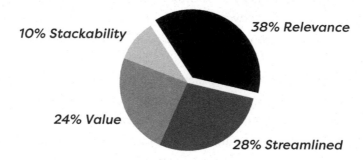

10% Stackability

38% Relevance

24% Value

28% Streamlined

Stackability

- Would lead to additional education or training in the future

Value

- Better value
- More benefit to my job or career advancement

Relevance

- Required in my field of work
- Better fit for my personal needs
- More applied/relevant to my work

Streamlined

- Faster
- Cheaper
- More convenient

Base: adults ages 18 and older, n=225.

Source: Strada Center, Public Viewpoint Survey, August 5–6, 2020.

a young woman we call Ronnie. At age fourteen, she dropped out of high school and soon thereafter became a mother. Ronnie eventually completed her GED and considered college, but her mother dissuaded her, thinking it would be a waste of time. Driven to get a degree but with no clear understanding of her options, Ronnie tried different routes until finally meeting a "coach" when she worked at Head Start. You can feel the confusion and uncertainty in Ronnie's words:

> I don't have other family members that are trying to take this type of pathway. So, it was hard for me to reach out to them because I was getting a lot of negative feedback because I wanted to go back to school in the first place. . . . Just, "why anybody would wanna go to school, it's just a waste of money," like [they were] kind of convincing me to get a trade. . . . So, it was hard for me to find that connection [to advice and support] in my immediate community.

Figure 3-6. **What Types of Training and Education Options Most Appeal Today**

Since the onset of the pandemic, Americans have expressed a consistent preference for nondegree and skills training options

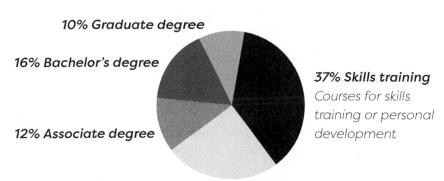

10% Graduate degree

16% Bachelor's degree

37% Skills training
Courses for skills training or personal development

12% Associate degree

25% Nondegree credential
Certificate, certification, or license

Base: adults ages 18 and older, n=5,272.

Source: Strada Center, Public Viewpoint Surveys, April 15–August 6, 2020.

According to Ronnie, the coach who triggered her first step "sat me down and asked me, 'Well, what do I want? What are my goals?' And I recognized that nobody had ever asked me that before, sitting on that side of the table."

Personalized Wayfinding: Navigating Enrollment and Sustaining Participation

While many workers question the value of continuing education and training, they are clear about what they want from it should they decide to enroll: greater financial stability and a better life for themselves and their families. But they have concerns about cost, logistics, and their ability to succeed. They need information and guidance to navigate their options. Apprehensions generated from past experiences help explain why so few enroll in currently available options.

The data surveys and focus groups are eye-opening but not surprising. They illustrate what workers and prospective workers are looking for and, importantly, what programs can do to help them navigate enrollment and sustain participation. It is here that personalization truly kicks in. The personalization practices of leading organizations that address the apprehensions voiced by aspiring learners can be grouped in three general areas:

- Application criteria that allow program officials to determine readiness to participate

- Assessment processes that further a deeper knowledge of the applicant/learner and facilitate the right placement

- Program configuration where coaches provide solutions to needs, such as tuition, wraparound services, and/or other logistical challenges.

We delve into these practices throughout the book because they are building blocks of the program-level design principles upon which a more equitable and effective skilling system depends. In the examples that follow, we look at organizations that use application criteria to determine tightness of fit and others that assign individuals to program tracks or interventions based on in-depth intake assessments.

We also look at the role coaches play in bolstering self-confidence by providing individualized learning and "life needs" supports. Taken together, these practices have a formidable compounding effect. By ensuring programs are the right match for an individual, by assigning learners to tracks or interventions appropriate to their preparedness, and by addressing the personal issues that impede participation and learning, organizations create conditions for success, reducing rather than reinforcing self-doubt.

Application: Tightness of Fit

Many organizations rely on their application processes to assess learners, not just on capabilities but also on whether they are ready, willing, and able to participate given the skilling content and time commitment required of them. Where the fit is poor, participants are not likely to succeed, with each failure aggravating the feelings of inadequacy that research shows are all too prevalent.

i.c.stars, Pursuit, and Year Up are sectoral skilling programs. i.c.stars and Pursuit concentrate on the tech sector; Year Up focuses on tech as well as several other sectors. Their application criteria are strikingly similar. Each requires that applicants have a high school degree or GED, be at least eighteen years old, and not exceed an income threshold. Importantly, they require candidates to be "available to attend internship 8AM–8PM, Monday–Friday for 16 weeks" (i.c.stars) or "committed to participating for the full length of the Fellowship" (Pursuit) or "available five days a week (M–F) for the full year of the program" (Year Up).

Even though these organizations provide stipends, direct resources, and referrals to resources, they recognize that every applicant's situation is unique. Personal challenges that go beyond the program's ability to address make participation difficult for potential attendees. Listening, responding, and personalizing in these instances may mean postponing enrollment while aspiring learners address the logistical barriers they face, or it may lead to placement in programs where success is more likely, or at least not problematic, from the outset.

Pathways for Advancing Careers and Education (PACE) is a

multisite project evaluating the effectiveness of employment and self-sufficiency strategies funded by the Department of Health and Human Services' Office of Planning, Research, and Evaluation. Abt Associates, conducting an evaluation for PACE, describes Year Up's approach this way:

> Year Up undertakes a comprehensive assessment of its students' academic and nonacademic strengths and barriers. . . . The majority of applicants move . . . [after completing their application] to a one-on-one interview with program staff. The interview provides another opportunity for staff to assess applicants' strengths, motivation, career interests, reasons for applying to the program, and any barriers that might present challenges for their performance and persistence in the program. Identification of most barriers does not automatically render an applicant ineligible; rather, this process assists staff in determining whether, with available Year Up support, the applicant is likely to be able to meet the demands of the program. As part of the interview, staff may inquire whether the individual has stable housing, a reliable childcare plan, and a transportation plan, among other factors perceived to support program participation. In some instances, applicants may work with the program's student services or academic staff to address areas of concerns before the program will make an eligibility decision. . . . Individuals who are not admitted are provided with feedback as to how they might improve their application for a subsequent cycle (e.g., steps to address barriers to participation, additional exploration to determine if the program is a good fit for their career interests).[3]

Failure breeds failure. While some are failures of personal responsibility, as some politicians claim, many more are failures of circumstance. For many people, the obstacles they face make program completion extremely challenging. Personalized matching based on individual needs and circumstances addresses the problems inherent in a one-size-fits-all system. An effective workforce system recognizes the diverse skilling needs and lived experiences of those it is designed to serve. A well-designed response accommodates disparities by bringing together multiple organizations that work in concert, focusing on different segments within the population.

Assess: Starting on the Right Path

Multitrack organizations use their intake-assessment processes to assign participants to the paths most appropriate for their goals, establish realistic expectations, and identify barriers that may adversely impact success.

Capital IDEA

Capital IDEA is now more than twenty years old and evolved from the shared vision of the local business community and Austin Interfaith, a multiethnic group of public schools, faith-based organizations, and unions. Capital IDEA underwrites the cost of postsecondary tuition, books, and fees for aspiring leaners interested in obtaining an associate's degree or its equivalent in select industries with living-wage jobs.

The agency provides resources such as childcare, transportation, and emergency assistance. Participants are paired with "career navigators" who support them on their academic journey. Applicants must be eighteen years or older, qualify as low income, have a high school degree or GED—and be willing to commit to full-time school.

Executive Director Steve Jackobs has been with Capital IDEA since its founding in 1998. During one of our visits with him, we asked him what makes his organization so effective. He spoke of its in-depth knowledge of the labor market, ongoing commitment to its students, and meticulous vetting and onboarding process.

Most individuals apply to Capital IDEA with a particular career in mind. As part of their application, Capital IDEA takes them through a preliminary "career exploration" review. Key to this step is matching the applicant's expectations with the career track they have chosen. Once applicants affirm their desired area of study, Capital IDEA begins its in-depth assessment process. This includes:

- Verification of a GED or high school diploma. When an applicant has neither, Capital IDEA refers them to an organization where they can obtain one.

- A personal budget review process. Although Capital IDEA provides funding to cover training and related costs, applicants must demonstrate that they can cover basic, month-to-month living expenses before being admitted.

- A three-hour career profile assessment that evaluates temperament, learning style, math and reading proficiency, and other related areas. This allows Capital IDEA to identify early on if someone has chosen a degree path unlikely to lead to success, or to determine whether an applicant needs further training prior to entering a postsecondary program.

Individuals who have a high school diploma or equivalent but do not demonstrate a high school level of reading and math proficiency are referred to an intensive twelve-week academy run by Capital IDEA and modeled after a similar Air Force program.

After the assessment process, candidates are either admitted or told they should come back at a later time. No one is rejected outright. Those who make it through the vetting process must take one final step, which Jackobs describes as, "probably our secret sauce." In a thirty-minute "affirm your commitment" meeting with staff, participants agree they will communicate frequently and openly, commit a high degree of effort to the program, and give back to the community upon completion. In return, staff affirm their commitment to the participants. They promise to cover all training-related expenses that come up and to partner in resolving personal and programmatic complications that arise along the way.

Jewish Vocational Services

Mark Elliott, president of Economic Mobility Corporation, believes that Jewish Vocational Services's English for Advancement (EfA) program is the first adult education program for English-language learners that has shown statistically significant employment and earnings impacts. In a recent interview published by Arnold Ventures, Elliott said that "JVS' relationships with employers open doors for people that I don't think would be possible otherwise."[4] EfA is one of many programs JVS offers. Others include sectoral training, job placement, financial coaching and education, refugee and immigrant services, and services for employers. A later chapter focuses on how JVS uses its English-language classes as a vehicle for advancing students' economic mobility.

Prospective students have multiple avenues through JVS. They all begin with the same first step: assessment. In EfA, assessment starts with a discussion of applicants' career aspirations, what type of work they have done and want to do, as well as their skills and education level. The process includes an evaluation of prospective students' English-language proficiency and a candid conversation about their personal circumstances.

This highly individualized approach allows JVS to assign students to the appropriate level English class. It also allows staff to identify the barriers that may impact a student's ability to participate. And it allows staff to set expectations for what students can accomplish and in what time frame, given their speaking ability and career aspirations.

If someone comes in hoping for a specific job—one they may have had before they immigrated to the United States—but their English-language skills won't permit it, staff have a frank conversation about realistic expectations and how to plot a viable path to their end goal. "It's a partnership, and we don't want to set people up for failure. That's crushing," one said. "We've seen too many come in after having wasted time in another program. We're not saying this is out of reach for you, we're saying that by joining this program, this is what we can help you with right now."

In striking a balance between aspirations and expectations, JVS simultaneously helps students achieve their goals and maintain their sense of self and self-confidence. The combination of supports and customization of responses can happen only one-on-one. A JVS staff member describes the situation in the following way:

This very often happens for immigrants in the healthcare setting, people who were nurses and doctors in their home countries. Their English is limited, and so they're not going to be able to do that

here, not yet. It's very hard for them to think about doing direct pa-
tient care (hygiene, feeding, etc.) . . . I say to them, "What's going
to make you happy? I'd love to help you get there. But first we need
to improve your English skills."

Amy Nishman, senior vice president of strategy and one of the
architects of EfA, explains why the agency modified its assessment
process to delve into people's personal lives and determine the right
intervention for the right person at the right time in their lives:

> When I looked back at the enrollment process for our skills train-
> ing programs, I saw that we were losing students who ended up
> having some life event that we didn't know about. How much did
> we ask in the beginning about their childcare situation, their hous-
> ing situation? And it turns out, we weren't asking those things,
> or we were only asking them as yes or no questions, like do you
> have a place to live? Yes or no. And do you have childcare? Yes or
> no. And then things would fall apart. So, we began asking more
> in-depth, open-ended questions, like tell me about your living sit-
> uation. When an applicant is also a parent, we ask them to show
> us their childcare plan. With a more in-depth conversation, we're
> able to understand what the student's real situation is.

Program Configuration

The next step in the personalization process involves configuring the
services necessary to remove the barriers that typically stand in the
way of enrollment and program participation.

CUNY ASAP

In April 2020, just as U.S. cities began to feel the effects of COVID,
Harvard's Kennedy School presented its much-acclaimed Innovations
in American Government Award to City University of New York's Accelerated Study in Associate Programs (ASAP). Harvard rarely highlights a thirteen-year-old program such as ASAP with its Innovations
recognition, but what drew the judges to CUNY's program, which has
benefited 60,000 individuals, was the way it personalizes services to

help students overcome the multiple barriers they face—and how it does so at scale.

How does a program as large as ASAP personalize support to the thousands of students enrolled at any one time? How does it help predominantly first-generation college goers, most of whom have been out of school for years or whose prior experience in school left much to be desired? It assigns every ASAP student an adviser. Advisers act as conduits to those things that can be personalized based on need—resource referrals, academic guidance, tutoring, emotional support, career development assistance. And they explain those things that cannot be personalized—prerequisites, degree requirements, course assignments.

We met several times through the COVID-imposed filter of online conversations with Donna Linderman, the associate vice chancellor for academic affairs and the leader of ASAP for most of the past decade. We asked about the program's success and to what extent it "got personal." We found her comments about the roles of advisers to be particularly insightful:

> The program is highly personalized. The central relationship is between the advisor and the ASAP student. Every student that comes into the program works with one assigned advisor who stays with them from start to finish and really gets to know that student—not just as the person sitting at my desk a couple of times a month, but to understand what some of the barriers or issues that a student faces as they're moving through their CUNY degree. By establishing rapport and a close relationship, the students are much more forthcoming about the challenges affecting them. If a student has a job but there are issues balancing that job with full-time school and childcare, we try to help. Because they've established a relationship with their ASAP advisor, they can have an open conversation leading to such possible advice as, "Let's see if we could find you a job here on campus, or closer to home, or closer to your child's school." Sometimes the issues are sensitive, like, "I'm having trouble talking to a faculty member." Or "If Jose Louis is my advisor, and I feel close to him and I trust him, [and] if he coaches me on how to talk to that faculty member, I'm more inclined to do it."

These personalized relationships motivate students because they feel like "somebody hears them," Glenda Wallace, associate director of ASAP at CUNY's Medgar Evers College, told us. These relationships, coupled with the financial support students receive, are critical to their progress and persistence. The Harvard expert who judged ASAP for the Innovations Award wrote: "The program operates from an abundance rather than a deficit mindset." This "abundance" approach helps students overcome the confidence barrier by understanding their unique needs and circumstances and then addressing those needs on a personal level.

Personalized Learning Approaches—The Role of Technology

Personalization is expensive. Even ASAP's comprehensive model requires substantial funding from the mayor's office. Yet, new technologies, such as augmented reality and hybrid online and in-person teaching models, provide an avenue to affordable training. The flexibility associated with these technologies allows them to be combined with a variety of different types of skills and stackable certifications. The result: a more creative, customizable blending of components. Educators can tailor their teaching to the student's preferred eventual occupation, as well as when and where this teaching is received. Susan Patrick, an expert in education technology, addressed this issue in an article on K–12 pedagogy a few years ago:

> Personalization allows students to take ownership of their learning, giving them the opportunity to feel valued, motivated, in control. It also changes the dynamic between the teacher and the student. Personalized pathways bridge informal and formal learning; it doesn't matter where or when students learn, but when they bring the knowledge to be assessed, the system has a way of being ready to assess and credential all learned knowledge, from inside and outside the school."[5]

These technologies allow a straight-line connection between workplace and classroom, and they facilitate personalized learning. Instructors can more closely manage a student's progress with data-driven recommendations on helpful new content. Students, in turn, receive more relevant training.

Beau Pollock, president of Trio Electric, a Houston electrical contractor, tells us he had to build out a classroom that looked like a worksite to make his company's training more worthwhile and entice prospective apprentices. It was a costly but necessary investment for which technology may increasingly provide a substitute.

We thought of Pollock when Purdue Mechanical Engineering professor Karthik Ramani and his colleague Josh Plue told us about their National Science Foundation grant to apply augmented reality to workforce training. Their approach should allow for greater personalization and create opportunities for hands-on experiences, but less expensively and for more individuals than Pollock can reach.

Ramani underscores the potential of technology-aided training. "One of the best ways to transfer hands-on skills is through the traditional one-on-one apprenticeship model," he says. "However, it is costly and not scalable. Workforce education in manufacturing has traditionally been low-tech, relying on in-person teaching sessions, one-on-one apprenticeship, written manuals, and perhaps a video."

In his effort to extend technology-enabled training, Ramani has formed partnerships in areas such as welding, and he has begun experimenting with offering workshops for minority students on the South Side of Chicago. He concludes with the observation: "Our strategy is to augment what's available and figure out the means to train people quickly for industry-specific work, so that the companies themselves reduce the cost of training workers. The traditional one-on-one is transformed to one-to-many for customized training at higher scale."

Plue is using augmented and virtual reality to teach young men and women in a rural Indiana county the skills necessary to fill open and critical electrical jobs, in what may prove to be an evolution of Pollock's physical classroom.

Personalized Self-Service

So far, we have discussed the important ways in which organizations configure service delivery around the learner. Another approach involves developing or making available tools to help that learner make better decisions on his or her own behalf. The need for this information is underscored by research showing that fewer than one in three adults without a post-secondary degree say they have a good understanding of career and education pathways.[6] Most need information on the skills that different jobs require. They want data on how much these jobs pay. They need to know where they can find the courses and training programs that will help them acquire the skills they hope to develop.

The material they seek must be communicated in ways that are both easy to access and easy to understand. Without better information, learners will continue to find it difficult to configure the solution that works best for them. Unfortunately, most workforce systems do a poor job of making job and skilling information available in a useful form. In chapter 8, we address the question of how the market can provide better data to learners for purposes of decisionmaking. Both the quality and the presentation of the data matter. Workers, by themselves or with the help of a navigator, should be able to personalize their decisions with the aid of reliable information on the likelihood that a specific program will lead to a particular job for "people like me."

Understanding

To sum this up, we return to Dave Clayton, senior vice president of consumer insights for Strada Education Network. He knows the survey data on the American workforce inside and out.

> When people believe in a big idea but don't take personal action, it tells you that the devil is in the details. People need greater clarity and confidence on the details. We must give them a clear sight line between education and work outcomes. We must answer their questions. Will a local employer really hire me with a spe-

cific credential in six weeks or six months? Can I be a successful student? How will I pay my bills, care for my children, stay sane? How do I choose the program that is right for me?

The design principle of listen, respond, get personal, sits at the heart of Clayton's comments. At the aggregate level, we must understand what people believe about the value of education to move them from inaction to consideration. We must understand what they need to know to allay their fears and overcome their material concerns to move them from consideration to action. For program providers, personalization applies across functions, processes, and stages of engagement. It includes how organizations assess and place individuals, how they guide participants through their options, and how they support learners and help remove the barriers that make participation and completion challenging. Personalization does not mean that everything must be provided by a single organization. But it does require cross-sector collaboration to ensure that the information that facilitates personalization as well as the necessary array of supports are available in the region. Without listening and responding to what workers and prospective workers tell us, we cannot hope to construct a system that works better for them.

4

Support Learners, Remove Barriers

Even enthusiastic aspiring workers face logistical and psychological hurdles that adversely impact their ability to participate in programs and opportunities. In this chapter, we highlight the multiple ways in which exemplary organizations work with individuals to overcome the simultaneously profound and mundane hurdles that challenge their participation and completion. We look at how organizations, through a combination of direct supports, referrals, and coaching, help learners navigate their way through the often unfamiliar territory of postsecondary education and training. We also look at how these same organizations work with participants on career preparedness and job placement. Support and coaching, as program leaders themselves attest, are necessary, if not sufficient, drivers of program outcomes and the fourth of our ten design principles.

Even as we highlight the necessary work of high performing organizations that help individuals overcome barriers of racial bias, poor transportation, unaffordable childcare, housing insecurity, lack of access to understandable employment and training information, we recognize these obstacles also operate at the systems level, affecting entire populations growing up in poverty. Even if organizations can help learners overcome some of these barriers on an individual basis, that does not relieve local leaders of the need to address them at a community level. After all, what we identify here as a barrier blocking the way of an aspiring worker generally afflicts most low-income families and their neighbors.

Table Stakes

When we began research for this book, we set a challenging bar for choosing which programs to profile. We looked at only those organizations whose work had been evaluated by third parties and had been shown to deliver specific outcomes. We hoped that, by understanding the key factors driving their success, we could extract principles applicable to the design of a more effective regional workforce system. The design principles we developed frame this book. We also thought we might uncover some secret sauce heretofore undiscovered; of course, that turned out to be overly ambitious. What we did find, however, was that the best organizations operationalize common program elements in an exceptional manner. Coaching helps students solve financial and social challenges, navigate unfamiliar institutions, and secure necessary wraparound services.

Financial support comes in many forms: no charge for program participation, tuition and fee waivers, book and uniform allowances, stipends to help full-time learners offset lost income or the ancillary costs associated with attendance. Transportation support is always high on the list. Some organizations provide program participants with bus cards; some offer transportation stipends, sometimes as an incentive and sometimes as a matter of course. Because access to childcare frequently constitutes a barrier to participation, most organizations refer participants to childcare providers. Others help with registration. One organization with which we spoke builds in time between program acceptance and start date to allow participants to arrange childcare on their own. While the subsidies vary, they share a common goal: to reduce the barriers that stand in the way of participation and completion. Subsidies address the concerns of working-age Americans and aspiring learners who cite cost as one of the chief obstacles to their enrolling in further education or training.

In addition to transportation and childcare, most organizations maintain comprehensive referral networks in domains such as housing, health, mental health, finances, and domestic abuse prevention. Delivery methods are tailored in a variety of ways to the population served and the underlying philosophy of the organization. Boston's EMPath produces high-quality results by providing referrals. EMPath believes that the participants' follow-through builds their task completion capacity. Other organizations provide on-site social workers or case managers who take an active role in the process of connecting participants with resources. Still other organizations have on-site domain experts, such as financial advisers, who provide services directly to participants. In all cases, coaches play a variety of critical roles helping participants overcome barriers, large and small, tangible and intangible.

An Aside about "Coaches"

Nomenclature confusion reigns when it comes to the term "coach," so a brief aside is useful. Called coaches, life coaches, career coaches, advisers, navigators, career navigators, or mentors, organizations use a variety of titles to refer to staff members who help individuals overcome the immediate barriers that affect participation, as well as the systemic barriers that adversely impact their prospects. We make the following functional distinctions. Participant-driven goal coaching focuses on individuals' life goals and the actions necessary to achieve them. General coaching is designed to help learners navigate the challenges that make program participation and completion difficult. Career-related coaching focuses on pathways, preparedness, and placement. Not all organizations provide all types of coaching, nor are the divisions among the functions hard and fast. One coach may act in a single or in multiple capacities. The only distinction that holds across organizations is that career placement is typically considered a specialized function.

CUNY ASAP Sets the Standard for
Removing Barriers to Completion

Community college completion rates are notoriously low, even accounting for oddities in how the data are reported—in some places transfers to four-year colleges are considered "dropouts." The statistics are not surprising. Community colleges disproportionately serve students who are first-generation, have limited resources, or may need to work while in school; and for whom childcare and transportation, not to mention tuition and money for supplies, are challenges. These are some of the same individuals for whom we propose the skilling system needs to be retooled.

Among the ranks of community college initiatives, CUNY ASAP stands out. A study conducted in 2015 by MDRC, an organization that designs, evaluates, and provides technical assistance to organizations and policymakers, found that ASAP students graduate at more than double the rate of non-ASAP students, and that these results hold across all eight cohorts that have participated in the program as well as subgroups within each cohort. According to the study's authors, "ASAP's effects are the largest MDRC has found in any of its evaluations of community college reforms. The model offers a highly promising strategy to markedly accelerate credit accumulation and increase graduation rates among educationally and economically disadvantaged populations."[1]

We profile ASAP here for two reasons. First, because community colleges are an important part of the economic mobility equation in a fully developed workforce system. And second, because programs like ASAP furnish an instructive model for how to help students and, by extension, individuals in other programs, most effectively overcome the barriers that stand in the way of participation and completion.

From the Mouths of Pre-Teens

When we first meet, Johnny is at home on Zoom. His granddaughter pops into the frame periodically throughout the conversation. Each time she does, he patiently and successfully distracts her. As grandparents, we are impressed; as researchers, too. We have heard something of Johnny's story from ASAP leadership. He got his GED, then an associate's degree (LaGuardia Community College), then a bachelor's (New York University), then a master's in organizational leadership at CUNY Herbert H. Lehman College, where he is now an academic adviser.

We ask Johnny about his life before ASAP. He shares his story. He dropped out of high school, went to work, became a father. Johnny recounts a conversation with his son, a pre-teen at the time. "I want to be just like you," his son announced. Ordinarily, Johnny says, those are precisely the words a father wants to hear. Not so with him, at least at the time. His son told him, "I don't think I'm gonna finish high school because you didn't." Johnny stepped back, horrified—his description, not ours. His son believed his father to be a success. What his son did not realize is that "behind the scenes, I was working 70 to 80 hours a week. I had no security; I had nothing to fall back on." Johnny's tone shifts. "I ran to school; I didn't want him to follow in my footsteps." Johnny registered for GED classes. That "was supposed to be the end of it." Turns out, it was just the beginning.

"A Three-Pronged Safety Net"

Donna Linderman, associate vice chancellor for academic affairs at CUNY, previously served as university dean for Student Success Initiatives and ASAP executive director, a position that now reports to her. In our conversations, she describes the components of ASAP's program as being "a three-pronged safety net that wraps around every student we bring into the program." If that sounds even slightly paternalistic, trust us, nothing could be further from the truth.

As Linderman put it, more than once, "The university's core mission is upward mobility. We do that through educational attainment and helping students get the skills to realize their potential." When asked to describe their students, she says, "Overwhelmingly, our students see themselves as degree-seeking and future-degree-earning students. They have high aspirations for themselves. . . . They care deeply about their families and their communities. . . . Thirteen years into the program, I continue to be impressed by their . . . tenacity, their intelligence, their passion for education." Johnny fits this bill.

The three core components of ASAP's program include financial scaffolding, academic guidance and support, and what ASAP refers to as its "connected community."

Come for the Financial Help, Stay for the Rest

As Linderman describes it, ASAP's goal is to remove barriers. They offer financial supports to help students "gain and maintain academic momentum" and, critically, to help them attend and stay in school full time. Supports include textbook assistance, transit cards, and tuition waivers for students whose costs are not fully covered by financial aid. These help students overcome real barriers that would otherwise make participation and completion a very steep climb.

According to Johnny, they serve another purpose, as well: "They open the door and shine a light on the ASAP program," he says. "It's what made me want to follow up. I was going to get this free Metro-Card. Once I was in the door, and I saw the other resources, that's what kept me there." Although ASAP does not use this precise terminology, the concept of "environmental modifications" discussed in chapter 2 is embedded throughout their approach. In the case of Metro cards, the simple act of offering transportation assistance removes both a tangible barrier and a mental impediment to forward momentum.

For CUNY, though, financial supports include more than just those directly associated with the program itself. They include helping the students access internships, research, and other credential opportunities. To a significant degree, Linderman's pride in ASAP rests on how it helps CUNY achieve its mission of moving large numbers of students to the middle class. To accomplish that objective and help graduates get jobs with family-sustaining wages requires "at least one internship on their résumé and, ideally, [that] they have a micro credential or a certificate, so it's a degree-plus," she believes. Attention to these connections serves a vital role, underscoring the fact that even a program as comprehensive as ASAP depends on cross-sector collaboration among other funders, providers, and employers.

Advising

The central goal of ASAP's academic and advising supports is to ensure that students move through their degree programs in a timely manner. From day one (figuratively speaking), students are assigned an adviser who sticks with them throughout the program. Advisers assist with academic scheduling and planning, help students navigate an unfamiliar world, and coach students on how to have conversations with faculty members, advocate for themselves, and view tutoring as a plus, not a stigma.

Advisers also help students think through their long-term goals and develop strategies for achieving those goals. These are trusted relationships—the kind that create the space for students to grow. Linderman calls advising "the heart and soul of ASAP. Over and over, we hear students talk about how their adviser becomes a cheerleader, a family member, someone who will give them tough love if need be. Someone who will encourage them."

In addition to "intrusive advising," coaches sometimes find themselves helping students overcome more personal barriers because, after all, as Johnny says, "Life gets in the way." Advisers assist in arranging other supports that might include access to childcare, a job closer to home to avoid a long bus ride, or help understanding other assistance programs. Because of the connection between advisee and adviser, Johnny says, "I never felt like I was rushed out of the office and never felt like I was just a number. That's what kept me coming back. I had my spot on the second floor and was able to talk to my adviser. Even if it was just to check in just to see if everything was OK. There was always somebody that really, really helped me feel comfortable." When he needed help because his mother was sick, he felt comfortable asking for advice on resources and a place where he could study without distraction.

Peer Supports: ASAP's Connected Community

The final, critical component of ASAP, upon which its success rests more than any other factor, is the connected community it facilitates for students. By formally designing engagement opportunities for them, ASAP structures occasions for its participants to come together, meet one another, program staff, and faculty, and to understand the options on their college campus. For example, CUNY promotes a connected community by "block scheduling" first-year courses, which enables participants to take classes with fellow ASAP students. Johnny relates the critical importance of his peers:

> It's like the old saying goes, "Show me who you hang out with and I'll show you the type of person that you are." Being with these individuals pushed me forward. Cohorts are a bridge. At first, I felt like I was going to get lost in the shuffle. But if you remove that doubt, all of these feelings of community help bridge that gap, because you don't want to do it alone. I know students who do try to learn on an island. It never works out. I've always said my most valuable resource besides ASAP staff and resources was literally students who had the same issues as me. And we spoke the same language.

Peers learn by exchanging shared experiences. They see how others with similar backgrounds deal with both day-to-day tasks and bumps in the road. They observe their friends processing similar issues, which helps all of them gain insight. These interactions complement advising and come in many forms, from formal sessions to informal exchanges. ASAP, in addition to all the other services it provides, carefully configures a strong foundation for peers to gain insights and confidence from each other.

ASAP's use of data powers its success in everything it does, including execution of its three-pronged safety net. The program uses data to preempt problems, intervene proactively, advise students, and evaluate outcomes. By relying on data to manage the program, ASAP can evolve as it learns more about what its students need to be successful.

A few examples make these points come alive. ASAP collects data on actual and attempted credits, earned GPA, retention, adviser-meeting attendance, use of tutors, collection of transit cards, and participation in ancillary services. It uses the data to create, and measure progress against, benchmarks.

By looking at patterns over time, ASAP has developed an early warning system that answers questions like, Did so-and-so meet with her adviser? or Did he pick up his metro card? Advisers reach out to students not hitting benchmarks, preempting problems before they become crises. Data and evaluation are the foundation of ASAP's continuous improvement. For instance, ASAP has evolved the role of its career and employment specialists as they have better come to understand the aspirations of their students. Specialists no longer focus as much on career placement, for example, as most students want a four-year degree. Now they help students think through their long-term career aspirations and the best path for achieving those goals.

We ask Linderman to tell us which components of the ASAP program are most critical. She compares the solution to a Jenga game—the comprehensiveness of the program provides the key to its success. She worries, "If you pull one component out as more or less important, the whole thing may fall." We ask again, pressing Linderman to be more specific about the secret sauce of the program. Her coy deflection reveals much about the program: "You should talk to our participants." So, let's take one more look at how ASAP supports learners with a particular focus on some of the more subtle ways it helped Johnny.

Taking the First Step

Johnny brought his history, his motivations, and his doubts to CUNY, just as all of us do with whatever new engagement we consider. Many of the successful programs we feature begin with outreach to a prospective learner to get them to enroll—to overcome their disinclination or confidence gap. When CUNY adviser Talia Castillo presented to Johnny's GED class at LaGuardia Community College, she explained ASAP's financial benefits and how they are bundled together and coordinated with personal advising. That prompted Johnny to tap into the part of himself that wanted more. When he first enrolled in LaGuardia's GED, he had no intention of going further. He thought he had too many responsibilities, that he was too old. But as he observed:

> Putting everything under the ASAP umbrella made it quite appealing. Here's this program that really removes a lot of the obsta-

cles that were in the way. I transitioned into the ASAP program at LaGuardia—they made the transition seamless. They helped out with the paperwork; they helped me sign up for financial aid. I literally had no issues transitioning over. And those same services helped me excel when I was in the program because I didn't have to worry about getting to school, getting to work, [or getting] textbooks, and I built a real relationship with my adviser.

This is another example of how ASAP modifies the environment, and, in this case, organizational processes, to remove barriers to participation and completion.

Even after succeeding at CUNY's two-year program, Johnny harbored doubts. He went to the transfer services office with a friend who wanted to explore nursing programs. The transfer adviser asked, "What about you?" Johnny told her he had a 3.9 GPA but no money and could not afford to go to NYU for a four-year degree. The transfer adviser told him about a community-college transfer program that came with paid tuition. "I applied, and I got it. That was an experience." ASAP opened a new world for Johnny. It helped him see himself as capable in academia. He knew he was good at his job, but school was different. ASAP gave him confidence; as he sat side-by-side with other students, he realized, "I, too, have some intelligence." His confidence mirrors the strong belief ASAP has in its students and the asset development advisement model they deploy.

Between his bachelor's and his master's programs, Johnny did outreach for the Fatherhood Academy. Now he is an academic adviser at Lehman College, which is part of CUNY. When asked what local leaders should do to support learners or programs like ASAP, Johnny offers the following: Too often, institutions aren't even aware of the array of programs that would benefit their clientele. He counsels leaders to take their programs on tour to make connections. Hold sessions in public housing and probation and public assistance offices. Information and outreach must go beyond an ad on the side of a bus. Talk to people and help them understand their options. Do not always go for the quick fix. Do not ignore adult learners. As Johnny puts it:

I know that everybody wants to take the low-hanging fruit, which are the high school students, and help them transition to school. But there's an untapped market out there. And if you really make it appealing to these adult learners, nobody wants to spend their lives without a bachelor's degree. A lot of individuals will take convincing because they don't see the need or the value until after they are enrolled. I was one of those.

So Many Stories Unwritten

There is no question that Johnny always had it in him to succeed. In our conversation, he confessed to having been "a very good student" as a child, of being told he was the smartest person in the room. His bosses at the limousine company were encouraging; he carried a GED course catalogue around in his backpack well before enrolling. But he dropped out of high school, feeling himself drawn to work rather than to education. He got caught up in life. He needed something to take him out of his comfort zone. A conversation with his son "sparked" his journey, and ASAP resources made it possible for him to bring that journey to fruition. This is not to take anything away from Johnny: he is bright, capable, driven, but we suspect he is not alone.

Too many community college students enroll without a clear sense of what is required to earn a degree in a timely manner. Too often, they lack the resources they need to support themselves and their families while they are in school. They lack access to consistent, high-quality advice to guide them. Schools require many students to take developmental education courses in reading, writing, and/or math, courses that do not count toward degree requirements and that, in and of themselves, produce obstacles as students struggle to gain and maintain academic momentum. Students frequently exhaust their financial aid before completing the necessary credits required for degree completion.

As a result, many do not persist, and degree attainment remains elusive. According to ASAP officials, although U.S. community colleges enroll more than 7 million students, only 20 percent of first-time full-time degree-seeking students earn a certificate or associate's degree within three years of entry. ASAP prides itself on doubling the completion rate of its students.[2]

We chose to profile ASAP because it embodies foundational principles in the design of a more equitable workforce skilling system. Intermediaries, whether academic, public, nonprofit, or private, must be cognizant of the many barriers that stand between individuals and opportunity. And so, they must consider how best to mitigate the effects of those barriers, either directly as a building block of programs or by ensuring cooperation across providers.

———————

In cities across the country, there are millions of learners like Johnny from challenged neighborhoods for whom two- and four-year college success would be more attainable with ASAP's model of integrated supports and academic and life coaching. Just as those students with ASAP, these individuals would benefit from both academic and "life-coaching." Researchers from the Antwerp Management School, in an article on the "Coaching Cube," note that development or life coaching, also known as personal or in-depth coaching, requires the highest engagement level as it "takes a broader, more holistic view, often dealing with more intimate, personal and professional questions." Examples of this type of agenda are important career decisions, work-life balance, and learning to cope with emotions in the workplace.[3]

Capital IDEA

There are many coaching programs around the country. Highly successful organizations anchor advice on data—about the educational institution, the learner, and the labor market. They get up close and personal with their advisees—it is not a perfunctory exercise. They must be believable to those they coach and influential enough with the educational institutions to make a difference. This fusion of activities produces meaningful success for participants of Capital IDEA.

Analyzing the Labor Market in Real Time

Capital IDEA's core mission is to move low-income adults into good-paying careers by supporting their pursuit of post-secondary degrees or certificates from other institutions. Capital IDEA conducts local labor market analyses to ascertain which occupations are growing and likely to lead to middle-income jobs. Its board of community and business leaders provides input to program managers in order to facilitate quick responses to market changes. Capital IDEA also conducts ongoing research to figure out the total package of skills someone needs to succeed in a job or sector identified as "growing." This includes the soft skills necessary for high performance. Capital IDEA uses the information it collects to closely examine and adjust the curricula of its training partners to verify that the identified skilling needs are being met.

Clear-Eyed Understanding of Participants

Capital IDEA serves primarily unemployed and under-employed adults. Two characteristic qualities repeatedly come up when staff describe Capital IDEA participants to us. "They're people that want to change their lives. *But they don't know how* [italics ours]. Or they don't have the means to do it, but they have a dream. They want something better for them or their families."

"They don't know how." Herein lies a critical message: Access alone is insufficient. Many of the individuals enrolling in community college, certificate programs, or training programs are entering a new world, a world they must navigate while managing their finances and their home lives, often without the support of family and friends. Whether it is as obvious as tuition or as subtle as recognizing the difference between constructive criticism and anger, these individuals face barriers they are often ill-equipped to address. Capital IDEA front line staff members told us:

"Some are trying to overcome their own insecurities."

"They may not have parents who are supporting their dream because they've never reached that far themselves."

"They just don't have a good support system and sometimes things break."

"They've never had to navigate the academic system. It's kind of a maze."

"They are frightened."

"They haven't been taught to communicate correctly . . . something someone says sounds negative . . . they give up."

Staff turn these very personal insights into coaching advice.

Committing to the Coaches

Capital IDEA staff, to a person, call their "career navigators" the key to their success. Like her boss Steve Jackobs, executive director of Capital IDEA, Eva Rios-Lleverino has been with Capital IDEA since its beginning in 1998. She sums up how critically important coaching is when she says: "You can give someone all of the money in the world, but if you're not guiding them—if there is no one there when the journey gets tough—then how are they going to really succeed?" Career navigators help people through the stresses and complexity of what is typically a multiyear training process.

From the very beginning of their relationship with Capital IDEA, navigators are available to students "anytime, for any reason." They are the infrastructure and the support system that so many participants lack. They help remove the barriers that stand in the way of participation and completion. They help with academic planning: class selection, registration, test requirements, how to communicate with a professor. They help with financial planning: budgeting, credit scores. They connect participants to resources in the community: rental assistance, food stamps, clothing for their children, domestic violence services. They intervene in a crisis. They provide encouragement, motivation, a place for students to vent. "They act as a cheerleader. . . . They get on you when you're not doing what you're supposed to. They follow up with you when your child needs counseling," says Rios-Lleverino. Or, to paraphrase Tiffany, a 2008 Capital IDEA registered nurse graduate, "They really invest in you and your family and give you the support and things you need to succeed."

Incorporating Early Warnings to Improve Outcomes

Like CUNY ASAP, Capital IDEA has developed an early warning system to make its coaching more responsive to individual needs. They use participant-centered algorithms to determine whether a student needs more or less attention. The system flags vulnerable students for follow up. For instance, if someone is experiencing housing instability, mental health issues, or transportation problems, navigators step in to provide emergency support without waiting for regularly scheduled meetings. Their goal is to preempt problems that may lead to students dropping out of the program.

William Askew Jr., a program manager with Capital IDEA, describes the process in more detail: "We've learned that our students typically struggle in three areas: academic, financial, and situational needs. So, we've created a 28-question survey that has an algorithm on the back end that helps us predict risk. Every semester, we survey our students. We know that if the student answers in a particular way, they may be at risk, and [this] tells our navigators this is something to look into."

InsideTrack

Not every student has access to supports like those offered by ASAP and Capital IDEA. An adviser who has the time to deeply understand the student and who can bundle that advice with resources and referrals that help overcome barriers produces more success but at a higher cost. We looked for other, somewhat lower touch, models and found InsideTrack, which supports nontraditional college students with coaching services.

A personalized student coaching service for college students, InsideTrack has assisted 2 million students, many of whom came from vulnerable populations affected by financial stress, food and housing insecurity, domestic violence, mental health, and other critical issues that interfere with college success. The nonprofit works directly with educational institutions to increase their enrollment, retention, and matriculation rates by providing coaching, capacity building, and training. A mentor ("coach") contacts students at the beginning of a semester and invites them to participate in the voluntary program. The resources to overcome their barriers often are found in the institution that contracts with InsideTrack to offer the advice.

Students who participate receive outreach on regular occasions for up to two semesters by a coach who helps identify and address perceived obstacles to the students' course completion, such as work schedules, family responsibilities, or financial obligations. Coaches who maintain caseloads of 75 to 150 students also support the students in developing skills from time management to self-advocacy. Stanford University researchers Rachel Baker and Eric Bettinger, in a randomized trial, found improved retention and completion from InsideTrack's individualized student coaching.[4]

Back to Brain Science

Although it does not usually come up in the literature, Jackobs from Capital IDEA makes a powerful observation about the impact of poverty and the role coaches can play in helping students overcome their initial reactions. Jackobs says his managers have noticed a significant mindset shift that takes place in participants throughout the program, typically around the eight-month mark. It is apparent in the way people react to hardship, discrimination, or confusion in the workplace. He describes it this way:

> If you're a poor person and you get in trouble, what you do to survive is grab your kids and run to safety. If you're a professional and get in trouble, you have resources [or] avenues [available] to bring those things to someone's attention and expect a fair resolution. It takes about eight months for someone to [make this mental shift and] realize that the new environment is different. If they get lost or scared, they shouldn't run. They should get a navigator, share it, and get some advice on what to do.

The trauma of poverty often produces a knee-jerk reaction toward a fight-or-flight response in the face of hardship, but the stability of the program's support structures helps participants appreciate the give-and-take of professional life. You can see these program characteristics play out with Tiffany, who highlights the importance of Capital IDEA navigators: "We had meetings every week with our navigators. It was an expectation when we signed up for the program. We were accountable for our time. They helped us succeed, gave us study partners if we needed them, helped us with issues at home, and sometimes they were just a shoulder to cry on. You do your part, but it's the extras that make a difference."

Avoiding Hammer and Nail Solutions

Many potholes can derail a person on the journey to a better life. Yet these obstacles are not insurmountable, as we see from programs like ASAP and Capital IDEA. Addressing the real barriers that block successful program participation—some financial, some logistical, some psychological—will open doors to greater mobility. An adviser needs to be involved enough to identify and help resolve the real problem, however.

We are reminded of a conversation Stephen had as he finished his last term as mayor of Indianapolis. He received a report from an appointed group of community leaders and experts on affordable housing and homelessness. This very good, well-written, and exceptionally well-laid-out report had dozens of pages of housing recommendations but little if any advice related to the underlying factors that produce housing insecurity. In government, and in the social sector, for that matter, solutions are too often siloed. If resources are limited and a citizen is in distress because they cannot afford available housing, should a city address that by building more housing or, say, for instance, by focusing on job creation, better education, domestic violence relief, or more affordable childcare?

Successfully helping those struggling to improve their lives and overcome obstacles placed in their way requires a coordinated regional response and, often, funding and services from multiple partners. The goal is not simply to produce more ASAPs but, rather, to draw attention to its approach so that a community can create and manage cross-sector networks that collectively do the many things CUNY accomplishes.

Community coordination of the full suite of services demands more than just a traffic cop directing people to various resources. Rather, it requires advising and coaching that recognizes that people enter the world of post-secondary education in various states of readiness. For some, it is an entirely new world, one they need help navigating.

Logistical and financial barriers challenge even the most enthusiastic person. Advising that supports the learner, that opens access to a variety of resources, can be provided through one of many CBOs, employer HR departments, hospital social workers, child protection service workers, community colleges, workforce investment boards, faith-based organizations, shelters, and more. An organization does not have to put together all necessary services under its own roof. Rather, it should determine its core expertise, which barriers it can directly help the student circumnavigate, and where referrals would make the most difference. That said, successful advising in the Capital IDEA or ASAP model is a core component of the program and not an incidental activity attached to something else.

Even high-quality advisers such as those we study here need an easy way to identify community resources necessary to overcome these obstacles. Coordination requires tenacity. Creating a network that supports a client means partners must be able to share relevant information about resources and needs—a problem fraught with real and imagined legal obstacles. An adviser helping arrange services needs to see inventory or determine it quickly—open childcare seats and vouchers to pay for them, community mental health or AA session openings, available tutors. A single view of the client is imperative when governments attempt to integrate service delivery across multiple providers from the public, private, and nonprofit sectors.

We began this chapter by observing that even the most enthusiastic learners face logistical and psychological obstacles that stand in the way of their participation in educational and skilling programs designed to improve their prospects. If we do not remove these barriers, we will not see the hoped-for outcomes. Linderman from CUNY sums it up, not just for her school but for all providers committed to removing barriers to participation:

> Every student is talented, uniquely qualified to realize their personal goals. Our job, as program staff, is to unlock that and support the students toward it and to push them sometimes. To keep them on track. Financial resources in isolation . . . are not good enough. It has to be part of a comprehensive approach, to help students identify their goals, move towards them and to support them in that process.

From CUNY ASAP, Capital IDEA, and others, we learn the importance of key supports that, when provided broadly to interested learners, will help people along the path to upward mobility. Underlying principles include the following:

1. The process must begin with an overture by someone—a nudge by a program official who can connect with the prospective student.

2. Financial supports not only are critical but help catalyze the first step.

3. Academic and life-coaching advisory services need be tightly connected.

4. Students have little in terms of backup and emergencies will arise that, without careful advice and temporary resources, will derail progress.

5. Advisers need to be able to locate important support services not available from their own institutions.

6. Continuing access by students/workers to peers with similar backgrounds and on a similar trajectory reinforces positive steps.

7. Career advisers need real-time job information.

8. Prospective students need confidence, which comes from accomplishing clear goals based on realistic but high expectations.

9. Advisers and their institutions benefit from data that preemptively identifies problems and suggests solutions.

We feature Capital IDEA and ASAP because they provide exceptional examples of how advisers unlock the potential of those they help through advice and resources that allow nontraditional students to overcome barriers. We feature them and the design principle they embody so that more communities can incorporate their approach into their regional offerings.

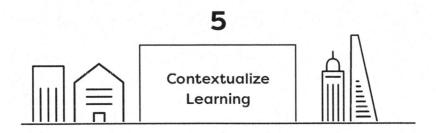

5

Contextualize Learning

One of the consequences of a husband-and-wife team writing a book together is that our blended family stories find their way in. One of our children—a young man of exceptional intelligence—rarely found his coursework relevant while enrolled in a four-year college. He left school and later registered in an electronics class offered by Vincennes University, where he studied math and how electrical systems work. He ended up wiring his own mock aircraft cockpit as part of the experience. From a disinterested, mediocre student, he evolved into to a straight-A student who, today, has a successful career in the aviation sector. Relevance sparked persistence.

Caught in a Bind

In a prior chapter, we looked at national survey data of Americans age eighteen and older fielded by Strada Education Network's Center for Consumer Insights. We spoke with Dave Clayton, senior vice president of the center, about the surveys. He told us that people need to see a direct line between education and immediate career prospects.

Relevance is the most important factor driving their interest in continuing education, and more of those surveyed preferred skills training or certifications to degree programs. Aspiring learners, a term Strada applies to a subset of the population, look to the practical benefits of further education or training. For them, a better quality of life, paying bills, and taking care of family motivates their interest in enrolling.

The sad reality holding back many adults for whom occupational training would provide a pathway to greater mobility is that they lack the basic English, math, and reading skills necessary to be successful in such programs. Researchers at the Urban Institute evaluated Accelerating Opportunity, an initiative designed to help adults with low basic skills obtain occupational credits through community and technical colleges. The evaluators observed that "the U.S. faces persistent literacy challenges . . . nearly one in five American adults displayed low literacy levels, and nearly one in three displayed low numeracy levels."[1]

They note that high school graduates are often underprepared for post-secondary education and, consequently, community college referral rates to remedial math (up to two-thirds of students) and reading (one-third of students) are stultifying. It is not uncommon for vocational and career and technical education "instructors to complain that their students don't have the required skills to perform adequately in these classes."[2] These workers and prospective workers need to build basic as well as occupational skills.

Many of the people we met in our travels lack the required reading, writing, and math skills that ought to come with a high school education. For them, remedial or developmental education is a necessary leg on the journey toward greater mobility.

Relevance and Time

Most adults enroll in adult basic education (ABE), GED, or ESL classes because they "want better pay and better jobs."[3] However, participation and completion rates in these classes are notoriously poor. This is, in part, because, as emphasized by Columbia University's Dolores Perin, "Students may not be motivated to learn the skills taught in developmental education courses because they do not perceive them to be directly connected to their personal educational goals."[4]

Further compounding the problem are the financial pressures

most adult learners face. These pressures steepen the price of participation. Strada found that aspiring learners make a calculated tradeoff when deciding whether to enroll in adult education or training courses, weighing their long-term benefits against the short-term challenges of lost wages and difficulties meeting family responsibilities.

Other research has shown that extending education with remedial courses makes would-be graduates less likely to persist. The longer the path to higher skills for adult education students, the greater the likelihood of attrition, especially if the basic courses are required prior to offerings of what the learner considers more relevant technical skills. The answer for many of these students lies in contextualizing ABE and career and technical instruction.

Why Contextualization?

Contextualized teaching and learning (CTL) encompasses a variety of instructional and pedagogical strategies "designed to link the learning of basic skills with academic or occupational content by focusing teaching and learning directly on concrete applications in a specific career context that is of interest to students."[5] A large body of theory informs CTL. Studies show that it accelerates learning and improves motivation, persistence, retention, program completion, and student success.[6]

While much of the literature on contextualized learning as it relates to workforce development focuses on ABE and career and technical training in community colleges, we observed the dynamic at work in many of the successful organizations we examined. Economic concerns drive participation in these organizations. But individuals arrive with multiple skilling requirements based on their life circumstances and tailored to the opportunities they seek. Rarely is one-dimensional job training sufficient.

This leads us to the fifth of our ten design principles: contextualized learning. Effective skilling curriculum combines core concepts, factual content, and basic and business skill development in ways that are relevant to participants. Education and training must, to greater or lesser degrees depending on participants' needs, contextualize learning.

Contextualization in Action

Peter Callstrom, CEO of the San Diego Workforce Partnership, notes that the old-school approach of standalone career centers with little connection to K–12 or community college must change. He points with pride to the Workforce Partnership's shift toward helping educators contextualize their teaching around meaningful work experiences.

Sarah Burns, director of research application at the Workforce Partnership and a former high school math teacher, views contextualized learning as central to the partnership's mission. "I've seen how a student's motivation can change after meaningfully connecting a geometry lesson to a career as an aerospace engineer, and I've seen how participating in an award-winning debate team can drive a student to pursue a career in public policy," Burns says. Conversely, she has seen "students with incredible potential drop out because they never found their personal answer to [the question], 'Why are we learning this?'"

In "Contextualizing Adult Education Instruction to Career Pathways," a Texas Education Agency manual for educators interested in contextualizing ABE, the authors note that "the result of classes or assignments that don't connect with a student's academic or career goal is often attrition, lack of persistence, and a demoralizing lack of course success." Conversely, the report concludes that contextualizing adult basic education "to workforce development can lead to better jobs by accelerating students through a career pathway with embedded basic skills instruction and academic support.[7]

Jobs for the Future (JFF), which helped develop the Texas manual, has been a powerful force behind several important workforce and adult education initiatives around the country. We spoke with Amy Girardi and Rachel Pleasants McDonnell, both associate directors for JFF, the former with its postsecondary team and the latter with its community college redesign efforts. They have been engaged deeply in some of the nation's most sophisticated initiatives combining ABE and occupational skilling, two of which are profiled later in this chapter.

When asked about their outspoken advocacy for contextualized learning, their answers speak directly to the issues of relevance and time. Integrating ABE and occupational training creates a "coherent learning experience," McDonnell argues. "It's not a series of disjointed pieces that theoretically add up to a whole; it's a learning journey that makes sense."

They share that students tell JFF anecdotes like: "I tried to kick-start my education numerous times. Once I got into this program [combined ABE and occupational skilling], it was clear how the math and English I was focusing on was connected to my goals of becoming a welder or a nurse. It finally made sense to me."

Contextualized learning, McDonnell adds, "helps students meet their goals better than the status quo." Girardi concurs: "What makes contextualization in a career context all the more important is that it leads to something."

Students' experiences with contextualized learning are mirrored in the voices of their teachers. McDonnell and Girardi paraphrase teachers who say:

> I finally understand how to serve my students better. I understand how to connect the dots between these math skills and what they need to know for the job. We [technical and ABE instructors] are actually serving the same students; we have common goals; we can learn from one another. [They go on to add:] It is fascinating to see team teachers talk to one another about instructional strategies that promote student success. In the past they operated in siloes and wondered why they didn't get anywhere, [with] everybody coming at it from different angles.

Girardi views contextualization through the lens of adult learning theory. "It's foundational," she observes. "Teaching people skills or concepts in a vacuum doesn't work. Learning happens when you connect concepts that appear to be disconnected and, in doing so, form new ideas. Content is socialized and integrated into existing bodies of knowledge."

When learning is not contextualized, when it happens in a vacuum, "it hampers progress," Girardi elaborates. "Adult students have no time to waste. They need to advance quickly. Just teaching people concepts without tying them to something broader inhibits learning and is profoundly disrespectful to the adult learner." She ponders that thought for a moment and demurs: "That was a little dramatic." Maybe so, but it is also true.

In this chapter, we profile organizations—nonprofit and academic—that combine occupational skill development with adult basic education and/or career readiness training, using a variety of instructional strategies. Their intent: to create programming relevant to students' goals and to accelerate progression through training curricula where appropriate.

Contextualization in these organizations takes multiple forms. In some situations, it involves a fully integrated curriculum that combines more than one skill set into each lesson. Other times, it involves formal pathways that include building competencies in different areas. In still other cases, it revolves around team-teaching by instructors from different disciplines. Frequently, a combination of methodologies is employed.

We begin with examples of contextualized learning as adapted by three extraordinary nonprofits whose efficacy is widely praised. We also profile two path-breaking community college-based initiatives that formally link ABE to career and technical education. All these organizations use contextualization to ensure relevance, promote persistence, and accelerate success.

The Career Readiness Approach:
Jewish Vocational Services

Jewish Vocational Services (JVS) was awarded the nation's first workforce development Pay for Success contract, and for good reason. This relatively new form of procurement involves government paying a social service provider for results. Launched in 2016, the Pathways for Economic Advancement project targets adult English as a Second Language learners by enrolling them in JVS's English for Advancement program. EfA contextualizes English language classes with job readiness and workplace training skilling.

Results to date have been impressive. The authors of an interim report assessing the program's effectiveness based on a randomized control trial note: "Although EfA was implemented during a strong labor market, . . . its particularly large earnings effects for unemployed workers make it an important option for states and cities to consider as they develop policies in response to high unemployment."

Jerry Rubin, president and CEO of JVS, estimates that about 90 percent of adult English language classes taught in the United States are not designed to get people employed. JVS, in contrast, has been integrating English language classes and workforce development for decades. "We just keep getting better at it," Rubin says. His comment comes alive in the voices of Emily Chick and Laura Sevigny, managers of EfA instruction at JVS. Both are committed to JVS, and both are intimately familiar with EfA. They refer to "EfA 3.0" with evident pride, underscoring its evolution, which they attribute to JVS staff, whom they characterize as

> analytically minded, amazing people. One thing that [we] have seen in this program is that staff regularly check in to see, how is the program going? What's going on with the numbers? What are we doing that's working? And if something isn't working, what can we do to change it? Leadership is very good at identifying or knowing where things are and identifying where there's space to innovate or try a new strategy if one way isn't working.

We share this before describing EfA for two reasons. First, to reiterate what we have said elsewhere: the better programs we have observed constantly evaluate their effectiveness and adjust—sometimes significantly—based on what the data tells them. Second, Chick and Sevigny's comments echo a powerful scaling strategy that proved effective for the YMCA of the USA, where coauthor Kate led the Strategic Initiatives Fund charged with scaling programs across the Y's national network of 10,000 program sites. Implementing this "fixed versus flexible" strategy requires understanding which program elements are essential to driving outcomes in any location and which can be modified to reflect the unique characteristics of a particular community.

JVS has offered English language classes in one form or another since the mid-1970s. The EfA program, first offered in its current form in 2016, serves approximately 350 people annually. On its website, JVS markets EfA to prospective students this way: "Learn English to help get a new job! The English for Advancement program offers English classes and one-on-one job coaching provide[s] specialized training to help advance your career." Potential EfA participants apply to JVS, are screened for eligibility (described in more detail in chapter 3), assigned to an English language class based on their proficiency, and paired with a career coach who helps them with job placement.

EfA is a robust example of contextualized learning, which occurs in three ways. First and most prominently, the curriculum is divided into modules. The content of each module is built around a job in-terview question. Second, on an ad hoc basis, instructors incorporate employer- or sector-specific content into the classes. Third, elements of the classes are structured, and the pedagogy designed, to replicate the workplace in the United States.

Using Job Interview Questions to
Frame English-Language Lessons

The EfA curriculum is divided into twelve modules, each of which corresponds to a question likely to be asked in a job interview. Using the given question as a frame, classes focus on the vocabulary and grammar necessary to answer the question. This means, according to Chick and Sevigny, that instructors "are able to connect it directly to the workplace, to answering an interview question. And in that way, keep the curriculum very contextualized."

Modules one through six cover questions including: Tell me about yourself, or tell me about your past work experience; or describe your skills; or what is your availability for work? In the "availability" for work module, as one example, participants study English words for the days of the week and prepositions associated with time. As students progress through the more advanced learning modules, they encounter interview questions like Tell me about a time when you had a conflict at work and how you resolved that conflict. Answering these questions involves complex sentence construction, grammar, and vocabulary.

During class, students practice their skills doing mock interviews, either in breakout groups or full class sessions. Nuha from Sudan, whom we introduced earlier, confesses that when she began taking classes, she "tried not to talk," and that she was "scared to talk to people." We imagine Nuha's life in this country, not speaking the language, not knowing her way around, being afraid to speak. How difficult everything must have seemed!

But Nuha got a job, which, to her deep disappointment, COVID-19 eliminated. While we sometimes struggled to understand her, evidently her interview practice had worked. "My teacher gave me the interview question," she says. "That also helped me. Because if my teacher asks me an interview question, I'm not scared because this is my teacher . . . If I need to go to interview, the questions are the same. I practice those a lot of time."

Adding Depth through Ad Hoc Content

While taking EfA classes, each student partners with a career coach who helps them sort through their goals and figure out how best to achieve them. Coaches work with students to develop résumés, prepare for interviews, and apply to jobs. The coaches and nearly one-third of staff overall interact with employers, as well, providing a range of services, such as recruiting and training classes for incumbent workers.

Jacqueline Chernoble, who leads JVS's business services team, describes the work of the coaches and their impact on both students and curriculum. "Students work one-on-one [with] their career coaches," she says. "The coaches and their colleagues interface directly with employers. So, there's matching going on while students are building their skills. We have a continuous feedback loop with the coaches who are also informing the curriculum."

Because coaches face both ways, they have a window into employer needs and real-time knowledge of what students must be prepared to discuss in interviews. Instructors and coaches communicate regularly, allowing the former to make subtle curriculum adjustments as necessary. Occasionally, if an instructor knows that a portion of the class plans to attend a job fair hosted by JVS, they add relevant sector vocabulary to the curriculum. These small but contextually meaningful modifications add relevance to lessons.

Contextualizing the American Workplace

Among multiple other responsibilities, Amy Nishman, senior vice president at JVS, oversees the Pay for Success initiative Pathways to Economic Advancement. Describing how JVS contextualizes training, Nishman tells us: "We model the workplace whenever possible, so that we're teaching what it's like to work in the American workplace all the time." This modeling is reflected in structural elements of EfA, in its pedagogy, and in supplemental content provided to students.

Instructors take daily attendance and note when students miss class, come late, or leave early. They add scheduled, timed breaks. Why? Because students who may not be familiar with them need to learn "that a 15-minute break is a 15-minute break," Nishman says. Instructors prepare and conduct progress reviews to model how students might experience on-the-job supervision.

"It's a sit-down, on a scale of one to four. . . . Exceeds expectations, meets expectations, students learn what those words mean ... applied to taking initiative, or problem-solving, or multi-tasking." If students are sick and cannot come to class, they are expected to call in because that is expected workplace behavior. In ESL classes, most instructors use multiple-choice tests rather than other formats "because we have to help them know what a multiple-choice test is, because in some jobs or job applications, you have to be able to do that," she says.

JVS works backward to identify necessary workplace skills, many related to executive functioning, and builds them into EfA's pedagogy. These skills translate into assignments that reinforce time management, scheduling, and organization. Chick and Sevigny tell us about in-class "opportunities for collaboration . . . group work and pair work. So that we reinforce being able to work with other people, people that have different backgrounds than your own, who speak different first languages, who come from different cultures."

As discussed previously, JVS uses interview questions to frame the content of the modules. Using an "observe-reflect-practice" structure, students watch interview videos and conduct mock interviews. They dissect what they observe and assess not only what is said but how it is said, taking into account posture, eye contact, and, in the world before COVID, handshakes. Then they practice interviewing using what they have learned from their observations and group discussion.

Interview question modules are supplemented by modules on résumé writing, understanding your paycheck, and other work-related knowledge. These supplemental modules, like EfA's core modules, combine vocabulary and grammar with job readiness and workplace skills.

Emulating Business: Year Up

Coauthor Kate has held chief marketing officer posts in several organizations. She has relied on visual imagery to compel emotional reactions, to tell a story, to convey the essence of a brand. The landing page of the "About" section of Year Up's website opens to a picture of seven young adults. Beyond their race, beyond their affect, their clothes tell us something about contextualization at Year Up. Three of the young men wear suits, and a fourth has on a sport coat and khakis. Two of the women wear dresses, and one young woman has on wide leg trousers and a sleeveless blouse. They dress for the jobs they will have—IT, software development, financial operations, business operations, sales, marketing, and customer support. They dress for the success that persistence promises.

Year Up provides sectoral training to young adults between the ages of eighteen and twenty-four with a high school diploma or its equivalent. Students in the program receive six months of intensive training in their chosen occupational track, followed by an internship of the same length with one of Year Up's employer partners. Year Up has been written about extensively and appropriately lauded for its outcomes. Like JVS, Year Up infuses "business language, concepts and tools throughout daily activities."[8] Consistent with the research cited at the beginning of this chapter, students, staff, and employers say this infusion "helps motivate students to work hard and connect well with Year Up's employer partners."[9]

In virtually every aspect of its programming, Year Up emulates the business environment. Staff appropriate corporate nomenclature. They call Year Up "the company," they "pitch ideas," and they create "investment prospectuses" for fundraising purposes.[10] During the six-month intensive training period, in addition to technical skills building, students take a professional skills course that covers corporate culture and etiquette, including email etiquette. They take a course in written and spoken business communications. Students receive periodic assessments structured much like corporate performance reviews. Instruction in occupational skills classes employs project-based learning to provide real-world applications.

Upon acceptance to the program, students sign a formal contract with Year Up "specifying standards for professional behavior."[11] Described by one staff member as outlining the "rules to the game for corporate America,"[12] the contract sets expectations and behavior standards related to timeliness, attendance, professional dress, conduct, and completion of assignments.[13]

Adherence to this contract has real-life consequences for Year Up students, who receive a weekly stipend for participation. The stipend is connected to a point system based on what Garrett Warfield, Year Up's chief research officer, calls Year Up's token-based economy:

> Students have certain numbers of points. Meeting expectations earns them points each week; not meeting expectations, falling short of expectations or [receiving] infractions . . . translates into point losses, which translates to dollar losses. But that simultaneous, positive reinforcement and token economy system can mean a lot. It sets expectations really high, but not without the high support the program otherwise aims to provide.

Some Year Up students receive their technical training as part of attending community college, a newer iteration of the program. Warfield notes that you often can distinguish Year Up students from others on campus. "They're the ones who are suited up, looking like they're going on a job interview every day."

A Year Up student sums up the impact of the system by saying: "I like [the contract]. I think it holds every student accountable. If they didn't have it, everybody'd be doing what they wanted. I don't think that would be fair. Now that we're on internship, we're dressed professionally because of Year Up . . . not using slang, getting to work on time, actually turning our work in on time, too."[14] Year Up uses contextualization to model the business world students will encounter as interns. Exposure breeds familiarity, familiarity instills confidence, and confidence promotes persistence and, ultimately, success.

Contextualized Learning and Integrated Pathways: Goodwill's Excel Center

Joshua graduated high school early, with honors. He is a freshman at Ball State University. He is a soldier in the National Guard. "He's incredible. He's a great kid," says Katie Reigelsperger, who teaches students seeking a pharmacy technician certification nationally and at Goodwill's Excel Center charter high school in Anderson, Indiana. She recently left her job supervising, training, and managing a staff of pharmacy technicians at Riverview Hospital to teach at The Excel Center full time. She reflects: "As a society, we are taught to believe that if you didn't finish high school, and if you spent time in foster care, got pregnant when you were 13, and if your family were drug addicts or alcoholics or spent time in prison, then that's who you are. That's who you are destined to become."

It doesn't have to be that way, Reigelsperger tells us. She knows. She is Joshua's mother, and she got her high school diploma and pharmacy tech certification through The Excel Center.

The Excel Center is a charter high school that operates in fifteen locations throughout central and southern Indiana. The center recently expanded outside the state. Excel Center students attend school tuition-free, receive a high school diploma, and can earn occupational certificates and/or college credits. Childcare, coaching, and other supports are provided. Like many adult or young adult learners, prospective Excel Center students previously have hit a wall. "They can't provide for their families; they can't move forward without a formal education," says Miriam Henry, who directs The Excel Center in Anderson, Indiana.

Recognizing the dual goals of their students, a high school diploma and economic mobility, The Excel Center integrates ABE, career readiness, and vocational and/or post-secondary education into its graduation requirements and its core curriculum.

Students' pathways through The Excel Center include meeting the following requirements: (1) state high school diploma standards; (2) demonstrated employability skills through project, service, or work-based learning; and (3) post-secondary readiness competencies that include options like college-ready benchmarks, dual-credit classes, career-technical education, and state- or industry-recognized credentials.

The Excel Center partners with local community colleges and other providers to make credits and certifications available to their students. The Excel Center's graduation pathway means that those who complete the program leave with both a high school diploma (generally viewed more favorably than a GED by employers) and occupational or college credits.

In addition to its graduation requirements, The Excel Center further prepares students for work by contextualizing non-occupation-specific skills into their high school curriculum. As Henry explains:

> They take math and English and science, but these aren't necessarily job skills. They also need computer skills and to know how to run Microsoft Office and Google Suite. They need to work collaboratively, build customer-service skills, resolve conflicts, make presentations. So we build projects and assessments into their high school course [work] to help them develop the job skills that are going to set them up for success the higher they go.

Henry shares a chart showing precisely which learning objectives are built into students' course work. Level 1 classes in math, English, writing, and so on include contextualized learning objectives related to social emotional learning, study skills, and working with Google Docs. In level 2 classes like algebra, biology, and English 3 and 4, students use Google Sheets, develop presentations, work on essays, and take project-based learning assessments. In upper-level classes that include advanced math and English, history, and government, students are expected to work on group projects and presentations, and to practice public speaking.

Of course, the Goodwill school isn't just about contextualization:

it's about hope for the students and their families. Reigelsperger and Henry know one another. Henry taught Reigelsperger math when she first enrolled in The Excel Center. Now Reigelsperger teaches pharmacy tech to students at Excel Centers nationwide. Both women are passionate about what they do, emphasizing that their students want to give their "kids the best they can." Reigelsperger had a closing comment for us:

> You should have asked about Joshua. He was my motivation. Its where my story started. Both of my parents are dead; they died of overdoses and alcoholism. I don't want that for my children. I had Joshua when I was 13. I wanted to give him a different life than I had. He watched me go through The Excel Center; both my kids did. It set the tone for the rest of Joshua's life. He will tell you a big part of his wanting to be a better person and work hard was watching his mom.

We heard permutations of this story from many of the people we interviewed. Lest we forget, in creating a more effective, equitable workforce development system, we impact generations of individuals within the same family.

Contextualization in Community and Technical Colleges

Community colleges educate about 40 percent of U.S. undergraduates. Their principal mission is to provide either career education or pathways to transfer to four-year colleges. They also help students who lack adequate skills in English or math by providing noncredit adult basic education classes. In practice, few of the students enrolled in basic education in community colleges transition into college-level classes because, as discussed earlier in this chapter, they do not see that route as advancing their career goals. Consequently, meaningful pathways to good jobs are closed to many students lacking a high school education or adequate basic skills.

Curriculum Contextualization: I-BEST

The Integrated Basic Education and Skills Training program (I-BEST), launched to coincide with the 2006–2007 academic year in Washington State. It was developed to address the needs of prospective students and low-skill workers who would benefit from enrolling in occupational training or certificate programs but who lack the basic skills necessary to do so. Designed by the Washington State Board for Community and Technical Colleges, I-BEST has been replicated in other states around the country.

The goal of the program is to "increase the rate at which adult basic education classes and ESL students advance to college-level occupational programs and complete post-secondary credentials in fields offering good wages and career advancement."[15] To do this, I-BEST combines ABE and career and technical training classes. As a result, students do not have to postpone occupational training while they complete ABE, a delay that frequently results in their not enrolling at all.

Washington State requires occupational and basic skills instructors to be in the classroom together at least 50 percent of the time, although they have leeway in how they team teach. Often, professional or technical training curricula are modified to include appropriate basic skills, which allows I-BEST to contextualize ABE "using materials and examples from students' occupational field of interest."[16] Critically, I-BEST's coursework is embedded within the college's career pathway programs.

The strength of I-BEST rests on its foundational understanding of adult learners' motivations, given that the delay associated with noncontextualized ABE creates a barrier to participation. Abt Associates, in an evaluation for the Federal Office of Planning, Research, and Evaluation Administration for Children and Families, found that "the I-BEST programs at the three colleges [studied] increased participation in college-level courses, number of credits earned and credential attainment." Further, they noted that their "evaluation greatly strengthens the evidence that I-BEST can produce increases in receipt of credits and credentials."[17]

Integrated Career Pathways: Accelerating Opportunity

Accelerating Opportunity (AO) launched in 2011 in four states initially as a demonstration project. The program grew out of an interest in promoting greater use of integrated career pathways in community colleges. AO pairs basic skills with for-credit programs in high-demand occupations. It is no longer a demonstration project, and many states now fund AO-like programs.

AO differs from I-BEST in that it does not mandate team-teaching; rather, it requires participating community colleges to offer a minimum of two formal career pathways in different industries. The pathways must include both ABE or ESL and career/technical education, and must lead to college credits and marketable credentials.

By combining ABE and occupational training into formal career pathways, participating community colleges have been able to accelerate the rate at which underprepared adults obtain college credentials. Reporting on evaluations of the initiative, JFF researchers McDonnell and Lisa Soricone note: "In a rigorous, quasi-experimental study, AO was found to increase the probability of earning a credential, compared to non-AO students. In most cases, AO reduced the number of credits earned, suggesting more efficient course-taking and accelerated learning among participants."[18]

They add: "Significantly, AO changed the culture around perceptions of ABE students and their potential in community college. Adult education students are now seen as part of a strategy to help states boost college enrollment, meet employer needs, and achieve credential attainment goals." To this, we add that it also changes the trajectory of students for whom integrated career pathways meet both their occupational goals and their remedial education requirements without unnecessarily delaying completion.

The organizations profiled in this chapter contextualize learning in diverse ways: teaching English using career readiness as a frame (JVS); inculcating business culture into the fabric of the organization and its processes (Year Up); blending work readiness skills into entry-, mid-, and advanced-level classes in its charter high schools (Goodwill's Excel Centers); or through team teaching or braided pathways that marry occupational and ABE skilling in community colleges around the country.

While their pedagogy may differ, all these organizations embed skill building into a context that is relevant and meaningful to students, particularly adult students for whom continuing education is frequently a means to an economic end.

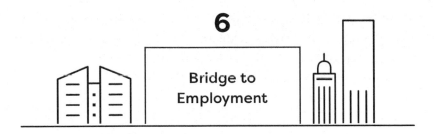

6
Bridge to Employment

Many people learn a profession by performing tasks under the watchful eye of an experienced colleague or by learning from someone whose role they wish to emulate. Those with little to no formal work experience and few role models need career readiness and job placement support, but they also need "on-ramps" that connect them to employers. For struggling workers troubled by doubts about their abilities and the opportunities available to them, bridges matter. Bridges connect individuals with a better future while, at the same time, providing the advantages of a training strategy featuring work-based learning.

This chapter's design principle—creating bridges to employment—describes best-practice programs that construct a way over previously impassable terrain for workers who lack experience and access to jobs or better jobs. "Bridges" is the fourth of our four program-level design principles (figure 1-2).

Many of the on-ramps that we profile—internship programs, apprenticeships, and sectoral training—take several months or even years to complete and are, in themselves, jobs. For some people, that presents a challenge. Poorly paid workers looking to move up often do not have the luxury of time and long-term ambitions. Immediate financial demands and family obligations stand in the way. For them, the connection between training and a job must be clear. The longer the period of training before placement, the more explicit the payoff needs to be.

William Askew Jr., a program director at the highly acclaimed Austin program Capital IDEA, explains the challenges of convincing potential applicants of the value of longer-term training:

> You can see these short term/midterm choices conflicts when a person has options. If an organization has funding for short-term training where the speed of placement is a measurable outcome, that competes with long-term training providers like us who say, "Let's work on getting you an associate degree, and then help place you in a higher wage job." We're trying to push students to get their associate degree and get living-wage jobs. But if a shorter training program tells them, "Oh, you can make $13 an hour," [sometimes] they leave and go make $13 an hour, versus waiting on the $25 or $30 an hour job a year or two from now. And they might stop our training. It works against us. So those outcomes compete against each other.

The programs described in this chapter connect individuals so closely to employers that they inspire longer-term planning. The bridges such organizations create take many forms but, in all cases, they include a combination of skill-building through experiential learning, access to potential employers, and job-readiness support and placement.

Internship Bridges
i.c.stars

Sandee Kastrul was a high school math and science teacher early in her career when she came upon one of her brightest former students doing janitorial work in a hotel for the minimum wage. Dismayed, she knew her students deserved better: They needed good careers, not minimum wage jobs. So, she committed to creating a program to provide training that would lead to more opportunity for promising individuals who otherwise lacked career paths.

Kastrul left teaching and, with a colleague, spent a year and a half researching effective technology training programs. The search ultimately led her to Milwaukee's Homeboyz Interactive, a faith-based recruitment training and job placement program founded by a Jesuit priest who worked with gang members. Kastrul and her partner thought the program, which trains youth to work in computer-related businesses, offered a model for them to follow. So, they adapted elements of it and started i.c.stars, a program that provides instruction in technology skills, leadership, and personal development.

Launched in 1999, i.c.stars is now well established in Chicago and has expanded to Columbus, Ohio, and Milwaukee. The program has improved the arc of progress for hundreds of students, both in their professional and personal lives; alumni have an impressive 82 percent job placement rate and, on average, quadruple the earnings they had before entering the program.

i.c.stars deliberately seeks out learners who demonstrate resiliency and critical thinking skills that have helped them overcome adversity. "Resilient people make great programmers, entrepreneurs and community leaders," Kastrul said. "They are able to identify problems, and they are able to ideate and create solutions."

The admissions process for i.c.stars is onerous. Applicants are given a packet of tasks that includes essay questions along with skills and logic tests. Then applicants are questioned by a panel of program staff, who assess their drive and authenticity. i.c.stars accepts only twenty students per cohort, usually from a pool of 200 applicants. Elizabeth Ferruelo, i.c.stars's chief revenue officer, calls the process a "pain in the neck by design." Once admitted to the program, learners must be all-in. Absences are not tolerated. Miss a class or a day of work without an acceptable excuse, and the student is kicked out of the program. i.c.stars delivers curriculum in four different ways. Three of its four instructional modalities combine experiential learning with traditional instruction and access to employers, creating on-ramps to permanent tech jobs or contract work (box 6-1).

i.c.stars interns spend sixteen weeks in "boot camp," working twelve hours a day, with a stipend to cover expenses. The first week of boot camp is devoted to team building and instruction in the fundamentals of leadership. On the last day of the first week of boot-

Box 6-1. **Four Ways to Learn**

- *Project-based learning:* Experiential learning that includes real-world work assignments and access to employers

- *Just-in-time learning:* Targeted instruction delivered by working professionals on subjects tied directly to interns' work assignments and on-the-job experiences

- *Classroom learning:* Traditional classroom instruction in programming and data fundamentals

- *Transformational learning:* Opportunities and events that introduce interns to employers, tech professionals, and others for the purpose of networking and social capital building

---

camp, the cohort is divided into four or five teams. Each team forms a consulting company that responds to RFPs issued by the cohort's corporate sponsor. These real-world projects can be solved only by using technology [experiential learning]. The interns spend the rest of bootcamp working on client projects, learning about technology and leadership, and networking with leaders, instructors, and mentors.

This is new territory for the interns. Kastrul gives us an example:

> Their client might say, "Next week, I want to see 20 user stories." And they're like, "I don't even know what a user story is." So, they go, they look it up. "What's a user story?" They bang their heads, they work together. They say, "This is what I've done, this is where I want to go. And this is where I'm stuck, and what I need." At this point, subject-matter experts step in (just in time) to help the interns with the technical skills they need to complete their assignments.

Interns hold regular meetings with their clients, during which conflicts among client and staff always erupt—by design. While the projects the teams address are real, the scenarios are scripted; they are designed to teach students how to respond to conflict. Interns must decide, in the moment, how to respond: Should they mediate? Should they let the loudest person win? "They've got to keep rolling with it," Kastrul says. The idea is to let interns experience the workplace in action.

After their "work day," part simulated and part real, interns return to i.c.stars's Learning Center, where they debrief with staff about the events of the day. Another form of just in time learning, the focus is on the scripted conflicts, which, over the course of the boot camp, cover some 300 learning objectives. Students also receive traditional classroom instruction in core technical skills such as JavaScript, HTML, CCS, C#, and SQL.

Boot camp culminates with "Career Month," during which participants write résumés, begin interviewing for positions, and work with i.c.stars's workforce development manager to find employment. After boot camp, graduates enter a twenty-month residency. During this time the organization supports them as needed with placement services and career and college counseling. Graduates get twenty-four credit hours from Indiana Wesleyan University, a private, four-year institution.

Along with hands-on experience, i.c.stars gives students multiple opportunities to meet and connect with business leaders, many of whom are also potential employers. i.c.stars dubs these events "transformational learning opportunities." Interns attend networking events and industry fairs with chief information and technology officers of tech firms. They are mentored by corporate sponsors and volunteers. And, in an i.c.stars signature practice, interns and business leaders gather together every day for "high tea." At four p.m., work stops, and "with sugar cubes and everything," a different business leader comes to the table to share his or her story over a pot of tea, Kastrul says. "By the end of the four months, interns have a Rolodex of 100 business leaders and technology leaders." Through these events, i.c.stars helps its interns build the social capital that so many of their peers lack.

i.c.stars' varied instructional approaches, and the many ways in which the organization provides students with crucial social capital, create bridges to employment and pathways to success. Kastrul speaks to the premise that we must construct a more equitable workforce development system when she says:

> From being in this industry for 30 years, I've learned that there are two things that separate great education from mediocre or crappy education. One is what we learn, and the other is who we learn with. By what we learn, I mean that when we answer questions at the back of the chapter and regurgitate information, we are learning to work on an assembly line. That hasn't changed much since the Industrial Revolution. However, when kids learn to come up with the questions themselves, they are not learning how to work in the assembly line. They're learning to be an entrepreneur, the leader of the plant, the innovator, the person who comes up with new businesses.
>
> The second part of it is who we learn with. If we go to school with kids whose parents are senators and CEOs, the opportunities that we have through our network are exponentially greater than if their parents work at the factory. And so, in our model, there's

two things. One is learning how to be a maker, an entrepreneur, how to ask questions, how to be a consultant, how to be a technologist. We bring the entire technology network to the student. So instead of it being one teacher, many students, it's one student, many teachers. And we're helping them build their social capital through our network.

We spoke with Christelle just as she finished boot camp. Her story illustrates how i.c.stars provides experiential learning and networking opportunities that help advance careers. Christelle lost her job as a stocking clerk in a Chicago shoe store shortly after the pandemic hit, in March 2020. Although she had earned an associate degree in math from Iowa Western Community College and had taken courses at the University of Illinois-Chicago, she was not confident about her future. "I had lost hope," she said. "I was at a place where I didn't see anything for my future."

One day, while scrolling through Craigslist, she saw an advertisement for i.c.stars. She did research on the program and decided to apply. "I viewed it as a job that paid you to learn," she said. "I mean, you want to give me a little bit of money so I can learn? Who would pass up on a program like that?"

During her boot camp experience, Christelle worked as a quality analyst for her student team on a client project for Accenture. Her team helped the company build a serverless web application that would allow Accenture employees to access the workplace safety information they need to return to the office after working remotely. Christelle said she learned how to use many technology programs. She also built the soft skills—empathy, interacting with clients and team members, and critical thinking—that will stay with her for years. "We're learning real-world things, in a setting we're going to be in after i.c.stars," she said.

Christelle believes the confidence i.c.stars instills in its students may be as important as the skills the students acquire. "This is the type of program that locates your potential, locates your passions and dreams and your abilities, and amplifies them," she said. "There are things you didn't know you were capable of, but you discover them." Thanks to her exposure to Accenture personnel while working on her client project, twenty-four-year-old Christelle was invited to interview with the firm.

Year Up

Gerald Chertavian visited with us at a Cambridge, Massachusetts, restaurant a few years ago to explain the rationale behind Year Up, the acclaimed program he founded more than twenty years ago. As CEO, Chertavian retains the wonderful blend of community activism and business entrepreneurship that has always driven him. His previous experience includes time with the well-known service programs of Ashoka and Big Brothers, as well as stints in banking and the start-up world.

Much has been written about the success of Year Up. Here we focus on specific aspects of the program, including its use of internships to build bridges to future prosperity. Participants spend six months at Year Up in learning communities where they receive technical- and professional-skills training in one of five sectoral tracks. Following this learning and development phase, students are placed in internships with employers in their chosen field for another six months. Interns work full time, four and a half days a week. They spend half a day per week at Year Up "processing" their experiences on the job with other interns while continuing with career planning.

Employers invest in Year Up on a per-intern basis to cover administrative costs and to support the program. In addition, employers provide feedback on the interns and input on how Year Up can improve its curriculum. For employers, the internships offer access to talent they might otherwise not have; for students, the internships furnish work-based learning and a bridge to the world of work in high-growth, high-opportunity fields.

In one of its many reviews of Year Up, Pathways for Advancing Careers and Education (PACE) notes, "Year Up encourages students to view the internship as an opportunity to gain hands-on experience with a leading employer, with the goal of earning a strong letter of recommendation or reference from their internship supervisor/host employer, and potentially a job upon graduation from the program."[1]

On its website, Year Up tells potential applicants that the effort "is about gaining access, getting your foot in the door, and making connections that count. You'll receive valuable, hands-on experience working at a major company as you further develop the technical skills you've learned." A Year Up participant sums it up this way: "I've really grown. That's what I mean by it changed my life. A year ago, I wasn't thinking about nothing like this, or being in contact with the people I'm in contact with or doing the things I'm doing. I feel like it's changing how I look at people now; how I look at situations."[2]

Garrett Warfield, chief research officer for Year Up, has been in the social science research field for some twenty years. He describes himself as "Year Up's internal nerd." He explains: "Everything we do is to improve the program, using research, iterative formative evaluation studies, things that we might tweak and adjust, and see if they're helping or not. We also have big-picture studies that seek to prove or test if we're delivering on our mission. And we work internally with [Year Up] teams, helping them get the information they need to do their jobs really well."

Warfield's response to our question about what drives Year Up's success is unequivocal: "Absolutely number one, and this is Year Up's unique value-add across workforce programs, is our connectivity to employers. They guarantee internships. You [students] join this program, and you make it through the classroom phase. You're guaranteed an internship. It's a sustained work and a learning opportunity with a financial component. It's from the internship that the bulk of the strong outcomes in studies on our program derive."

When we ask Warfield what about the internship makes it so vitally important, and whether it has to do with motivation, he responds:

> It's definitely a motivator. But the critical thing is, it's the start of their career path. About four years ago, we started shifting our strategy not to just sell the internship but to sell the job after the internship with corporate partners. It turns into day one of a long and meaningful career with an employer. At least 40 to 50 percent of those internships are going to lead to jobs. To students, the promise of a career path beyond an internship is so meaningful.

Apprenticeship: Bridging to Regular Work

Apprenticeships come in many shapes and sizes designed for a variety of workers. They offer one of the more common experiential learning bridges. Some combine school with on-the-job learning. Others feature initiatives set up by unions or businesses to provide transitional learning opportunities. The U.S. Department of Labor describes apprentice programs as employer-driven, "learn-while-you-earn" models that combine the jobs and training.[3] Apprenticeships vary in length, depending on the needs of the student/worker and the complexity of the job itself. They typically last between one and two years.

In some situations (though not enough), employers enter into arrangements with local educational institutions to develop pipelines of qualified employees. Nationally, more than 90 percent of those who complete such programs stay with the employer where they did their apprenticeship. Some states provide tax credits or formal certifications for programs. In other states, the process is more informal. Nationally, union construction jobs provide among the most well-established apprenticeship pathways into work.

Apprenticeships can be incorporated into secondary schools' vocational programs or into community colleges' degree and certificate programs for workers seeking to advance from low-skill jobs. In the United States, research indicates that registered apprentices out-earn similarly situated individuals without this opportunity.

Enthusiasm for apprentice programs has been growing across sectors, from manufacturing to healthcare, finance, and technology.[4] One program, the Federation for Advanced Manufacturing Education (FAME), began in 2010 as an experiment featuring Toyota Motor Corp and its need for middle-skill jobs. Now 400 employers nationally host FAME apprentices of all ages who split their week between the factory and the classroom. After graduation from community college, participants generally stay on in the company, earning more than individuals with the same degree but no apprentice participation.[5]

TRIO: Apprenticeships Bridging School to Full-time Work

The journey of Guadalupe Maldonado illustrates the power of a well-designed apprentice program that involves a range of community institutions. Guadalupe was just a sophomore in high school when she discovered a way to learn new skills and advance her education while earning money at the same time.

She and other students at Northbrook High School in Houston were called into a conference room and told about a new pre-apprenticeship program coordinated by TRIO Electric, the Spring Branch School District, and other partners. Guadalupe said she had no idea what to expect, but after hearing from TRIO and school district leaders, she was intrigued. She signed up for the program at the beginning of her junior year. It was not a traditional classroom experience. The program combined hands-on learning with practicing and mastering the skills required to work in electrical contracting. "It was learning by doing," she said.

Guadalupe remained in the program for the rest of high school. After graduating, she took a year off from school but continued to work with TRIO. Later she resumed her education at Houston Community College (HCC) while continuing to work as a purchasing agent with the company. Today she works full-time at TRIO and takes her online community college classes in the late afternoon. She plans to spend two years at HCC and then transfer to a four-year institution to complete a bachelor's degree in construction management.

In the course of her training, Guadalupe has earned four certificates representing different skills she has mastered. She also has earned a decent wage. The only cost to her has been the $20 she had to pay for a state-required electrical apprentice license. "Honestly, you are getting taught how to be an adult," Guadalupe said. The program "gives you something you can have in your back pocket. If I want to go and be a project manager, and it doesn't work out for me, I'm OK. I can always come back and become an electrician. I have all these certificates."

Fatima Perez, another Northbrook student in the pre-apprenticeship program, said it appealed to her because she has always enjoyed working with her hands. "Getting to be an electrician was not something I had thought of," she said. "But it opens a lot of doors."

By the end of the program, Fatima will have received 8,000 hours of training over four years. Upon graduating from Northbrook, she started taking online courses through Brigham Young University while continuing to work at TRIO. She is particularly proud that she took advantage of an opportunity few women get, in a field dominated by men. She was one of just three women in her TRIO cohort. "I personally don't think I can see myself doing anything else," she said. "It's kind of a girl power thing. There's no man out there who can do the job better. I'm doing just as good or better than the guys."

Guadalupe and Fatima also show us the importance of outreach. Getting learners to take their first steps onto a bridge requires more than posting a notice or offering a traditional vocational education course.

Beau Pollock is the youthful and earnest-looking CEO of TRIO Holdings, the electrical engineering and construction company that recruited Guadalupe and Fatima into its electrical pre-apprenticeship program. Pollack said he decided to create the apprenticeship program because he was frustrated that his ability to expand was hampered by an insufficient talent pipeline. "We needed to grow and diversify our business," Pollock said. "After years of going to the traditional outlets and resources that were supposed to be producing skilled labor . . . we realized there was just a big disparity in what was being taught versus what we needed as employers."

Successful apprenticeship programs require institutions not only to think differently about how they educate and place students but also about how they recruit them. Pollock decided that the best way for him to solve this latter hurdle would be to go to the schools and meet prospective students face-to-face. In school settings, with a focused message, he believed he could bring opportunity alive by making it tangible to the students, many of whom come from lower-income neighborhoods, use English as a second language, and would be the first in their family to be afforded such an experience. As Pollock explains:

> They may not view the job of an electrician as a skilled job, or they may not want to take a step that looks like an admission they won't be going to college. Usually, we go and make presentations to stu-

dents who are identified by the counselors as students that would benefit from this program. But for many years, young men and women who would have been great employees have been brainwashed into thinking college is the only option. And even if college is not for them, they don't take the steps to prepare for a good job early enough. It's not until their senior year, second semester, they realized that college was not the option that they thought it was going to be.

Pollock also notes that in his school presentations he makes sure to convey that he is confident future apprentices are fully capable of completing the program and landing a good-paying job. As he puts it:

One [challenge] is what gives them confidence, persistence by helping them understand that they could take this step and be successful when they have seen a lot of folks around them not be successful. The second is, "I got to take care of my younger brother, how do I get there and do the job training and get back and help Mom?" Their families have such a limited set of support services, and that may affect them. So, they need to factor in what the opportunity means and how realistic it is they can get to the finish line. That's usually the hook, when they see the trajectory of how much they can make, either as an intern or once they graduate. That's usually when their eyes light up, and they become super-focused and fill out the interest cards.

Most students do not receive enough tailored counseling to help them with difficult decisions about which postsecondary step to take. Through an affiliate, TRIO Education, Pollock has created an industry-initiated pre-apprenticeship partnership with school districts and community colleges across the state of Texas. One of its K–12 partners, Stafford Municipal School District (SMSD), rethought its apprenticeship offerings under the leadership of superintendent HD Chambers. A veteran of thirty-five years teaching and serving as an administrator in Texas public education before becoming Stafford's superintendent, Chambers's words aren't couched in academic jargon or abstract principles. They bespeak common sense. Chambers fights "so that kids who are not on a college trajectory will not be labeled failures. They can do good work and have a good quality of life from jobs requiring technical skills but not four-year degrees."

Chambers's mission of changing secondary-school apprentice programs began when he read the influential 2011 report on career and technical education, "Pathways to Prosperity: Meeting the Challenge of Preparing Young Americans for the 21st Century."[6] It was then that Chambers began pushing back against established ways of doing things. He focused on improving both advising and training, as well as integrating the two more tightly.

Chambers believes one does not need to be a licensed counselor to be valuable to students. It is more useful, he says, to deploy someone who knows the world of work. The large caseloads and need for advisers who know the work world better leads Chambers to conclude that "if you're going to put as much money and effort and importance on this as we do to prepare students for a meaningful post-secondary opportunity, you need to invest in the adults who can help them do that."

TRIO's success in providing pathways to students relies on several important building blocks: a convincing narrative for the student, a realistic classroom with relevant training, a tangible job opportunity, contextualized learning, and supportive advice along the way. More efforts need to pay attention to these components.

City Hall: Apprenticeships in the Public Sector

Through its innovative Targeted Local Hire Program (TLH), Los Angeles combines some of the best features of an apprentice program with a transitional support initiative. The one-year apprenticeship provides on-the-job training while serving as a gateway to long-term employment with the city. City officials developed the program before COVID to provide an upward path for those from neighborhoods without many opportunities and to set an example for other employers. Some of the people who were recruited into the program are shown in figure 6-1.

TLH combines on-the-job learning with training; for example, community college classes that lead to commercial driver's licenses. Importantly, it provides an alternative pathway to the traditional civil

Figure 6-1. **City of Los Angeles, Personnel Department**

Source: Classification Division, Workforce & Service Restoration, Targeted Local Hire Program, https://lalocalhire.lacity.org/targeted-local-hire-program.

service exam, which often deters less literate individuals as well as those who do not have the opportunity to prepare for an unfamiliar test. Apprentices spend the first six months of the program acquiring skills on the job. During the second half-year, individuals who receive positive evaluations obtain a probationary civil service classification. Before COVID-19 hit, approximately 1,000 graduates successfully completed the work phase and acquired civil service designations, including administrative clerk, gardener/caretaker, and animal control officer.[7]

According to Miguel Sangalang, who championed the initiative when he was Los Angeles deputy mayor:

With Targeted Local Hire, we were looking to fix our shrinking workforce. We ended up breaking just as many things as we fixed. But in a good way: For our residents, we broke common barriers to good-paying, steady jobs; for our departments, we broke traditional molds of hiring and found passionate, hardworking Angelenos. It's been amazing to see people thrive in the program. We've had a few who went through TLH in entry-level positions that are now managers in big departments in just a few years.[8]

Tech: Apprenticeships that Fill a Competitive Need

Apprenticeship programs can be targeted not just at preparing people for entry-level jobs but also toward increasing the supply of needed skills in a regional economy. The Northern Virginia area is one of the hottest in the country for cybersecurity professionals, and a substantial workforce deficit exists. A program developed with the State of Virginia and the Department of Labor provides registered apprenticeship options with Peregrine Technical Solutions LLC for students who attend the University of Virginia College at Wise or Tidewater Community College.[9]

The Center for Urban Futures, a think tank in New York City that promotes policies "to reduce inequality, increase economic mobility, and grow the [local] economy," highlights technology apprenticeship programs as a significant opportunity. At the time it issued its 2018 report, over 90 percent of New York City apprenticeship programs existed in building trades and manufacturing. Only three programs registered with the state at the time of the Center's review involved tech occupations. In 2019, the New York City invested $5 million into 450 apprenticeships, which is a start but nevertheless a small amount considering the size of the city's tech sector. The State of New York has authorized a $2,000 apprentice tax-credit program for "in-demand" jobs other than construction.

Noting the gaps in hiring minority IT workers, the Center observes:

> There's little question that a traditional four-year college degree remains the most common credential for people in the city's tech workforce, and expanding access to the tech sector for lower-income New Yorkers should include new efforts to boost college success. But given the costs in terms of both time and money required to earn a four-year degree—and competing demands like family obligations and the need to work full-time to cover living expenses—many New Yorkers could benefit immensely from alternative paths to stable careers.[10]

These observations, although specific to New York, apply throughout the country where open tech jobs exist, but absent an apprentice program or other bridge, the opportunity for such jobs falls unevenly by race.

Obstacles to Expanding Apprenticeship Bridges

Apprenticeship programs looking to expand continue to face challenges. Many employers have been slow to appreciate their benefits, preferring to rely, when hiring, on proxies such as postsecondary credentials. Likewise, traditional vocational education has been slow to change what worked in the past but may not be adequate for the future. Many states have a cumbersome registration process.

Understandably, parents do not want their children tracked into vocational education or apprenticeships if they believe college is the better option, or if they do not have confidence that the high wages associated with a certain trade are truly obtainable. Students and parents need more information to make this important decision. Curricular relevance is another significant obstacle. In Houston, employers had to assist with teaching when conventional vocational education teachers did not have sufficient familiarity with the skills required for a particular trade.

Bridging through Intermediaries and Partners

Staffing agencies create another bridge to long-term employment. They hire and do the necessary administrative work to prepare a person and place him or her on the site of an employer. In some instances, these placements are for tough to fill IT jobs where demand has surged. Other forms involve longer-term placements for workers who need assistance. No one does the latter category better than Goodwill.

Goodwill: Training Employees with Contracted Work

Most people know Goodwill as a retail store or a place to drop off second-hand furniture and clothes. We have come to know Goodwill Industries International as one of the largest and most creative suppliers of skill development and employment opportunities in the country. Its programs employ over 100,000 workers annually.

Goodwill does many of the things characteristic of high-performing organizations, including the provision of wraparound services and coaching. Yet, what stands out most about the organization is its willingness to take a "risk" with individuals more traditional employers too frequently shy away from. Whether these employers base their rejection on intentional or unintentional profiling, people with physical disabilities and young Black males suffer. Since it is hard to know what jobs are in demand in any given community, Goodwill relies on advanced labor market information and insights gained from local businesses.

Goodwill provides a direct bridge to employment by hiring workers, putting them on its own payroll, and furnishing services under contract to third-party companies. Goodwill knows its employees possess assets and takes responsibility for managing them. The exceptional Goodwill of Central and Southern Indiana illustrates this model.

On the near east side of Indianapolis stands something almost unheard of given the neighborhood's hardscrabble reputation—a new 47,000-square-foot commercial building that houses a manufacturing plant for a national company, Cook Medical. Cook contracted with Goodwill to recruit, train, hire, and manage the employees. Cook chose to locate the endeavor in one of the highest-unemployment neighborhoods in central Indiana and targeted recruitment at young Black men.

An impressive outreach effort to that end hinged on partnerships with local churches and the state legislative Black Caucus. These intermediaries, respected in the community, played the role of translators (as described in chapter 8), using their influence and standing in the community to attract participants. Even the prospect of a good job and good pay in an interesting field requires translation and targeted outreach with many young men and women of color who are more accustomed to a cold shoulder than a fair opportunity.

Applicants for the Cook/Goodwill jobs, many of whom do not have a high school degree, have often logged time in the criminal justice system. The average employer has difficulty helping employees whose life circumstances are challenging. However, through a wide array of wrap around services, Goodwill takes pride in helping people knock down barriers as they navigate life and work, ultimately finding success. In the words of Goodwill Indy CEO Kent Kramer, "Cook Medical sees this project as a way to give back and provide jobs in a community that has seen commerce, manufacturing and jobs leave for decades. And do it through a social enterprise partner like Goodwill."

By taking on "risk" that many companies will not, Goodwill simultaneously provides experiential learning and earning for hard-to-place populations.

Pursuit: Partners in Tech

It is tempting but unfair to stereotype Jukay Hsu. While he fits the profile of many social entrepreneurs, his path has been anything but typical. Growing up in Queens in a working-class immigrant family, he attended the famous high-performing Stuyvesant public high school, where he sat not far from the World Trade Center disaster on 9/11. A volunteer, a student, a rifle platoon leader; from Harvard to the Army back to Harvard, back to Queens, Hsu moved between worlds, all the while thinking about the people he knew growing up. "Blue collar workers and low-income communities weren't part of the city's civic tech growth." His concern for the people tech left behind mixed with an ample dose of entrepreneurial spirit led Hsu to found Pursuit, a social impact company. Pursuit provides four-year intensive training and placement to help individuals from low-income backgrounds, particularly those without college degrees and New Yorkers of color, get their first jobs in tech.

Pursuit partners with companies such as Uber, LinkedIn, and Citi to identify, recruit, and train nontraditional workers to become software engineers. Students awarded a Pursuit Fellowship begin by enrolling in its core program. The curriculum is built around three threads: in-demand coding and computer science skills; industry read-iness and leadership; and personal development. After completing the core, students, now job candidates, are eligible for full-time engineer-ing positions, typically with one of Pursuit's partners. Pursuit acts as a bridge in that its pipeline into specific employers is clear, and its record of near universal placements makes the program compelling. In interviews, Hsu and Zac Smith, chair of Pursuit's operating board, identified a few key components of their effort.

Both Pursuit officials homed in on how they help produce the per-sonal growth that is as necessary a component of their on-ramp as the technical training itself. Hsu argues:

> Our secret sauce, and what we're really doing, is actually teaching professional skills and cultural elements in addition to the techni-cal. Anyone can learn how to code online for free. But people have barriers that cause them not to enroll or complete whether finan-cial reasons or other constraints. We design our selection process to encourage, demonstrate, and build the right belief system. A critical part of our Fellowship program is instilling those beliefs, asking people to do things that they did not think they could do before.

Hsu's commitment to those in the program remains deep and re-alistic. "If you've up leveled from the warehouse to engineering, you are entering a brand new and unfamiliar environment. We want to ensure that even if you don't have a college degree, are a person of color, or are from a different background, you have the on-the-job tools to succeed."

This sense of realism shows through in separate conversations with both men. The organization's dedication to helping low-income workers improve their incomes from an average of $18,000 to $85,000 comes with a cautionary note regarding how they position their fel-lows. Smith tells us that if Pursuit emphasizes the candidate's poverty background to the employers, they run the risk of stigmatizing their trainees: "It's telling HR departments to expect someone different. Even though 70% of the people we serve are Black or Hispanic, and almost all reside in low-income communities, for us, it's about economic mobility. Our audience mirrors the ethnicity of New York City and we present our candidates that way to the employer so as not to taint the first impression. They have the talent, not the résumés or diplomas."

Organizations like Pursuit face a short-term/long-term tradeoff like that of their clients. Longer-term, more intensive help produces better results that cost more to deliver—but dosage matters. Most of the on-ramps described here require participants to commit many months, often years. They are not quick fixes. Pursuit's solution to this quandary combines philanthropy with an innovative funding model now used by a few universities.

To provide a fellowship with no loans and no upfront costs, Pursuit fellows enter into an income-sharing agreement, which aligns the interests of Pursuit and the learner. Funded by impact investors, Pursuit fronts the costs of training and career development services. Upon employment, fellows repay Pursuit a percentage of their earnings for a set amount of time. If a learner's income drops below a certain threshold, or she stops working, she pays nothing. If the program does not produce results, Pursuit bears the direct costs of its failure. Because their incentives are aligned, Pursuit offers participants an additional three years of career support, including mentors from the companies they join.

As board chair Smith puts it:

> What really is important about the Pursuit approach is that it's not one and done. . . . It's a journey, you're going to up level over time. The first one or two steps are to get your first job. But that's not the end, it's just the beginning. Some people might want to get a different job or need the support of our community to help them get into another network or learn other skills.

Pursuit creates bridges to employment by preparing fellows with the right personal and technical skills and partnering with employers to hire students who successfully complete training. The organization views the bridge they create as the first of many on the way to economic mobility for participants.

Sectoral Bridges

When manufacturing dominated the economy, employees stayed with their employer for most if not all of their careers, moving up the ladder of pay and opportunity. We contrast these employees to hundreds we encountered in our research and over the course of our lives who find themselves, despite experience, without a way to ascend either where they work or in their chosen field. For many individuals, sectoral initiatives, facilitated by intermediaries, create critical bridges from one company to another in the same industry. These training programs bring multiple employers together to erect industry-wide ladders, helping, for example, an orderly in one hospital find a job as an X-ray technician in another medical facility.

One 2010 analysis of several existing efforts found that workers participating in organized sectoral programs experienced substantial increases in hours worked, in wages, and in the likelihood of getting benefits and sustaining employment.[11] Sectoral collaborations can make the market work more effectively for underemployed workers who earn lower wages and struggle to create their own ladders upward. In comprehensive programs, multiple employers join together through a third-party organization to offer some combination of job training, skill development, workforce readiness, apprenticeships, mentoring, and job finding services, with an agreement by employer partners to hire from the pool of those completing training.

Sectoral bridges reduce the market friction that impacts both the employer and the prospective employee. Employers need to increase their talent pipelines while reducing their recruiting, screening, and training costs. Employees need to know that program participation increases their access to good-paying jobs and greater mobility. Sectoral collaboration improves outcomes for all parties.

In 2012, major Chicago philanthropies launched the Chicagoland Workforce Funder Alliance (CWFA), a particularly effective sectoral initiative set up to create bridges between employers and ladders within specific industries. The Alliance's mission is to "collaborate with employers and other workforce stakeholders to increase employment, earnings and racial equity for underprepared workers in the Chicago region."

CWFA now involves more than thirty funders. One of its activities includes the Chicagoland Healthcare Workforce Collaborative, which brings together employers and underemployed populations and adapts training to emerging workforce trends. Partners to the healthcare collaborative include large providers, like medical centers associated with the University of Chicago, the University of Illinois, and Northwestern University. Other partners include NorthShore University Health System, Cook County Health and Hospital System, and Malcolm X College.

This program succeeds, in part, because its partners have adopted common job-classification nomenclature and job-specific skill requirements. The collaboration has established training standards for each skill. Employers in the partnership understand that it is in each of their best interests to support common skill-based training and to hire from those who complete that training.

Like many of the leaders and program directors with whom we visited, Alliance director Matt Bruce spent time in an AmericCorps program, in his case in a Head Start program called Jump Start. He also served as a data analyst for the well-regarded Ounce of Prevention Fund. He explains:

> The thing that we think has the most traction is working with employers in groups and trying to get them to collaborate with each other and learn from each other. Some of the employers have changed how they pay for training for incumbent workers. Previously, some of them would only hire based on degrees and they wouldn't allow for certificates. So, we started pilots, and they learned through working together that they needed to make policy changes.

The Alliance, through its support of the Chicagoland Healthcare Workforce Collaborative, has created new pathways and on-ramps to better jobs. Bruce points to medical assistants as one example:

> Hospitals have staff who are in non-clinical roles, who don't have a pathway, and the hospitals have a need at the medical assistant level and above. If you can get out of working in the cafeteria or

working in a support position, you can get into career pathways. The hospitals had not done this before. None of them were sure at the outset that they could put together enough candidates on their own for a whole cohort to train, say, 20 people. But they thought they could, as a group of hospitals, together join in establishing a recruiting and training cohort. When you get them at the table, they realize that they do not compete in this space because they're not poaching employees from each other.

Bruce emphasizes the importance of configuring services around what the data show as critical skilling requirements. He also uses the data to determine where the Alliance should invest its collective resources in training for jobs likely to grow in the future, which in turn presents opportunities for those employees wishing to add a skill-based post-secondary degree.

Combining coaching, support services, training, and a clear route to a job—or a better job—to bridge a client to the future is a recipe for success. A lessons-learned summary concerning career pathways from the highly respected nonprofit JFF reinforces the idea that critical components include pathway entry, integrated training, and career progression. Importantly, JFF concludes, "prior reviews of career pathway studies have tended to bifurcate education and employment outcomes, but we think this is a mistake."[12] Bridges that facilitate career progression help individuals continuously add stacked credentials or certificates for better opportunities.

High-performing sectoral initiatives combine many of the best of our design principles. They involve multiple stakeholders joining together through the good work of an intermediary. They use data to identify growth sectors and jobs in their region. Their efforts focus on stackable skills—providing training that augments the experience of employees already working in the industry in entry-level positions. By hiring workers who graduate from the applicable programs into better jobs, participating employers create strong incentives for participation. And employers, by virtue of having helped to craft the training, know that graduating employees have the requisite skills. Best of all, hard-working individuals have an on-ramp to upward mobility.

7

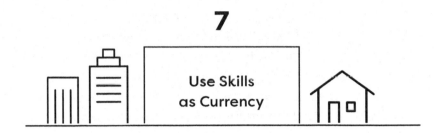

Use Skills as Currency

The Problem and Opportunity

During our interviews with i.c.stars, we met Chicago native Ernest Roberts, who graduated from the program more than two years ago. After moving to Mississippi with his mother at age sixteen, Ernest learned from his stepfather how to build houses and do construction but was not interested in pursuing that trade as a career. He went to work in a warehouse, married at age twenty, got a divorce, and fought a custody battle over his son before, at age twenty-six, "alone and depressed," he moved back to Chicago. "I decided to come back home and start completely over," Ernest said.

Technology had always fascinated Ernest, so when a family member who was an i.c.stars graduate told him about the program, he was immediately intrigued. "From day one, I knew this was what I wanted to do," he said. "I felt I had to be here."

Ernest spent two entire days working on his application. Before he completed the program in November 2018, he had landed a job with a company, Options Clearing Corporation (OCC), whose recruiter he met at one of i.c.stars's afternoon teas.

Ernest had worked at OCC for more than two years when we spoke with him. As a site reliability engineer, he works with development

teams to create and enhance the software delivery process by simplifying the user's experience, establishing best practices, and creating
cloud solutions. Ernest's success is emblematic of how people without
four-year college degrees can use skills as currency.

Another such individual is Graciela (Gracie), whom we met
through Charlene Haymond-Bussel, director of career planning and
placement at Olive-Harvey College in Chicago. Prior to enrolling,
Gracie had been working as a loader for a Chicago-based company
lifting plastic material onto semi-trailers. "The only female on the
team among men, I was lifting from the lightest to the heaviest plastic
material, bending, and at times crawling into tight spaces," she said.
"It was a simple job, but not the easiest on my body."

In 2020, in her words, Gracie "took the bull by the horns" and
enrolled in Olive-Harvey, one of the City Colleges of Chicago. "I did
not want to let fear and intimidation take over me, and to be clueless
in terms of not knowing how to properly function a forklift," she said.
"Taking this course was the best decision I ever made!"

Gracie now works for a major corporation, making more money
than before and handling responsibilities that include both forklift
and office work, all made possible by the forklift certification she received from Olive-Harvey. When asked how her life has changed, she
replies: "Just the simple fact that when you are determined to achieve
something, even if you are afraid, it can really impact your life in so
many ways, that makes you feel beyond this world!" She quotes hip
hop artist Notorious B.I.G.: "Stay far from timid. Only make moves
when ya heart's in it. And live the phrase, 'sky's the limit.' "

This chapter focuses on the Ernests and Gracies, individuals who
lack four-year college degrees but can move up the economic ladder
with the right guidance and training. Our next design principle operates at the system level (figure 1-2). It advocates using skills as the
currency for training and advancement, and to better match learners'
skills with better-paying jobs.

A 2018 Brookings Institution paper focuses on an important
segment of middle-skill jobs, calling them mid-tech, and including occupations such as computer network architects, network support specialists, and computer systems analysts. These are jobs that
often do not require a bachelor's degree. Pre-COVID-19, more than

900,000 workers occupied mid-tech occupations, and more than 38 percent of these workers did not have a bachelor's degree. At the same time, 17 percent, or half a million, high-tech workers with jobs such as programmers and security analysts also lacked a bachelor's degree.[1]

Given the rapid growth of highly skilled and mid-skilled jobs, the demand for qualified candidates cannot be met by college graduates alone. According to Harvard's Peter Blair and Byron Auguste, the pipeline of four-year degree candidates will be short by at least 25 percent, and the number of college graduates cannot be increased sufficiently to meet the new and burgeoning demand.[2] As the changing nature of work continues to require more skills and baby boomer retirements accelerate, the shortfall in available labor will increase and present a dilemma—but also a substantial opportunity. Auguste's nonprofit Opportunity@Work focuses on how mid-skill jobs can produce better careers for Black workers without college degrees.

According to Blair, "While some of these new occupations (e.g., data scientist) may require skills (e.g., statistical methods) which are typically acquired in advanced formal education, a large number (e.g., application developers and administrators for enterprise software-as-a-service platforms such as Salesforce, Workday, or ServiceNow) are learned not in formal education, but mostly on the job or in credentialed skill training designed by the SaaS companies themselves."[3]

In this chapter, we focus on strategies that elevate regional skill-building (not just degrees) to help lift workers into better jobs, including those referred to generally as middle-skill jobs as well as the subset called mid-tech jobs. A path upward does exist for aspiring workers, although it is not a prescriptively narrow technical path. These middle-skill jobs often are hybrid in nature, requiring both digital and non-cognitive or soft skills, and they are projected to grow twice as quickly as the overall labor market.

"In the ever-changing modern economy, having a narrow skill set may not be sufficient to ensure long-term success," says Matthew Sigelman, CEO of data company Burning Glass. "Ironically, despite being some of the most technology-driven and data-enabled jobs, they are also, in a way, more human—that is, more dependent on judgment and creativity."[4]

As the contours of the workforce shift, skills like participating in teams and working through problems have received greater emphasis. Likewise, the ability to exercise judgment has taken on increasing importance. Soft skills further critical thinking and behaviors that boost the likelihood of being hired. In one study, skills such as qualitative analysis, teamwork, and communication were the most important factors impacting which applicants received offers.[5]

An effective regional collaboration that uses skills as currency needs to coordinate action across various stakeholders. Skilling the pipeline requires changing the distinguishing characteristics of the local economy from one that focuses exclusively on providing jobs, into one that also emphasizes building specific, matching skill sets. This includes addressing the following:

- *Employee needs:* Determine current and predict future workforce skills needed.

- *Employer needs:* Assist employers in identifying the skills they need and how they can secure talent using skill-based hiring.

- *Training and education needs:* Tailor training and education to match predicted future workforce skills needed.

UNCF and Atlanta: Focus on Equity

The market currently places many obstacles in the way of a skill-based approach. More often than not, employers recruit based on educational attainment, and job postings often do not identify the detailed skills workers need. Often employees cannot document and employers cannot discern applicants' existing skills. Thus, the suppliers of training and education miss the opportunity to craft training for the most relevant additional skills. Here we focus on how regions can build labor pipelines for those who possess a work history but find themselves trapped in lower-paying jobs.

In 2019, Harvard's Kennedy School hosted a program for ten large-city mayors dedicated to excellence in their K–12 schools. The program had a distinguished advisory board of past and present national, state, local, and nonprofit leaders. Among them was one of the people who authored the preface of this book, Dr. Michael Lomax,

CEO of the United Negro College Fund (UNCF). He brought to the mayors a deep understanding of the lives of young people of color, as well as a broad institutional background, having served as president of Dillard University in New Orleans, as literature professor at UNCF-member institutions Morehouse and Spelman Colleges, and as chair of the Fulton County Commission in Atlanta.

Lomax cautioned the group not to forget the large number of young adults from urban environments who do not earn four-year college degrees. He suggested that the mayors include, as part of their mission, an analysis of opportunities for those not earning college degrees to ensure that they too can secure meaningful jobs. Without an intentional strategy and set of supports, non-college-educated candidates—especially those of color—cannot easily break through ceilings imposed by college degree requirements.

While pondering the Lomax challenge, the mayors' group recognized how little attention is paid to coordinating efforts to upskill the sizable population of those with identifiable talents but no postsecondary degree. To address this issue, UNCF and the mayor's office in Atlanta began a pilot project that provides a blueprint for a system that better prepares both workers and employers for skills-based employment.

Existing career pathways discriminate against minority workers without degrees in two ways. First the college degree requirement disproportionately leaves out significant portions of the Black community. As Blair and Shad Ahmed put it in a *Wall Street Journal* opinion piece, degree requirements embed into the labor market "the legacy of Black exclusion from the U.S. education system—namely, the anti-literacy laws that made it illegal for Blacks to learn to read, the separate and unequal schools that kept them from catching up, and the limited progress since then on policies designed to remedy racial discrimination."[6] In addition, young adults of color in urban high schools lack access to adequate counseling, which, if present, would lead to more students acquiring post-secondary credentials that match their interests and build on their skills.

The Atlanta project was led by UNCF's Julian Thompson, a graduate of Morehouse College and Harvard Law School. After getting his J.D., Thompson joined the highly respected City Year service move-

ment, and later took a staff position with the city council in Philadelphia, his hometown. At UNCF, he had been running leadership
programs for presidents and board chairs of Historically Black Colleges and Universities. Thompson combined his ability to work with
senior officials and his passion as a community organizer when he
joined with the mayor's office to organize a broad array of regional
stakeholders for the Atlanta/UNCF project.

The partners to the Atlanta project—including schools and universities, employers, the Chamber of Commerce, workforce organizations like WorkSource Atlanta, technical schools, and the United
Way—convened to address skilling as a way to increase equity and
opportunity. According to Thompson:

> The conversation centered on both a regional conceptualization of
> the need for skill development and the insufficiency of the current
> offerings. First, it's really clear that you have to be much more dy-
> namic if your real goal is to make sure that everyone has the skills
> they need for the workforce. Second, if you're going to empower a
> region to do well at reskilling or upskilling, you need to focus on
> a network approach.

The Atlanta project benefited from its extensive use of real-time
regional data, which identified growth sectors and skill opportunities. The data also allowed participating organizations to identify job
categories that are in decline and/or pay low wages with little upward
opportunity. Importantly their analyses helped participants to identify which skills gained from low-paying jobs could be applied to other
jobs with greater potential.

The first set of findings from the Atlanta team, when presented to
the mayors' education leadership group at Harvard, sparked the interest of leaders from all over the country. Data visualizations showed the
most in-demand competencies and how they aligned with the skills a
displaced hospitality worker, for example, might possess (figure 7-1).

The Atlanta cooperative then set about convincing regional stakeholders to use a common skill-based language. To facilitate completion of this goal, UNCF worked with data analysis company Emsi to
identify in-demand regional skills and to create a skills-based résumé-

Figure 7-1. **Skills Required for Successful Transition**

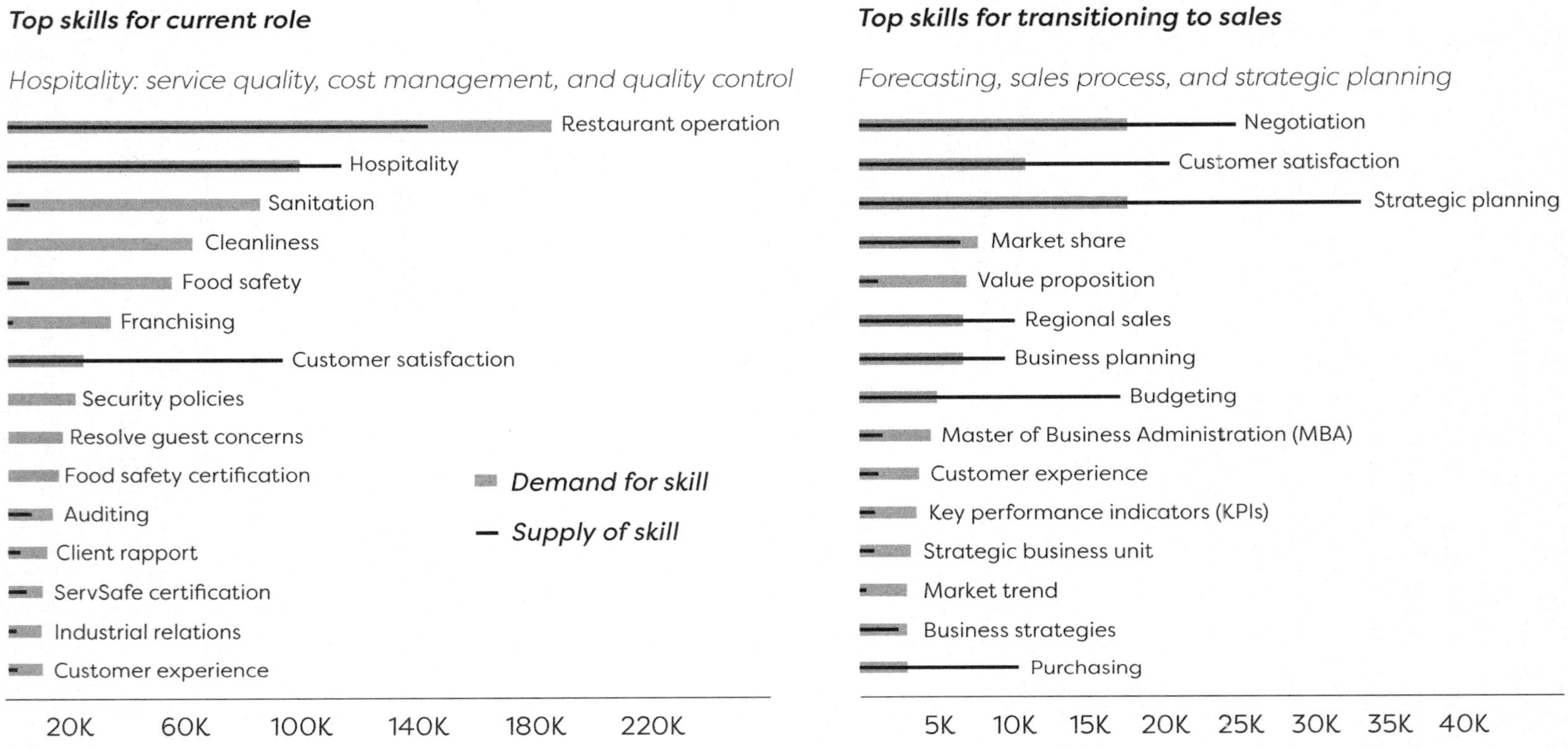

Top skills for current role

Hospitality: service quality, cost management, and quality control

Top skills for transitioning to sales

Forecasting, sales process, and strategic planning

Legend:
- ▇ *Demand for skill*
- — *Supply of skill*

Source: "Atlanta MSA Regional Skills Analysis," Emsi, July 2020, www.economicmodeling.com/wp-content/uploads/2020/08/Final-Report.pdf, p. 26.

builder tool. Training and education providers needed to design relevant programs to augment existing skills; job seekers needed to write their résumés to emphasize said skills; and workforce organizations needed to identify and respond to skill gaps. This language focused on skills, not job titles. For example, a software engineer for an auto manufacturer requires different skills than a position with the same title at Amazon Web Services.

Cooperative efforts like Atlanta's need leaders like Thompson. We have heard him give presentations on several occasions, among them to the large cities' chiefs of staff and chief data officer groups at Harvard's Kennedy School. His ability to combine the dispassionate command of data with the passionate advancement of his cause—the intersection of equity and opportunity—sets him apart.

Focusing on skills and opportunities necessarily involves issues of equity. The data show that Black workers in growing sectors such as healthcare are overrepresented in lower-paying roles and underrepresented in higher-paying roles. Leaders looking for policies to close the equity gap can see the problem and possible solutions in the data. For example, the skills data reveal that good healthcare jobs provide an ideal place for focused talent development. Expected growth in these jobs—coupled with training, education, and better career advice—could begin to reduce the imbalance.

Local leaders in Atlanta, with the help of UNCF, have set out to tackle an important challenge: creating sustainable, equitable growth by identifying opportunities for excluded populations, particularly some in the Black community. "What will be interesting here is how a municipality that's interested in influencing those skills spaces can use a data source that has a focus on equity in order to center what they hope will be a priority," Thompson said.

Walmart: Focus on Mobility

The Atlanta skilling effort required coordination across multiple players. A single large or medium-size employer may apply similar principles internally to support job advancement even while participating in larger regional initiatives. Walmart's skill-based efforts require it to work through an internal taxonomy of skills for its stores, including field work and supply chain. The mass merchandiser uses corporate data analytics to help identify the skills needed for a given role, which are then associated with a credentialing program to validate skill acquisition.

Walmart's Live Better U (LBU) makes it possible for hourly employees, for $1 a day, to attend any of seven learning providers, five of which are universities, and to enroll in a range of programs, including IT, pharmacy, supply management, and business management. Walmart covers tuition, books, and fees. For associates taking ESL and high school completion courses, the big box retailer pays 100 percent of the costs. As of 2021, more than 25,000 employees participated in LBU programs. The company works with participating universities to make sure their curriculum teaches skills relevant to promotion opportunities for employees.

Walmart partners with Guild Education to provide academic counseling to its worker-students and with the credentialing app Badgr to allow associates to attend courses virtually and accumulate stackable badges that demonstrate preparation and qualifications for a new job.

Components of a Skill-Based System

A review of organized skilling efforts by leading employers like IBM and Walmart and community efforts in Atlanta and San Diego suggests several components necessary to create more upward mobility based on skills.

Use Real-Time Local Data

Better pathways to middle-skill jobs using actionable regional data create opportunities for students and guide the development of modules that will fill in necessary training gaps. Many programs are overly dependent on Bureau of Labor Statistics data about unemployment, job growth, and wages. The data are insufficient, according to AEI expert Brent Orrell. "While traditional LMI [Labor Market Information] is extremely helpful and an essential component of labor market analytics, it is also very limited in the amount of detail it captures, especially at the local level."[7]

He further notes that official reports often use terms with which most people are unfamiliar, potentially confusing job seekers. Instead of relying just on BLS data, advancing a skilling agenda requires real-time regional data powered by machine learning that translates job and résumé postings into regional skill clusters. That information helps employers and employees understand the skills they need.

In Atlanta, Emsi provided the data services that configured regional highlights from almost 100 national sources involving 170 million job postings. MIT "future of work" experts Sanjay Sarma and William Bonvillian underscore that insufficient "information is available on employment options, job location, skill requirements and ways to acquire new skills." The U.S. labor market information system is broken, and both workers and employers are largely flying blind, the professors conclude.[8]

Use Analytics to Skill Gaps

Building this system starts with a landscape scan that describes in detail the skilling opportunities available to jobseekers. Analytics should help a region uncover skills that will open opportunities and assist local companies in maintaining their competitive advantages while serving to attract new businesses by focusing on developing the necessary skills.

This data-driven exercise should incorporate and analyze:

- The in-demand skills that employers need.

- The skills that aspiring workers have.

- The supply of training and education from local institutions. For example, are existing offerings over- or under-producing the skills needed for the market in that region?

- The demographics of the skill landscape by racial, gender, and other characteristics.

The resulting skills gap analysis will paint a detailed picture of opportunities in the local economy based on the difference between the demand coming from employers and the supply (or lack thereof) of specific skills in the workforce.[9]

More standardized language concerning skills will help leaders determine needs across industries. For example, accounting or book-keeping skills are needed in a multitude of industries. Thompson of UNCF observes that "if you have a tool that shows you that your hospitality skills might partially qualify you for a certain type of job in a manufacturing plant, then you can supplement those skills to unlock new relationships and opportunities." The Atlanta project used a tool called SkillScape that allowed stakeholders to better understand career pathways and make decisions informed by the data.

Consider the night manager of a hotel restaurant as one hypothetical. She may very well possess a decent set of skills related to managing money but needs additional training to prepare her for a higher level financial job in another industry. "Stackable" skills and related certifications potentially can produce substantial upward mobility, but only if the training and education providers as well as the local employers use the same language.

Figure 7-2 demonstrates employment growth sectors in Atlanta ranked in terms of thousands of projected new positions. Atlanta's analysis identified software development, management, nursing, and IT support as growth areas. It also highlighted where demand for specific jobs would exceed the projected supply of appropriately skilled labor, as shown in figure 7-3. Using analytics can help a regional group identify needed skills and with more precision point to places where workers can secure the necessary training.

Create Personal Skill Records

As a worker moves from job to job, better documentation of the skills obtained while employed and augmented by training becomes necessary. Employees can digitally record their work and training accomplishments in a verifiable form that can be shared with employers. The U.S. Chamber of Commerce, in its T3 Innovation network, labels this type of effort as "learning and employment records" (LER).

LERs use technology—sometimes blockchain—to create interop-

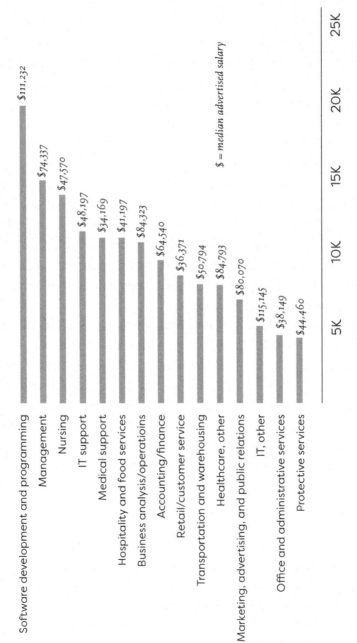

Figure 7-2. EMSI Skills and BLS Employment:
Top Growing Sub-Career Areas for the Atlanta MSA, Projections 2019–24

Software development and programming — $111,232

Management — $74,337

Nursing — $47,570

IT support — $48,197

Medical support — $34,169

Hospitality and food services — $41,197

Business analysis/operatioins — $84,323

Accounting/finance — $64,540

Retail/customer service — $36,371

Transportation and warehousing — $50,794

Healthcare, other — $84,793

Marketing, advertising, and public relations — $80,070

IT, other — $115,145

Office and administrative services — $38,149

Protective services — $44,460

$ = median advertised salary

5K   10K   15K   20K   25K

Source: "Atlanta MSA Regional Skills Analysis," Emsi, July 2020, www.economicmodeling.com/wp-content/uploads/2020/08/Final-Report.pdf, p. 13.

Figure 7-3. **EMSI Skills: Upskilling Opportunities in the Four Target Career Areas**

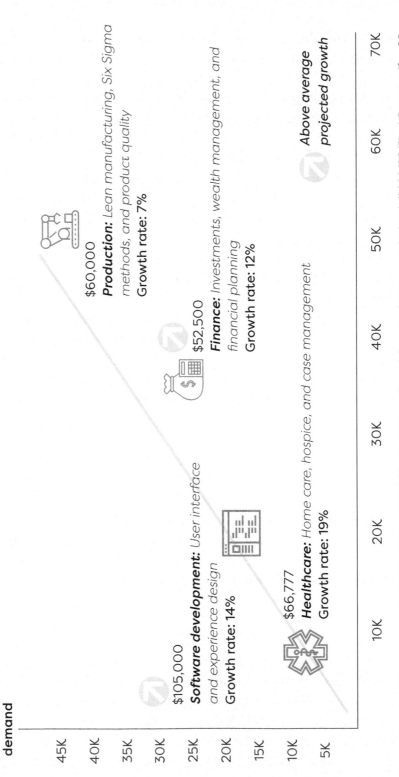

Estimated demand

45K
40K
35K
30K
25K
20K
15K
10K
5K

10K   20K   30K   40K   50K   60K   70K

$105,000

Software development: *User interface and experience design*
Growth rate: 14%

$66,777

Healthcare: *Home care, hospice, and case management*
Growth rate: 19%

$60,000

Production: *Lean manufacturing, Six Sigma methods, and product quality*
Growth rate: 7%

$52,500

Finance: *Investments, wealth management, and financial planning*
Growth rate: 12%

Above average projected growth

Source: "Atlanta MSA Regional Skills Analysis," Emsi, July 2020, www.economicmodeling.com/wp-content/uploads/2020/08/Final-Report.pdf, p. 20.

erable, verifiable, and portable records keyed to different work areas, including cybersecurity led by IBM, retail led by Walmart, and healthcare led by Salesforce. These LERs benefit learners, educators, and employers, all of whom can use the information to build stackable skills. Developing LERs also helps drive the important task of creating a standard language or currency of skills, and that standardization, in turn, facilitates LER adoption.

Two significant LER efforts involving blockchain are now underway. One, the IBM Learning Credential Engine, includes such organizations as the National Student Clearinghouse, Western Governors University, and Central New Mexico Community College. The IBM effort uses blockchain to create a cumulative, verified chain of a worker's credentials, tying together their education and experience and the skills they have built.

The other major undertaking, the nonprofit Velocity Network, consists of major corporations and has the goal of providing governance over a system that enables "trusted, private and secure exchange of career credentials" among individuals and organizations. The network plans to establish and manage a rulebook and framework that supports users of decentralized protocols, all built in an open-source environment.

The promise of these efforts lies in their ability to record skills from traditional higher education and other training providers, including employers, and to merge them into a single, verifiable record. If widely implemented, they would dramatically advance skill-based hiring, and would substantially cut down on the difficulty facing employers in evaluating the experience and education of workers, especially those who lack traditional degrees.

Working toward Equity

Hiring focused on skills elevates capabilities over degrees and, in part, compensates for a system that makes it more difficult for Black workers and other people of color to acquire four-year diplomas. People of color disproportionately lack the traditional educational qualifications needed for high-quality jobs. For example, 35 percent of white adults have a bachelor's degree or higher versus 21 percent of Blacks and 15 percent of Hispanics/Latinos.[10] Utilizing alternative, skill-based pathways helps to offset the ill effects of these inequities.

The Atlanta effort analyzed the Metropolitan Statistical Area (MSA) to find equity gaps by looking at levels of Black employment and pay. Black workers were somewhat underrepresented in the most common middle-skill areas and overrepresented in the lower-paying categories (figure 7-4).

The Atlanta partners and the mayor's office collectively used data identifying existing racial disparities with the intention of establishing responsive corrective measures. Informed by data, local officials planned how to tailor training that narrowed or closed equity gaps by helping workers to secure better jobs for which they were qualified by skill, not just by formal education.

Byron Auguste, in his writing and through his Opportunity@ Work initiative, highlights the racial imbalances that result from insisting on attainment of unnecessary degrees. Starting with the 70 million STARs—workers he classifies as "Skilled through Alternative Routes"—he narrows in on the approximately 7 million Black Americans who have skills and who, based on their current roles, could transition to jobs that, on average, pay 70 percent more than what they are currently earning.

Viewing the employment picture through an equity lens spotlights specific opportunities for this group of STARs. It also allows regional leaders to address racial inequities related to career ladders. Some low-wage jobs serve as a step up on a ladder. Other low-wage jobs are merely lateral steps to other low-wage jobs. The Atlanta partnership analyzed Black representation in jobs with low wages and little or no upward career mobility to identify employees who might be good candidates for upskilling to position them for a new career path.

Dane Linn, vice president of immigration, workforce, and education for Business Roundtable (BRT), leads the organization's Multiple Pathways initiative, an effort to pave the way for skill-based hiring involving over eighty employers. He refers to one of their surveys, in which three-quarters of employers cited advancing equity as an important factor in their participation. Josh Bolton, BRT's CEO, agrees that by emphasizing and rewarding worker skills both in the recruitment and the promotion process, employers have found that demon-

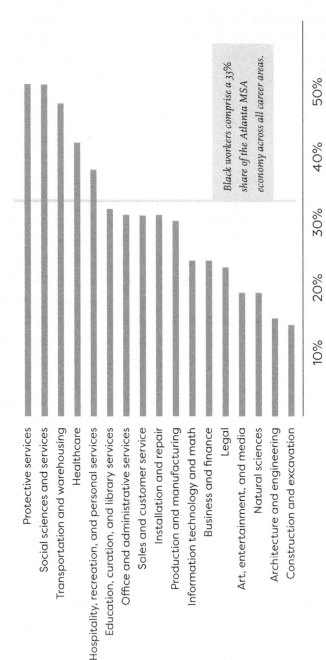

Figure 7-4. **EMSI Skills and BLS Employment: Current Black Employment by Career Area Compared to Black Employment Share of Workforce (2019)**

Protective services

Social sciences and services

Transportation and warehousing

Healthcare

Hospitality, recreation, and personal services

Education, curation, and library services

Office and administrative services

Sales and customer service

Installation and repair

Production and manufacturing

Information technology and math

Business and finance

Legal

Art, entertainment, and media

Natural sciences

Architecture and engineering

Construction and excavation

Black workers comprise a 33% share of the Atlanta MSA economy across all career areas.

10% 20% 30% 40% 50%

Share of employment

Source: "Atlanta MSA Regional Skills Analysis," Emsi, July 2020, www.economicmodeling.com/wp-content/uploads/2020/08/Final-Report.pdf, p. 13.

strated skills are often a better predictor of on-the-job success than traditional résumé listings.

Move Employers to Skill-Based Hiring

To achieve greater equity and remove inefficiencies in the labor market, employers must be convinced to adopt skill-based hiring practices rather than hiring and promoting solely based on degree credentials. A 2014 survey of human resource professionals conducted by Accenture showed that employers use higher levels of education as a proxy for employability instead of hiring workers based on demonstrable competencies directly related to job tasks.[11] Lack of information about the skills necessary for a specific job can make it difficult for workers to determine how to develop requisite qualifications.[12]

For both the learner and the employer, unclear data present serious obstacles. Education and training institutions offer almost 1 million different certificates and degrees,[13] but HR departments often lack the data to match those 1 million options to qualifications. Employees find it difficult to assess the relevance of a particular educational attainment to actual skill requirements. And employers, by not more intentionally recruiting based on skills, pass up the opportunity to create a system with more targeted pathways to the suppliers of education and training.

By using specific skills as a barometer for hiring and advancement, employers also create greater transparency in terms of how workers can acquire the necessary capabilities to move up and around the company. This allows companies to upskill and, thus, retain existing employees, instead of recruiting talent, at a higher cost, from competitors. It also opens up promotion opportunities for those in lower-level positions based on their work and learning.

BRT's Multiple Pathways initiative sets out a roadmap for recruitment, hiring, and promotions based on skills. The Roundtable suggests several actions companies can take:

- Rewrite job descriptions to focus on the skills needed to succeed in the job.

- Review existing assessment tools and adopt new standard interview processes to screen candidates and determine the level of skills required to perform the job.

- Develop and publish transparent job advancement pathways for the current workforce that can be navigated by meeting specific training milestones and skill acquisitions.

- Create and use training modules that teach employees new skills needed to meet job advancement milestones. Training can be delivered through on-the-job experience (for example, mentorships and apprenticeships), online learning platforms, and/or partnerships with external education and training providers.

- Recognize and reward employees who complete credentials or certifications valued by the company.[14]

Employers, especially large ones, can apply these techniques to their workforces by quantifying skills, augmenting them through training, and promoting employees based on the results. One way to slow turnover and reward loyalty is to promote from within.

Apply Badges

Certificates and badges have emerged as signals of achievement. IBM is one of the country's leaders in using skills to provide an alternate hiring pathway for what IBM refers to as "new collar" jobs. We asked David Leaser, senior executive for IBM's training and skills program, to explain how the company uses credentials to support advancement. Leaser explains that the call for action originated from then CEO Ginni Rometty and her passion to identify "new collar" as a concept that reflects changes occurring in the U.S. labor market. The old dichotomy of college degreed workers filling white collar jobs and nondegreed workers filling blue collar jobs no longer reflects reality.

IBM began by reevaluating roles that unnecessarily required a college education and commissioned an internal team to go through job descriptions and strip out degree qualifications where they were not needed. Currently, the company does not require a college degree for roughly 50 percent of its roles in North America. Once the company eliminated four-year degree requirements, it needed to delineate the right sets of skills for those hiring and those seeking to be hired for applicable jobs. The team developed a system to help prepare people for those roles.

Leaser took us, next, to a critical component of their matching and training effort, the IBM Digital Badge program, which he founded. His enthusiasm and the program's ease of use were evident, even on Zoom, as he walked through his personal digital wallet and its connection to his digital résumé. Badges and courses for IBM include myriad subjects, from programming and machine learning to communication and visualization.

Adquena Faine's journey illustrates the importance of skills and badging. She enlisted in the military and, when discharged, started but did not complete a college degree. Her words capture her situation and opportunity better than ours ever could:

> I had a series of life situations and found myself having to figure out a way to make ends meet. My daughter was six; I lost my home and was living in a hotel and driving for rideshare companies a lot. It was very demanding. It was taxing on my body to do all that. And what was the hardest is that it was taking time away from my daughter. I got to the point where I knew I had to do something different. I was doing online searches for taking a coding boot-camp. And I found Big Data University, which is offered by IBM. And it's a badging program. So, I'm thinking, okay, if I do this, maybe if I take this course and I earn this badge, I can apply for this apprenticeship program. And that's what I did.

Adquena's first badge was in data science, according to Credly, the national credential tracker. Her most recent of five total badges include enterprise design thinking, data science, and cloud object storage. Adquena's badges led directly to her current IBM job. Near the end of our conversation, she leans into the Zoom camera with a wonderful sense of confidence and enthusiasm and exclaims that she is "excited to be at work, I'm excited about my job! If a time comes when I'm not excited, I can learn more and go somewhere else in IBM and grow with what they have given me. And the courses are free and no more student loans are hanging over my head."

Kelli Jordan, IBM's director leading career and skilling efforts, describes the company's groundbreaking goal to use artificial intelligence (AI) to go a step further and proactively suggest to workers badges that would augment their skills and prepare them for new opportunities. Her goal is to help "IBMers" understand the skills they have and those they might need as they progress toward their next career goal. She adds that as employees progress and build skills they improve their current performance, as well. Critical to IBM's success is its taxonomy, which allows it to use skills as a currency. The taxonomy gets more granular as it penetrates further down in the company and includes both job roles, such as project management, and specialty skills, such as Java.

Jordan explains the "inference engine" that uses IBM's AI-powered platform, called Watson:

> It helps us tag and make clear learning recommendations. We do benchmarking around scarcity of a skill in the marketplace to determine whether this is a skill that is readily available. We use that when we consider pay scales for skills, as well.
>
> The inference engine helps us translate particular jobs into the skills associated with them. Our inference capability is looking at the digital footprint of every single IBMer using millions and millions of documents and source files. It comes from roughly two dozen different sources, anything from a résumé to completed badges. We look at our patent databases and public repositories in GitHub for our technical IBMers. That digital footprint is then analyzed to determine how much skill a person might possess. If we see skill gaps using the taxonomy, we show employees on an internal platform the skill data that will help them build a career path. They can see those learning recommendations. They can navigate that career journey using all of the data that we have at our disposal, helping them make informed decisions about where they should invest their time when they're thinking about growth and development.

IBM integrates its digital badge program into its inference engine learning experience platform. It relies on open badge architecture, pioneered by Mozilla, that ensures the badges have value and meaning, and uses tags to connect IBM badges with the open-architecture badges.

Leaser reports that the badging results have exceeded his wildest expectations in terms of employee response. They've provided value to IBM as an employer, as well. IBM has seen triple-digit increases in employee/student enrollments, completed courses, and pass rates. Three-quarters of managers found badges motivated employees to develop current skills.

The IBM story is a remarkable one. The company issued a digital badge every twenty seconds in 2020. Since 2015, the overall program has issued roughly 3.5 million digital badges across 195 countries to both internal and external earners. Within IBM alone, over 1 million badges have been earned in the past five years.

Badges also help individuals find jobs when out of work and when they move among employers. We met Coletta, who found herself without a good job or up-to-date experience. Her bridge to a job was a badge she received from an online course. It created a new start for her. She recounts:

> I had hit one of those patches in life where everything fell apart. Consequently, I lost work contacts while I took time off to care for family situations. Then, after a few years of various jobs, I wanted to get back up and rolling because everything had settled down. I couldn't find a job and, at my age, over 50, they looked at me funny, assuming I was too old. I did everything I could as far as updating my résumé and making it look good.
>
> Nothing worked. I wasn't finding any decent jobs. All employers saw was my spotty experience for the past five years. They didn't recognize the 25 years before that of outstanding experience. Those 25 years just didn't matter. I needed some way to make those 25 years relevant again. The one thing that kept coming up was to go back to school, go back to school. Okay, fine, but I've been out of work, and I don't have a lot of money, I can't pay for school. The other thing was, what do I do?

Then I saw a post on Twitter about what was then Big Data University. I thought that even though I might not get any kind of data science job, showing that I could take on high-level technical subjects and do them on my own would enhance my résumé.

Upon the completion of courses that provided her badges in big data foundations, data Hadoop foundations, data analytics, and cloud development, Coletta took a contract job with Microsoft, a company that valued her tenacity and self-improvement—demonstrated by her securing badges—as much as it did the substance of the courses she took.

To the learner like Coletta, badges enhance the use of skills as a currency. And the fact that, increasingly, universities such as Northeastern provide badges associated with more formal classes enhances their usefulness. Badging paths works for students and corporate learners hoping to advance their careers, and for lifelong learners looking for new opportunities or the chance to freshen up dated skills, as was the situation with Coletta.

Badges serve multiple purposes. In addition to quantifying skills as a currency for companies, they motivate employees to look for ways to improve themselves while also providing recognizable authentication. Badges make it possible for individuals to connect the skills learned in college courses with on-the-job experience, making it much easier for universities to create stackable skills and for employers to make decisions based on skills.

Use the Skilling and Credentialing as Currency across Institutions

Skills as a currency when coupled with shorter-term credentialing and training open up doors to higher paying jobs. Yet as noted in a recent MDRC study: "While shorter-term credentialing and training programs have promise, many also present challenges for schools and students. Because these programs operate under a different system of governance from colleges' academic programs and have traditionally been divorced from those pathways, students encounter challenges applying their noncredit training toward academic degrees."[15] Connecting noncredit credentials with college courses will require an effort from these separate parts of the system to communicate and "tag" the relevant components.

Network Management

A region committed to more opportunity and equity by recruiting, hiring, and promoting based on skills needs a coordinated effort to succeed. The sectors and stakeholders involved, even if amenable to the concept, can succeed only through the use of a common language and an organized approach. The fragmented nature of the workforce "system" produces serious obstacles that cannot be overcome at the level of a single institution.

Regional collaboratives need to convince more local employers of the opportunities produced by broadening their current hiring and retention pathways, using skills as a currency. Even when employers are willing to augment a higher education credentials-based system with alternative skill-based paths, they need a way to determine which applicants possess what skills. Also, convincing a human resources manager to use a skill-oriented approach requires the ability to efficiently determine whether, in fact, a prospect has acquired these necessary skills. Otherwise, workers without bachelor's degrees still will face substantial barriers to entry.

To put this market problem in economic terms, Harvard's Blair says, "Some of the college wage premium and the stagnant/declining fortunes of workers without college degrees may be due to ineffective signaling of the relevant skills (which many non-college graduates acquire through work experience) rather than to differential skill levels *per se* between workers with and without BA degrees."[16]

Clear signals require standardization, which can be coordinated by: (1) an industry association such as National Institute for Metalworking Skills (NIMS), a nationally recognized validator of manufacturing industry credentials; or (2) a multiemployer national effort, like that of the U.S. Chamber, or local initiatives like the one in San Diego. However, moving to this model requires regional leadership to work out the best solutions for its community.

The San Diego Workforce Partnership relies on data to identify in-demand occupations expected to have high growth and job openings over the next five years. In conjunction with the County Office of Education, the partnership's CEO Peter Callstrom and his team created an essential skill rubric that helps orient learning and hiring around necessary skills like communication, critical thinking, dependability, and resourcefulness.[17]

Without a common language concerning skills, workers need to guess how the skills they possess prepare them for and match them to new opportunities. Callstrom runs one of the country's most outstanding workforce development boards. As the chief executive officer of the group, he brings, with his team, a big-picture approach to workforce when he emphasizes that lack of knowledge about sectors, specific skills, and in-demand jobs creates an "information scarcity [that] is a source of inequality. The skills gap is not a lack of talent. It is talent yet unrealized due to an awareness gap, an education gap and opportunity gaps. This inequity can be reversed with the right approach."

Many U.S. employers rely on the four-year degree as a blunt instrument for predicting success in the workplace. Others too often express a preference for investing in technology over investing in the hiring or training of employees. Compounding these factors from an equity standpoint is the fact that Black and Latino workers remain underrepresented in good jobs relative not only to population share but also educational attainment.[18]

Yet, across the United States, a myriad of organizations are producing important breakthroughs and advancing skill-based hiring. The Business Higher Education Forum brings together business and education in several markets to advance these themes. Universities across the country have taken several important steps. The Utah-based online Western Governors University, in particular, has played a leadership role in offering online, skill-based learning. Markle Foundation's Skillful project is working with states to create skills-based systems, including consulting with education providers and employers to prompt them to hire and train based on skills. Skillful also advocates for more government funded career coaching outside traditional education and workforce investment board offices, to better reach marginalized communities.

Another significant effort includes the SkillUp Coalition and its major partner, Jobs for the Future, which harnesses foundation dollars to provide job replacement information directly to individuals, especially those impacted by COVID-19. SkillUp efforts aim to develop local partnerships, connecting short-term credential-based training to jobs. They provide skill oriented virtual career coaching in conjunction with nonprofit Roadtrip Nation.

The work of the Business Roundtable provides an important and practical guide to regions as well as supporting specific involved companies. Dane Linn provided us the metrics used in the BRT Multiple Pathways project. The preliminary top-level metrics used by the BRT participants in the Multiple Pathways project, with a bit of modification, serve as an excellent starting point for a regional collaboration designed to advance skills as a currency. We modified what Linn provided, and suggest the following regional metrics as a starting point, shown in table 7-1.

Of course, other components and metrics can and should be added. For example, since 2018, the Bank of America's Pathways initiative with community colleges and partners such as Year Up, UnidosUS, and the National Urban League has resulted in the hiring of more than 10,000 employees from low- and moderate-income neighborhoods.

These important company-level efforts, however, need to come together in the broader community. Well-developed regional alliances that advance a skills-based infrastructure need a network manager to support a platform across stakeholders. Examine the role UNCF played, for instance. With its deep roots in Atlanta, UNCF took on the challenge of bringing together almost twenty different organizations to produce more equitable opportunities around skilling. The consortium grounded its work on actionable data that showed both opportunities and inequities.

Initiatives in Atlanta and San Diego and inside IBM demonstrate how the use of data creates value. These efforts, founded on skills as a currency, demonstrate the intersection of three important themes: identifying mid-tech jobs in growth sectors; using skilling as the language of advancement; and focusing relentlessly on equity. Community-wide organizing that promotes these three themes will help workers, especially those of color, gain access to jobs with better wages and clearer upward trajectories.

Table 7-1. **Preliminary Top-Level Metrics**

How many business, higher education, nonprofit, and government partners are engaged?	How many individuals have been impacted through these efforts? ▪ How many students have participated? ▪ How many apprentices have been brought on? ▪ How many new hires have been made as a result? ▪ How many employees have been upskilled?
How many new apprenticeship, internship, or credential programs have been created through this effort?	
	How many new hires have you made as a result of these efforts?
How many new courses or course curricula have been developed?	What diverse populations (underrepresented people of color, veterans, people with disabilities) have been engaged and how?
What HR policies and/or job description requirements have been reviewed? What changes have been made?	

Source: Business Roundtable and Business-Higher Education Forum, Workforce Partnership Initiative Site Convening (Washington, DC: BHEF, 2021), p. 3.

8

Commit to Transparency

For decades, public and nongovernment organizations frequently succumbed to the tendency to label activities as outcomes, and even then to present the results in a fashion that could not be easily used to motivate performance. As chair of the Corporation for National and Community Service (CNCS), the parent of AmeriCorps and Vista for almost a decade, Stephen faced these issues.

On one occasion, he asked what criteria the corporation's reviewers used to rank the entities seeking funding. The answer from staff was: performance. Their definition of performance? Whether the organizations excelled in the way they completed the CNCS applications, and whether they had previously closed their grants without exception. Contributions to the community or the quality of the experience for young adult volunteers were not considered, and CNCS lawyers interpreting government rules doubted they could be.

When, after 9/11, applications for AmeriCorps soared, many individuals interested in serving looked for guidance on which programs provided the best experience. But, again, no one captured that information, and the government lawyers did not think CNCS could require exit evaluations from graduating members to inform their successors. In response, an association of AmeriCorps alums took on the responsibility of conducting surveys of volunteers' experiences with organizations and then compiling and posting them online to guide decisionmaking.

Kate spent her career in the social sector tackling this very question. All too often outputs, counting people served or units provided, are used rather than impact or outcome achieved. It can lead to false assumptions of efficacy.

We thought about these issues during a recent conversation with Jerry Rubin from Jewish Vocational Services, who worried about federally imposed workforce performance standards that paid him based on the number of individuals completing a specific training course and not whether they received and held a job as a consequence. He wondered why he received a demerit if they got a job too soon and dropped out of his program.

Several factors aggravate this problem in the area of career development. The "system's" fragmentation means that no single entity has responsibility for compiling and publishing relevant outcomes. Parties frequently disagree often about what should be considered an outcome. As noted before, government contracts often reward completion of an act, rather than its results. Measures compiled for government and philanthropic funders are not usually expressed in a fashion that helps the learner or the worker—the consumer of training and education services.

This chapter focuses on the design principle of price and performance transparency—how the right data can be captured, used, and disseminated in order to turn aspiring learners into informed consumers. Vastly more individuals could reach their potential and improve their upward mobility if they made career choices with the aid of clear, easy-to-understand information from which they could calculate the return on an investment of training, skills, and degrees.

Applying this design principle and producing easily usable, transparent information would reduce much of the decision-related friction that impedes mobility. The coauthors provide an illustration of how inaccessible such data is, even to those who are relatively knowledgeable. Married to each other, together we have six adult children. Counting spouses, our family consists of ten adult learners and/or workers. At any one time, most of them hold jobs, but several are also consulting us about new jobs.

Given the multiple degrees and jobs the two of us have held, we are, presumably, in a better position than many to understand educational and job choices and tradeoffs. Nevertheless, after each family question concerning a possible change in career or a return to school for a certification or another degree, we reach a level of complexity where, even after substantial research, answers remain uncertain and relevant information opaque.

Our efforts to give workforce advice to our children and their spouses provide a window into the challenges and frustrations faced by those with less experience and knowledge. We find too much of the wrong information, not enough of the information we need, and way too much difficulty deciphering what we do find online. Upward mobility depends on a wider array of individuals being able to make decisions about precisely what schools, courses, or training will produce the skills they need to secure a particular type of job, and the pay and working conditions associated with that job. The current informational infrastructure makes this extremely challenging at best.

Markets with good information systems operate much more efficiently. A worker or learner trying to figure out the most practical steps to take now must sort through incomplete, difficult to access, and often incomprehensible local labor information. The complexity can produce uncertainty, which results in individuals not taking any steps. Or it results in them taking wrong, expensive, or wasteful next steps.

Complexities and inefficiencies challenge would-be college students and, even more so, workers without post-secondary education. These informational obstacles emanate from four compounding factors: (1) the lack of clear performance outcomes creates the benchmarking challenge; (2) the fragmented nature of the workforce "system" presents the curator challenge; (3) the poor user experience creates the UX or presentation challenge; and (4) the overall complexity and often unfriendly terminology within the system leads to the translator challenge.

Policymakers need to make sure the systems they design help learners and their families secure easily understandable information that aids in decisionmaking. Over the last decade, the number of learners who have relied on internet searches for advice has, predictably, increased. However, despite the array of accessible data, interested consumers still cannot easily understand their options in terms of what course or class sequences produce the skills required for a necessary credential. In this chapter, we look at ways that improved information can be delivered more effectively to consumers of education and training.

The Benchmarking Challenge

The presentation of outcome information for a course requires some agreement on the definition of workforce outcomes and the benchmarks of success. Outcomes should be agreed upon locally and collaboratively. Training and education providers, employers, and economic development groups will have separate definitions of institutional success, but in this chapter, we suggest that stakeholders should agree on performance definitions that relate to the workers' upward mobility.

Players in the workforce market—consumers, education providers, and employers—need high-quality information for the system to work in a fairer and more efficient way. As workers begin to understand and quantify their own skills, they need a system designed to help them determine how best to acquire the additional skills they need from a program in a location and at a cost that works for them.

The benchmarking necessary for a more efficient labor market requires an agreed-upon taxonomy of skills and a way to measure the value of courses or steps on the pathway to better jobs. As cities move to a more fulsome consideration of skills as a currency, they will need a currency converter—a taxonomy—to classify job descriptions and experience into skills, and to translate education and training curricula into skill sets. These changes will assist the employee searching for a better return on investment as he looks to develop the right skills at the best educational institution for his needs; one where successful completion sends a confirming signal to employers about his worth. A well-designed system will assist job seekers in creating résumés, communicating with employers using a common language, and making decisions concerning what might be best—knowing that the courses they take signal the right skill sets to the employers.

Employers should translate their postings into a skills-based language, and education and training organizations should provide information on the costs and financial benefits resulting from the courses they offer. Prospects can then evaluate which courses best help them close the gap between their skills and what they need for a better, more fulfilling job.

In addition, employers and employees alike need clear information on training quality. Employers face challenges with skill-based hiring because of the difficulty of translating jobs into skills and, in turn, determining which workers without degrees possess those skills. The further from a traditional background a worker is, the more obstacles employer and employee alike face in hiring and promotion decisions. The fact that skill credentials and degrees augment one another creates additional complexity.

Businesses can form ad hoc relationships in which they secure the information they need to advance hiring decisions. Some community colleges work to structure highly specific programs with certain companies, which provides the employer insights into the quality of program graduates. And some human resources directors know they can depend on graduates of a particular school or course, which gives them hiring confidence. These ad hoc successes based on experience or institutional reputation reduce hiring friction. But their very ad hoc nature also suggests how far we have to go in producing higher quality, transparent regional data that signals to worker and employer alike whether a particular course actually better prepares the learner.

Transparency requires that educational institutions and training providers translate courses and programs into the common skill-based language of the labor market. Useful, quality, scalable information can be generated from machine-reading of syllabi, and the conversion of that information into a skills-based language that resembles employer job postings. This process, in turn, provides signals to businesses and students that the coursework is relevant and valuable to the market.

Last, benchmarks that reveal outcomes allow more precise and tailored additional learning, which can be reconfigured as necessary to produce a higher return on investment. American Enterprise Institute's Mason Bishop points out that: (1) noncredit skills-training programs can be implemented and made operational more quickly than traditional, credit-bearing, two- or four-year degree programs, and (2) noncredit programs can be highly adaptable and responsive to employer demand. This agility results from and depends on an ability to document both existing worker skills and the skills taught in postsecondary courses; and this promises, in return, significant additional value in terms of upskilling mobility.

We asked Carol D'Amico, former community college chancellor and U.S. assistant secretary for adult and vocational education, for her recommendations on how a region might think about outcome benchmarks that would aid a consumer. She suggested answering these questions, which can apply to both degree and non-degree programs:

1. What kind of jobs do people with my intended degree get after graduation? By specific degrees by specific colleges.

2. What kind of jobs require my intended degree?

3. What is the job demand for my degree?

4. What is the starting salary for people with my degree?

5. What are the wages one year, five years, and ten years after graduation?

6. Do I need an advanced degree to achieve top earnings?

7. What do those who complete my degree think about the value of it?

8. How much is this degree, certification, or course going to cost me?

Transparency will provide opportunity and market efficiency, but it requires careful attention to definitions. Agreed-upon definitions of skills coupled with outcome information and costs will aid the worker as she or he pieces together job experience, training, and education to create a ladder to upward mobility. Students and their advisers alike will benefit from a more understandable and extensible language.

The Curator Challenge

To successfully implement the design principle of making career data accessible to users, an entity at the regional level is needed to help convert massive amounts of information to actionable data. The fragmented nature of government and nonprofit workforce efforts scatters the enormous amount of information about jobs produced by a market economy. The ability of a consumer to select the right path requires curation of critical information to reduce the noise currently associated with consuming that information.

Choosing the best training program or community college course of study can be dizzying to the uninitiated. As one would expect, universities, colleges, and training programs aggressively and effectively market their offerings. However, in the absence of a data-informed consumer/learner, marketing can lead to decisions that do not produce an effective return on educational investment.

To make the most impactful college investment, Philip Oreopoulos from the University of Toronto and Uros Petronijevic from York University stress that "Prospective students must give careful consideration to selecting the institution itself, the major to follow, and the eventual occupation to pursue. For any particular program at a particular school, anticipated future labor market earnings, the likelihood of completion, the costs and the value of any student debt must all be factored into the assessment."[1]

If one counts degrees, certificates, licenses, badges, and apprenticeships, there are close to 1 million unique credentials in the United States.[2] This huge array of choices represents only a fraction of the necessary information, as a prospective student must also try to find data, such as it is, concerning relevance, return on investment, and the skills associated with a particular path. Effective curation will make this daunting challenge easier for both the person interested in making a training or education decision and as the employer who attempts to evaluate a credential.[3]

The Presentation or UX Challenge

Whether oriented toward a single large employer or developed by a regional consortium, better "self-service tools"—those that a job seeker can use even without an expert adviser—need to be available. This allows searches to yield a relevant set of options with clarity about the likely return on investment.

Well-designed, user-friendly presentation requires simplification, standardization, and intuitive functionality. A learner should be able to easily determine whether a credential leads to a job, and whether success in that job will make upward mobility possible. A community attempting to help learners by presenting more salient information needs to be mindful that a large number of learners lack confidence and are reluctant to take that next step, according to surveys by the national research consulting firm Heart+Mind Strategies, and as reflected in figure 8-1.

Many of these doubters previously could not afford traditional post-secondary opportunities, received poor or no advice, and/or had bad experiences in the workplace. Confidence that additional edu-

Figure 8-1. **Barriers to Pursuing Education and Training**
Confidence

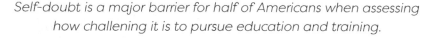

Self-doubt is a major barrier for half of Americans when assessing how challening it is to pursue education and training.

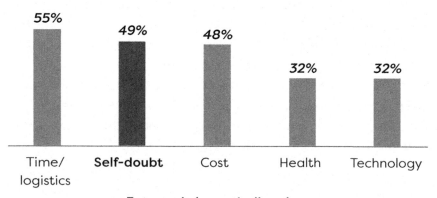

Source: Heart+Mind Strategies, www.heartandmind.us.

cation will "make me an attractive job candidate to a potential employer," dropped dramatically under the COVID onslaught, falling by more than 50 percent, according to Heart+Mind. Many nontraditional workers feel powerless to change their perceived inability to get a good job or advance their career believing that the system for hiring and advancement is not fair, that employers cannot or will not help them sufficiently, and that they lack the right skills. One in four Americans without a college degree say more education and training would make no difference in their ability to get a good job, as shown earlier in figure 3-3.

The critical information that connects training with a good job needs to be presented in a manner that aids and encourages the person who wishes to add a credential. Credential transparency allows consumers to make more-informed decisions. Simplified and visualized data are necessary but not sufficient. Information about the jobs that a person with a certain credential can obtain and the wages associated with those jobs is necessary if policymakers are to overcome the barriers potential workers see as standing in the way.

In order to make it easier for workers to access understandable information, the Retail and Hospitality Credentials Initiative of Credential Engine, joining together with and supported by the National Retail Federation Foundation, the National Restaurant Association, and the American Hotel and Lodging Educational Foundation, documents and publishes the credentials currently available in the retail, hospitality, restaurant, lodging, and related sectors. The goal of this initiative is to help job seekers and employers make choices regarding whether and how to acquire supplemental skills that will qualify them for more advanced jobs.

A self-directed application supported by AI allows workers to configure solutions to fit their needs. The most critical usability features include the ability of learners to control searches around their goals; to be able within the app to collaborate with peers, asking them questions and following their ratings; and to connect their discoveries to how completion will add value.

Around the country, various components of this user-friendly design exist. For example, the San Diego Workforce Partnership has developed an interactive online experience with a range of tools to support workers. It combines career information with labor market data and suggestions concerning where one can achieve critical skills. Unfortunately, few if any apps provide the full functionality that derives from regional data. Shared intergovernmental data present legal and technical issues, especially as different agency programs bring with them varying federal rules concerning access and use. States need to facilitate access to intergovernmental data in order to assist learners.

The State of Colorado's OnwardCO, in conjunction with Bright-Hive, a company that provides the tools and processes necessary for data stewardship, demonstrates one of the necessary steps in simplifying and consolidating data so it is more usable at the front end. Colorado's COVID-19 response site connects the state's residents with necessary services like shelter, childcare, or mental health, and also allows them to better understand retraining programs and employment opportunities.

Matt Stevens, director of data collaboration services for BrightHive, helps coordinate the effort. Stevens saw, from his past work, the power of bringing data together to serve people involved in the justice system, which is a "system" in name only, awash in discrete, siloed data. Colorado officials working with BrightHive sought to capture data-integration benefits that could be a first step to presenting better information derived from various agencies in a single place.

A taskforce of state agencies—including the Colorado Department of Higher Education, the Department of Human Services—Child Welfare Division, the Workforce Development Council, and the Department of Labor and Employment—contributed to and use the resulting data trust, which facilitates mutual sharing and learning among public and nongovernment agencies. Educational institutions and employers also contribute. The trust's quasi-independent structure allows it to manage how data is used and shared, as well as control who gets what sort of access. The employer and government information combined in OnwardCO is augmented with national data about topics like credentialing.

According to Stevens, a worker (or job seeker) can log in and go through a series of questions and an assessment to figure out what opportunities might be applicable to herself, using the real-time data in the trust. MyColorado allows some calculation of return on invest-ment, as it uses well-visualized information to show wages of people who completed programs. Data aggregators such as Burning Glass provide information on regional trends that add important, relevant, current information. The Colorado data trust may not yet provide the user all he or she needs, but it does take a big step toward integrating and coordinating critical data sets that must be part of simplifying any solution.

The presentation and functionality of such a system must ac-count for context and consider how communication strategies influ-ence behaviors. The creators must ask themselves, "How does the clarity, relevance, and visualization of the data help a hesitant job- or education-seeker make a decision? How does it motivate someone to take a step toward a better life?" Presentation requires an under-standing of context; it requires trusted local people and agencies to be involved in the design.

The Translator Challenge

For many people, access to well-presented, high-quality data is not enough. Making sense of the options and understanding the return on investment often require access to a person knowledgeable about such offerings who can help translate and personalize the data. When someone the nontraditional worker trusts helps translate, students process that information with more confidence.

Krystal Rawls's work at California State University, Dominguez Hills (CSUDH), a community-focused institution located in the South Bay area of Los Angeles that enrolls many first-generation students, demonstrates the power of a community-level translator. Rawls, a Ph.D. teacher and administrator, carries the fascinating job title of Workforce Integration Program Designer, which means she uses skill mapping to help students amass relevant qualifications and explore career interests. She explains the title and the importance of her job by reminding us that "stakeholders enter this higher-education con-versation with their own culture and history of relationships, which informs how they're going to interact. If we want to convince these students, then we have to acknowledge that we have previously inappropriately punished some of their communities, which affects their behaviors." Rawls's proximity to these students and her understanding of the way they may have been treated previously, whether in school or on the street, allows her to assist them in ways others could not.

Rawls helps students translate confusing job and course descriptions into understandable, contextualized information around skills in a fashion that builds confidence and strengthens decisionmaking. She takes data on which jobs require which skills, and then helps her students understand their options by connecting the information to the work-relevant skills they already have. She provided a wealth of insights and important context during our discussion:

> These students literally don't think they have talents. They're amazed at the numbers of skills they have that relate to jobs. They don't think waitressing is cash-handling. They don't understand how that skill can be utilized in other industries. And so, to see these skills build up from what they consider every day or cultural or family experiences, it really amazes them to understand that there is economic value in their experience. We haven't previously had those conversations about the economic value of their experiences that are cultural but not explicitly workforce related. And so you're not teaching a specific skill; you're teaching them this kind of range of hybrid skills that lets them both understand who they are and understand what they're capable of.

A terrific website with current and relevant information will produce value only to those who can understand its personal relevance to them. Rawls's narrative helps explain the gap. She tells of students surprised that she trusted them to make their own decisions. "That's the point: They don't trust themselves because society has not placed any trust in their experience or any value in that." Rawls emphasizes the gap these students face due to the deficit orientation inappropriately ascribed to non-white, first-generation college students. In order not to be penalized by their background, students need to understand "the language and jargon of the workplace to which they have not been exposed."

Rawls translates both ways: helping students understand opportunities and pathways and teaching them how to express their skills and successfully present themselves in a world where they have little experience.

Students and workers trying to decide what to do with their lives, or what steps to take next, ask various individuals for advice. These individuals can be institutional or formal, such as school counselors or employers. Or learners may receive the information on which they act from the media. The potential advice can come from informal sources, as well, including family, friends, and social networks. Even though low-income individuals may have access to fewer peers with applicable experience, they tend to rely on each other more than on formal sources, according to at least one survey.

While Latinos and white Americans rank colleges and universities as the most or second-most valuable source of advice about education and training, Black Americans rank them fourth, behind internet search, according to a recent survey taken by Strada's Center for Consumer Insights. The results suggest that organizations providing trusted counseling are not effectively reaching Black Americans.

Although real-time quality data is hard to come by, formal advisers are more likely to have access to it than friends and family. Nevertheless, the percentage of secondary students relying on high school or college counselors has declined by one-third over the last four decades. The younger the student, the more likely the information comes from an informal social network. Where one turns for help affects outcomes. Those who rely on work-based or professional sources for advice much less frequently have second thoughts concerning their decisions. In the words of David Clayton, the surveying expert: "A disconnect exists between the sources students most commonly consult for advice about selecting a field of study and the helpfulness of the advice they receive. In short, the most valued sources of advice—work-based—are the least used."

Bad or insufficient advice based on poor outcome data—or none at all—not only harms a student's future prospects, but it can also result in wasteful spending for a learner who chooses the wrong path, school, or major. At least some of the one-third of college-educated adults who work in jobs that do not require college-level training may have second thoughts about the path they choose or the debt they incurred.[4] This market inefficiency and lack of precision delays completion of education and training, and it translates into millions of additional study hours and billions of dollars in wasted tuition.

Regionally designated intermediaries or trusted neighborhood organizations can play an effective translator role when they have access to the right information and the right strategic cross-sector relationships.

Community Translation—Figurative and Literal

Central Indiana Community Partnership (CICP), which focuses on creating jobs in key industry clusters, is another example of an organization that helps translate data about opportunities. In the years following its formation, the partnership has launched sector-specific initiatives in life sciences, technology, advanced manufacturing and logistics, and agriculture biosciences. To pull these together, CICP created an initiative to increase connectivity among job seekers, educators, intermediaries, and employers. This initiative, called Ascend, concentrates on high school and college students of color as well as individuals from low-income backgrounds and supports them through the education-to-workforce transition. The network leverages an online platform on which Ascend staff compile important regional data that they then use to connect current students or recent graduates with a specific job, more education, or an internship or certificate program. The Indianapolis effort takes on both of the challenges featured in this chapter: It creates a better way to consume local data from academic institutions, skilling intermediaries, and employers. And it offers the professional advice of a translator who can counsel the user and help him understand his choices and connect him with the most suitable opportunities.

To make the digital tool as helpful as possible, Ascend worked with user groups to design technology that would support the various stakeholders in the system, including and especially the student. According to Ascend's president & CEO Jason Kloth, the data involves hundreds of employers and thousands of work-based learning opportunities and jobs. The technology captures the data at the skill and task level, as well as incorporating degree types that job seekers need. You can sense Kloth's experience with the nonprofit Teach for America program that places young educators in hard-to-staff schools and, formerly, as the deputy mayor of the city of Indianapolis, when he explains how Ascend brings job seekers, educational institutions, and employers together:

> By focusing on the actual skills that employers in a cluster of jobs are looking for, the characteristics of who is actually getting hired, and what's causing those matches to occur, we create a positive feedback loop. We can assist educational institutions and employers in helping job seekers make sense of the data so they can make effective career choices. This type of information will be especially helpful for career counselors, since the ratio of student to counselor exceeds 600 to one in Indiana.

Ascend's technology can eventually help offset this lopsided ratio by providing career counselors with high-quality information on good jobs and relevant training. Not every community needs to build its own software, but all of them do need to identify the most relevant skill needs among competitive job clusters and translate that data for employees and students, as well as educators and employers. Finally, communities must use this information to efficiently connect talent with available opportunities. Ascend shows us one such excellent approach.

Faith-based Translation and Connection

The most exquisitely configured data will not help a person who is not inclined to look at it. Sometimes, even getting a person to look at the available information requires a trusted intermediary who helps him understand the options and build the confidence necessary to take a step forward.

After designing a broad range of access points for those needing entry-level jobs or training, Indiana state officials worried that participation remained relatively low. Information on "free" training for programs in IT and healthcare that would lead to certifications for listed jobs did not stimulate the desired level of interest from under-employed workers. Radio and website promotions touting available training programs, even when coupled with information about jobs and earnings possibilities, produced tepid interest from individuals who might benefit from the offerings.

So, Indiana tried an additional avenue. Blair Milo, a former mayor whom Governor Eric Holcomb appointed as the state's secretary for career connections and talent, also served on the governor's Work-force Cabinet, a body dedicated to shaping education and workforce training. In those capacities, Milo reached out to faith-based organizations who could help struggling Hoosiers make sense of the data the state put together concerning their options. According to Milo:

> We're learning that connecting education and careers to those who would benefit is best done through local relationships, and some of the best of those relationships are with community and/or faith-based organizations. The role for a statewide workforce agency or organization is then more about compiling data and making it usable, [and] encouraging, facilitating and creating the conditions that foster such relationships—as well as the traditional mission of providing appropriate tools and education and training resources.

Milo referred us to a faith-based leader whom, in fact, we have known for twenty years—Jay Height of Indianapolis-based Shepherd Community Center. Height works with the state in helping to create opportunities for residents in his hard-pressed catchment area. In a post-COVID economy, he sees vacant houses and decay worsening alongside 35 percent unemployment. When we ask him about state resources, he immediately emphasizes his critical need for assistance.

But he affirms that his residents need local translators—people they know and believe in—to help them sort through and make decisions about the actions they should take. State programs arrive with a set of strange terminology and federal- and state-imposed bureaucratic language that puts off Shepherd's anxious clients. Quality information can be delivered through user-friendly technologies to some. For others, it needs a local translator like Shepherd.

We can see through Height and Rawls the importance of a trusted intermediary in translating critical information to people who doubt whether they have the right skills and who do not believe that the system is fair. Faith-based and community translators are even more necessary for those with little work context. Work-related experiences help a person make sense of job, training, and education options. That context comes not only from apprentice or intern programs but also from employers who have the wherewithal to act as translators concerning the relevance of potential training options.

A Role for Local and State Government

State and local government can help produce transparent performance data in several ways, including insisting on performance as part of their workforce contracts, specifying data that must be open and shared when public dollars are involved, and promulgating data formats that ease collection and use.

City and county officials now almost universally accept the responsibility of providing usable municipal data. However, most do not include the information described in this chapter. City open-data efforts should be expanded to include the education and training data mentioned here and should do it in a way that facilitates its use by residents. For example, the more advanced open-data cities incorporate user feedback into their curation function, so as to present data in a fashion that advances citizen use. In Chicago, city hall partners with Smart Chicago Collaborative's Civic User Testing Group (CUT) to make sure the user experience meets community needs. CUT is a 1,600+ member civic engagement program that invites Chicago residents to contribute to emerging technology "while providing public, private, and social sector partners with feedback to improve product design and deployment." Mayors and county executives could produce dramatic increases in upward mobility by assuming responsibility for curating a wider range of workforce data within the broader system, or they could appoint an intermediary to do so.

State and local government funds training programs and community colleges and serves as a conduit for substantial amounts of relevant federal workforce and TANF funds. Government should use its public interest in effectiveness to create a framework for sharing data that enhances performance. Local and state government should use their regulatory authority to advance outcome-based transparency in workforce development as it does elsewhere. Government today mandates that health inspector restaurant rankings be posted on windows in many cities to help consumers make informed choices. Local government pays someone to check the accuracy of meat scales and gas pumps to give shoppers confidence they have gotten their money's worth.

That government plays a role in advancing quality and price transparency to help its residents is relatively common. In 2004, North Carolina won the Harvard Innovations Award for its child care five star rating initiative that graded providers on quality to help parents select the right facility for their children. In April 2014, New York City mayor Bill de Blasio announced that his "Pre-K for All" offering would need to be in operation the following September; a key ingredient included providing parents with sufficient information for them to choose from among public schools and nonprofit providers.

Government's role in pushing this user-centric design principle forward includes insisting on performance-based transparency. Two plus decades ago, we incorporated the America Works pay-for-performance model in Indianapolis. But even now, years later, the *New York Times*[5] extolls the American Diesel Training Centers supported by the state of Ohio, in part because it relies on a performance contract model that is still way too underutilized. Why is that? These contracts with training organizations produce a rigor in measuring outcomes that simply would not occur otherwise. Regardless of whether the training organization receives its pay in stages or at the end, cities, states, workforce boards, and community colleges need to take responsibility for producing easy-to-use information. And that ease of use depends not just on the user experience but on the quality of the information.

Governors, mayors, county executives, workforce board members, and legislators need to challenge current funding patterns and insist that nonprofit and public organizations define, measure, and publicize performance.

Conclusion

We are reminded of a story in one of Stephen's earlier books, *The Twenty-First Century City: Resurrecting Urban America*,[6] which describes Indianapolis reform efforts. During one of his efficiency initiatives as mayor, coauthor Stephen met a longtime public employee working away in the sub-basement of the city-county building and asked the fellow what he did. The employee responded, "I test scales in butcher shops and measure gallonage at gas pumps."

When Stephen asked why this was a core city function, one of his advisers replied that no one else in the building produced as much value to the market as this employee. This function, the adviser pointed out, allows residents to buy a pound of hamburger or ten gallons of gas without needing to bring along weights or a one-gallon can. The Office of Weights and Measures made decisions easier for tens of thousands of local consumers.

Yet, now, in cities, with even more consequential decisions at stake, government and nonprofit partners play a much smaller role in producing commonly understood measurements related to career choices. It takes an enormous amount of effort for a worker to figure out what course will add which skill, and how that skill can be stacked with prior experience to qualify for a new job. And the worker experiences even more frustration when trying to determine whether the cost of the class, course, or degree will result in a reasonable return on investment.

Information inefficiencies make it difficult for employer and employee alike. The resulting friction especially harms those who have the furthest yet to go, or whose journey is the most circuitous. Without clarity in terminology and transparency, employers fall back on degrees as the proxy for qualifications—a proxy that discriminates against qualified workers with skills but not degrees.

Local leadership can scale opportunity and produce significant value by making good, skill-based data available to stakeholders—learner, employer, educator—which will lead to better returns on investment to learners and to greater regional productivity. Simply offering more training without this clarity increases the risk of wasted resources. Conversely, clearer information on how a certain course adds the skills that will take an employee on an upward path will build the confidence required for that person to do so.

We raise these options not necessarily to suggest that a single local organization should build an app or create a central marketplace but, rather, that local leadership writ large needs to figure out how to make data more valuable, accessible, and easy to use—to ensure that someone provides "weights and measures" support to learners, employers, and educators.

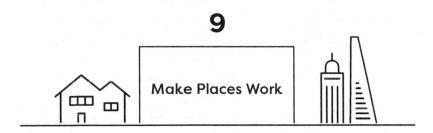

9

Make Places Work

We recollect the TV spots Kate produced for the YMCA of the USA in her role as executive vice president for strategy and advancement. As the camera passes over vacant lots, abandoned homes, weeds, and graffiti, a young adult voice intones, "I am here. Can you see me? 'Cause I feel like I am invisible. Like this whole place is invisible." The ad closes with words scrolling across the screen reminding viewers that when communities are forgotten, the Y remembers—for mentorship, for safe places, for opportunity, for childcare, for education, for a better us. While many see vulnerable communities from a distance, in the heart of those communities live people with the same hopes, dreams, aspirations, and talents as people everywhere.

Places cannot be ignored. Cities themselves and their systems need to be designed and managed to work. Look at that YMCA list of critical needs—safe places, mentors, quality childcare, and education. Mix in the absence of any reasonable way to get to work and top it off with regulations that forbid entry into certain trades and you get a system that makes it difficult not only to find work but to sustain employment. The individuals shown may be invisible to others, but poverty, segregation, and disinvestment make the challenges they face no less vivid to them. A part of the bargain that promises the American

Dream for those who work hard is a city—its civic and government sectors—that make it possible to work.

Cities cannot close the opportunity gap unless government, with support from the nonprofit and business sectors, consistently remembers these neighborhoods when it designs and provides necessary infrastructure. The basics—safety, education, civic space, municipal services like trash collection—are fundamental. So are transportation, childcare, and family-friendly policies. Such is this chapter's design principle. We do not propose to solve complex urban problems or comprehensively address urban zoning, transit, or design in a single chapter. However, any city interested in equitable economic progress must address these threshold issues. Bottom line, we believe a book on economic mobility would be incomplete without clearly connecting opportunity to livability.

This exploration starts with the reality that many workers face practical, day-to-day challenges that make it difficult for them to acquire or sustain living-wage employment. Some of these issues deal with like barriers to getting to work—disconnected transportation and few if any options for childcare, for instance. Another set of barriers stems from the use of licensing, which often unnecessarily restricts entry into a trade. And other challenges include policies that drive up living costs for low-income workers, essentially taxing their limited incomes with higher than necessary housing costs or forcing them to make longer and more complicated commutes.

Build Neighborhoods that Support Work

Any identification of barriers to economic mobility would be incomplete without noting those imposed by race compounded by place, whether these are the effects of legacy legal restrictions or the personal biases of today. Government-sanctioned bias helped produce the current concentrations of Black poverty through the use of zoning restrictions, racial covenants, mortgage redlining, the siting of public housing in the cities, and minimum lot sizes in the suburbs. These restrictions combined to force "Black families to crowd into undesirable areas where amenities were few, the housing stock was often decrepit or cheaply built, and the streets were lined with factories spewing industrial pollution," as Stanford's Jennifer Eberhardt describes it.[1] These conditions, according to urban expert Robert Samuelson, "predict lower intergenerational income mobility, adult incarceration, and teenage birth among children who grow up poor and undermine social mobility later in life."[2]

The Raj Chetty "zip code is destiny" reports and subsequent work generated by his Opportunity Insights Center shocked many when they came out. But the data confirmed what we have long witnessed in terms of the contrasts in physical and social infrastructure, violence, service delivery, education, and more among neighborhoods. Training, coaching, and apprentice programs help individuals fortunate enough to have access to those services overcome neighborhood barriers. However, city leaders looking to create long-term economic gains need to address the systemic effects that burden the residents of deeply impoverished neighborhoods. A city without a plan to strengthen its neighborhoods can never adequately close the equity gap.

In chapter 1, we spoke of the shrinking middle class. Here, we address the vanishing middle-class neighborhood. Deeply poor neighborhoods with fewer social supports from neighbors and community organizations greatly restrict their residents' job prospects and the possibility of productive futures for their children.

The American Enterprise Institute's Ryan Streeter identifies the "driving question of how to connect lower-income families to information, networks and relationships that lead to high-quality, opportunity-rich learning and job opportunities."[3] Job seekers who have stronger, wider webs of relationships are more likely to find work, and typically earn more than their peers without such networks. Neighborhoods transitioning downward find themselves trapped in a cycle that produces less community cohesion and, in turn, more crime. And those deteriorating conditions, in turn, affect job prospects.

Wayne State University professor of urban affairs George Galster defines these "social-interactive neighborhood mechanisms as including social contagion (changed behaviors, aspirations, and attitudes gained from contact with neighbors), collective socialization (conforming to local social norms through role models or social pressures), social capital (connections within and between social networks), and collective efficacy (social cohesion combined with a willingness to work together for the common good)."[4]

The absence of collective efficacy and socialization produces a wide range of long-lasting barriers to mobility. For instance, as Stanford's Caroline Hoxby and Harvard's Richard Avery document, low-income, high-achieving high school students often do not apply to top-tier universities for which they are qualified because no one in their networks, including their teachers, has any experience with such universities.[5] Living in a neighborhood where the local schools have higher graduation rates or a where more adult residents have college degrees sends strong messages that education is attainable. Neighborhood conditions influence long-term outcomes such as health, life expectancy, and adult income.[6]

By the same token, improved conditions powerfully boost a resident's confidence in taking new and riskier steps forward. In a study on upward mobility, Shigehiro Oishi of Columbia, Minkyung Koo of University of Illinois, and Nicholas Buttrick of University of Virginia note: "If people feel a great sense of belonging to their city, they are likely to apply for jobs outside their immediate neighborhoods and feel that they could work there. In contrast, if people do not feel a sense of belonging to the city, they might feel that they do not fit in and might not apply to jobs, for instance, in the downtown."[7]

Neither all lower-income neighborhoods nor all cities are the same. Some lower-income neighborhoods have more social infrastructure—and, therefore, more opportunity. In some cities, the economic gap between wealthier and poorer communities is smaller—which also makes a difference.

Workforce interventions, for the most part, operate at the individual level. But the effects described here are more systemic, occurring at the community level. Communities dominated by crime, decaying infrastructure, vacant housing, and limited positive relationships will suffocate the upward mobility of most who live there. These structural issues do not lend themselves to easy answers.

Yet, ignoring them comes at a high price that undermines many of the other promising steps toward upward mobility. Given how the physical concentration of hazards—environmental, social, and personal—produces long-term harm, how might local leaders respond? As a starting point, cities could add to the relationship capital that flows forth from safer, more walkable communities generated by investments in sidewalks, parks, and the removal of abandoned homes.[8] Improved community connectedness also can benefit from officials examining policies that price lower-income workers out of middle-class neighborhoods.

Of course, a neighborhood that does not offer families effective schools will produce long-term barriers regardless of everything else we discuss.

Make Housing More Affordable and Available

One culprit in the saga of the vanishing middle-class neighborhood is housing costs that prevent more socially and racially diverse neighborhoods. In 2019, even before the massive impact of COVID-19, 31.5 percent of American households paid more than 30 percent of their incomes for housing expenses, and even more of their income in the twenty-five highest rent markets. HUD defines families who face challenges paying for other necessities as "cost-burdened." Seventy-two percent of households with incomes below $15,000 paid more than 50 percent of their income on housing.[9] African American-led renter households were one-third more likely to be rent burdened than white households.[10]

Cities across the country are addressing this problem in various ways, including revising housing codes, increasing the required percentage of affordable housing in new construction, and implementing strategies to mitigate the effects of gentrification. Since the focus of this chapter is local design and how it supports or erodes work, one approach that would make a difference is highlighted: increasing the supply of affordable housing.

In a National Bureau of Economic Research Working Paper, Chang-Tai Hsieh of the University of Chicago and Enrico Moretti of University of California, Berkeley estimate that land-use restrictions have cost the U.S. economy between $1.6 trillion and $2 trillion in lost productivity and output. That translates to a yearly increase in wages of $8,775 for the average worker.[11] Governments increase the cost of housing by using zoning to limit the number of living units on a lot while increasing lot sizes. Similarly, onerous building codes raise prices.

Local leaders in some places are now beginning to address these issues. For example, many cities allow more market rate units on a site if the developer commits to additional affordable units. In New York City, former mayor Michael Bloomberg helped launch the "mini-apartment" movement when he authorized very small residences on the East Side of Manhattan. These units allow workers to make a decision about what best fits their needs: live closer to work in a smaller apartment or farther away in a larger residence.

Minneapolis was the first major U.S. city to eliminate single-family zoning in an effort to increase housing supply and density, reduce housing costs, and create more racially and economically integrated neighborhoods. Other cities, including Atlanta, San Diego, Austin, and Pinellas County (Florida), have created expedited approval and review processes for new projects, which bring down costs.[12] These reforms illustrate the broad range of tools that can be used to improve the life of urban workers, and they should not be ignored as part of a larger strategy.

Officials face difficult choices in that not every urban neighborhood can be comprehensively rebuilt—especially those with a large number of vacant lots. Galster offers evidence of the adverse consequences of individuals living in neighborhoods with more than 20 percent poverty. He finds that "independent impacts of neighborhood poverty rates in encouraging negative outcomes for individuals like crime, school leaving, and duration of poverty spells appear to be nil unless the neighborhood exceeds about 20 percent poverty, whereupon the externality effects grow rapidly until the neighborhood reaches approximately 40 percent poverty."[13]

Thus, mixed-income communities present opportunities in terms of relationships, exposure to a broader array of activities, and higher levels of investment in resources aimed at building a brighter future for individuals. And as we have seen, proximity to those with careers provides not just positive role models but greater access to employment.

Chetty participated in a King County, Washington, initiative that provides one answer. The housing authority provided Section 8 vouchers to families and counseled them on the positive aspects of moving to more middle-class neighborhoods. The experiment convinced more than half of the families to move, and those families achieved mostly positive outcomes.[14] Poor residents should be able to move, just like those of us with more resources.

We have long been conflicted about choices between people- and place-based strategies, worried that the cure for some might further the disease for others. Helping one family get out of a battered neighborhood potentially results in one more vacant house and one less involved resident. Restoring neighborhoods and their civic and physical infrastructure is complex and will be expensive. To grow fairly, city officials need to target their interventions and build on the assets that exist in all communities.

The Cost of Making Ends Meet

Local policies can more easily and immediately make a difference for workers by helping their time and money go further. In at least three specific ways, the nature of a city's policies can affect costs in such a way that work does or does not make financial sense. A substantial part of a worker's income goes for childcare, transportation, and housing. To the extent that urban policies artificially drive up those expenses, they "tax" work and drive down the benefits of employment, as can be seen in figure 9-1, a detailed 2017 budget created by the California Budget and Policy Center for a family of four. The center estimated that a family of four in California needed approximately $75,000 to make ends meet.

Better municipal policies and services enhance net income by lowering expenses, including the opportunity cost of getting to a job.

Transportation

During a bus strike in New York City some years ago, we met with a group of workers in Queens who, without convenient access to subways, worried about how to get to their jobs in Manhattan. City and state regulations sharply limited the availability of vans, shuttles, and commercially arranged shared rides. The strike highlighted the tran-

Figure 9-1. **Cost of Making Ends Meet, Two-Worker Families**

Two-Working-Parent Family	▼	

Statewide Average	▼	

Annual Total	**$75,952**	

Basic Monthly Budget		
Housing and Utilities	$1,568	24.8%
Food	$773	12.2%
Child Care	$1,300	20.5%
Health Care	$522	8.2%
Transportation	$556	8.8%
Miscellaneous	$787	12.4%
Taxes	$824	13.0%
Total	**$6,329**	**100.0%**

Source: Sara Kimberlin and Amy Rose, "Making Ends Meet: How Much Does It Cost to Support a Family in California?" California Budget & Policy Center, December 2017, https://calbudgetcenter.org/resources/making-ends-meet-much-cost-support-family-california/.

sit dependency of these workers, especially given legal restrictions on who can provide transit service to them. Even without a strike, the lack of multimodal solutions that more smoothly integrate bikes, buses, Uber/Lyfts, small vans, and scooters causes workers to lose work time.

Chetty and his Opportunity Insights team found that average commute time was one of the strongest predictors of upward mobility in neighborhoods across the United States.[15] Distance to a job is inversely related to one's chances of being hired; in short, employers seem to be biased against people with longer commutes.[16] Researchers at the Brookings Institution found that a typical metropolitan resident can reach only about 30 percent of jobs via transit in ninety minutes, and that job access by neighborhood differs considerably across metropolitan areas.[17]

Officials in one city layered maps of neighborhoods with substantial numbers of underemployed individuals over maps of concentrated job opportunities (such as the airport area) and then evaluated how easily a worker in those neighborhoods could get to those jobs. They found that transportation problems reduce economic mobility in so far as they both impose physical barriers to work and drive down the value of work by driving up the time and cost of getting there.

COVID-19 brought visibility to essential workers who kept public services, hospitals, logistics systems, and food services available; however, it did not bring much visibility to the often-difficult routes these essential workers take to work. A forty-five-minute commute with a transfer or two each way turns out to be a substantial tax on a person earning $15 or less an hour. Across the country, cities began experimenting before COVID-19 with various ways to help address the substantial barriers that poor transportation creates for struggling workers. Transit services in most regions remained relatively stable even though from 2000 to 2015 almost half the growth in poverty occurred in inner ring suburbs, increasing commute times for lower-income workers.[18]

Supported by Bloomberg Philanthropies Mayors Challenge, the South Bend, Indiana, Ride Guarantee program aimed to spark economic mobility by improving transit mobility. Both employers and employees contribute to a fund that supports the rides. Employees can take up to twenty rides a month with Lyft/Uber/carpool. The first two rides cost one cent each, while the next eighteen rides cost a total of $4. The rides must start or end at the participant's workplace. The city's research showed that employees who used this service worked extra shifts, and employers reported less turnover.[19] The multiyear plan included service through 2021, but COVID-19 disruptions to work and concerns about shared vehicles slowed down the rollout. Betsy Gardner, who reported on the project for the Harvard Kennedy School DataSmart project, sums up the before and after situation with a worker who exclaimed: "I had to walk home at 11 at night over five miles, and now that this is available, I don't have to walk anymore!"

Careful research led by South Bend program director Aaron Steiner discovered interesting nuances in the second year of the program. Steiner, in a 2021 report, "concluded that our current Ride Guarantee program is a good solution for individuals who face temporary or moderate transportation insecurity, and less so for those facing chronic or severe insecurity." The Notre Dame Pulte Institute for

Global Development that supported the research found in the second year a 10 percent increase in hours worked by those in the program compared to other similar workers, but less impact on absenteeism.[20] These second-year results, though affected by COVID-19 concerns about shared rides, continue to support the proposition that better transit produces more work.

Upward mobility increases as the number of jobs that can be reasonably accessed goes up. Too many cities rely exclusively on fixed route public transit from bus stops. In the words of Zachary Wasserman, chief strategy officer at the micro-transit provider Via, "poor bus service, both in terms of network coverage and frequency, limits the 'job shed' that a particular individual can access." In Wilson, North Carolina, the micro-transit service increased coverage from 40 to 100 percent, expanding access to more jobs than when the fixed-route bus was the only option.

Too many cities remain dependent on obsolete bus routes and outdated rules concerning equipment and operations. New "mobility officers" in cities need more authority to restructure services. Too few cities give mobility officers real authority to consider how various modes can be woven together. Even fewer charge the true cost of parking in commercial centers, which would provide additional resources to support programs similar to that of South Bend. Seamlessly integrated mobility options can and should be offered to workers.

Of course, moving jobs into neighborhoods is an important approach, as well. Economic development policies should provide incentives to attract middle-skill jobs to areas within reach of low-income neighborhoods. Clearer data sharing requirements by transportation regulators would allow policymakers to assess commuting patterns and diagnose place-based inefficiencies. Ride shares, scooters, buses, taxis, and shared bikes all produce important data that would improve planning. As transportation patterns fall into place coming out of COVID-19, city leaders will need to reimagine transit.

Childcare

Few issues affect decisions about work more than the ability to find quality, affordable childcare for children five and under. A 2019 survey found 63 percent of parents said they made career or workplace changes to afford childcare, with more than half of mothers choosing or being forced to scale back hours to save on childcare.[21] Higher childcare subsidies from government significantly increase labor force participation and employment rates among low-income mothers,[22] and the "majority of non-working, prime-age poor women cite home and family responsibilities as the primary reason that they did not work in the past year."[23]

High-quality pre-K plays a critical role in the lives of children, but that discussion is outside the scope of this review. We pay attention here to the often overlooked benefit of how additional years of early childhood learning supported by local education dollars assist struggling parents in finding and sustaining jobs that make financial sense. Upward mobility requires a worker to take the first step; if that step is too high or too steep, then no amount of skill-based support will help. The federal government and some states subsidize childcare, and several cities, following in the footsteps of Denver, now support preschool.

The federal contribution is increasing. The CARES Act included $3.5 billion in emergency funds for the Child Care and Development Block Grant. And the Biden administration released $39 billion in funding for the childcare industry from the American Rescue Plan that will go through the states and then to educators and providers. Combined with more flexibility allowed to states, continuing increases in federal funds will address some of the deficit. However, to truly make upward mobility possible, more local officials will need to join this effort with resources and advocacy.

Allow Workers to Work

Most of the efforts featured in this book assume an employee/employer relationship. Advancing economic mobility should extend, as well, to facilitating options for those interested in starting their own business and to others who want to work in a trade that requires a license.

When deputy mayor in New York City, Stephen heard complaints from residents at community meetings who were interested in going into a trade but found the licensing requirements and related expenses too onerous. The young man in the Bronx who wanted to be a plumber could not maneuver his way through the thicket of passing two licensing tests, then finding someone to take him on as an apprentice, and then completing seven years of experience before receiving the master plumber license he wanted.

Labor expert Diana Furchtgott-Roth has observed that by protecting established, older workers, the government's occupational licensing requirements make it hard for the young to enter the workforce as entrepreneurs, thus leaving them with fewer job opportunities.[24] This conclusion corresponds with that of a 2015 White House Council of Economic Advisors report[25] that found lower-income workers are less likely to be able to afford the tuition and time measured in lost wages associated with fulfilling a licensing requirement.[26] One Arkansas-based study found that a 40 percent reduction in the number of jobs that required a license would reduce the poverty rate among African Americans in the state by 2.1 percent.[27]

For electricians, plumbers, beauticians, crane operators, and dozens of other positions, licensing requirements often do more to protect incumbents than consumers. Regulations related to health and safety, of course, are necessary. But in many cases, consumers can find out more about the reputations and quality of work of vendors from Yelp or Angie's List or Facebook friends than they can from regulators.[28]

A broad reconsideration of state and local licensing restrictions, many originally influenced by political and not safety purposes, will produce opportunities—especially for workers of color who are not part of the groups lobbying to keep restrictions in place. A range of policy options should be considered, including:

- Allowing out-of-state reciprocity among licensing requirements.

- Examining all requirements, A-to-Z, to see if they are truly necessary for health and safety.

- Reconsidering whether formal training should be required for those who can pass exams.

- Evaluating whether tests are constructed in a fair and impartial way.

- Providing a way to waive fees when formal training is involved.

Cities and states interested in providing ladders of opportunity should set up commissions to review occupational licensing requirements with an eye to the above approaches for the purpose of allowing more persons to safely participate in a trade.

Provide Services to Those with Criminal Justice Involvement

Populations facing particularly daunting obstacles need more structured and longer-lasting supports. One such group includes the approximately 8 to 9 million people[29] under custodial control—including those held in jails, prisons, or community corrections facilities or who are under parole supervision. Arrest, conviction, and incarceration all reduce the odds of getting a job.[30] Even released felons who secure employment struggle with job stability. Criminal justice involvement reduces employment stability, in part due to the nature of the jobs themselves, many of which are day labor jobs.

A Pew Foundation summary of research concluded that incarceration carries enduring economic repercussions and that "former inmates work fewer weeks each year, earn less money and have limited upward mobility. These costs are borne by offenders' families and communities, and they reverberate across generations."[31] The long-term economic impact of incarceration is an earnings drop of 40 percent over their lifetime.

In several ways, judicial systems needlessly create obstacles to work. For example, millions of Americans de facto lose their job when they lose their driver's license for unpaid traffic tickets or other fines and fees. Most individuals drive to work, and even more need to show a driver's license as a condition of work. In fact, a recent study found that, in Phoenix, more than half of the people who lost their licenses also lost their jobs, making it more difficult for them to support their families and contribute to the local economy."[32]

A project sponsored by What Works Cities mentions, as one example of this phenomenon, the city of Durham, North Carolina, where one in five residents had a suspended or revoked driver's license, 80 percent of whom were African American or Hispanic. Recognizing the negative cascading effects, the city—in partnership with the district attorney's office, courts, and other stakeholders—launched an effort called the Durham Expungement and Restoration (DEAR) program. The program identified minor traffic charges and fees that could result in loss of one's driver's license. The effort ultimately resulted in the dismissal of more than 50,000 traffic charges against 35,000 people.[33]

Even those charged but not yet convicted of a crime suffer consequences. The deciding factor about who is jailed and who is released is often the defendant's ability to pay, which, in turn, more adversely impacts the job prospects of the most vulnerable. Nearly half of Americans have less than $500 for emergencies. If they get arrested, they are more likely to go to jail. If they remain in jail, they are more likely to lose their jobs. Once they are out of jail, to varying degrees court fees, victim restitution, and child support also present serious obstacles for the former inmates. These obligations are relatively large for individuals in marginal circumstances and often create a sense of hopelessness for formerly incarcerated job seekers. Creative counties have found solutions for many of these obstacles. Some county officials avoid unnecessary short-term pre-trial incarceration by applying non-cash-bond options and using data analytics to discern who should be diverted from jail to treatment for underlying mental health or substance abuse issues.

In addition to financial penalties, a conviction record itself produces an enduring obstacle. More than 150 cities and counties have adopted "ban-the-box" policies, which refer to stopping the practice of requiring job seekers to check the box on an employment application asking about previous criminal records. These efforts increase the chance that an applicant will get a callback. However, recent studies show ban-the-box policies do not necessarily increase the likelihood of a job due to the biased way young Black male applicants are often treated in the employment process irrespective of information about previous justice involvement.[34]

All in all, though, policies like reviewing fines and fees, halting license suspensions for minor matters, banning the box, and providing incentives to employers to hire previously incarcerated individuals can help eliminate barriers that stand in the way of jobs and can create additional opportunity.

Federal Policy

Because federal policy plays such an important role in supporting work, we mention it here even though the focal point of these chapters is local action. Federal policy determines the structure of benefits for those not working, work supports through tax and benefit policy, and many of the rules for unemployment compensation. It funds and sets the rules for a workforce system.

One critical federal program, the Earned Income Tax Credit (EITC), rewards work by making it more valuable. The COVID-19 relief bill (American Rescue Plan Act of 2021) expanded EITC to include lower-income working adults not raising children as well as some younger adults age nineteen to twenty-four who aren't full-time students. Some states add their own EITC incentives concerning state taxes to further raise the value of work. Many cities engage nonprofit intermediaries to do outreach to increase the percentage of eligible workers who file for the benefit.

Greater flexibility in major federal benefit programs would give families the ability to handle the choices they face between jobs. Similarly, federal rules that control the terms of state unemployment insurance programs and increase the portability and flexibility of the program also would be helpful. The U.S. Chamber of Commerce has pointed out the antiquated nature of unemployment insurance, suggesting that the system be modified to cover more circumstances. The chamber advocates expanded unemployment programs to cover short-time or partial claims and stronger support of reskilling for in-demand positions.

Local action at the system level matters. Livable neighborhoods produce opportunity through relationships. City policies affect how much it costs and how much time it takes to get to work. Local and state laws control and determine the rules for participation in many trades and professions. And the actions of city hall and nonprofits affect neighborhood livability. A city that addresses upward mobility in terms of both workforce and community can produce short-term and long-term impact.

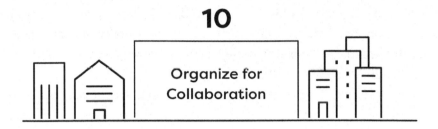

10

Organize for Collaboration

Today's workforce development system does too little development in part because it too little resembles a system. As a consequence it does not produce equitable outcomes. A regional economy contains many institutions that affect aspiring workers. In this chapter, we address the last design of our principles: the imperative to collaborate and the need for an intermediary that serves as a network manager to bring together cross-sector stakeholders. This final design principle force-multiplies the previous concepts and takes them to scale.

Involved local institutions suffer from a lack of perspective on the region's needs and often have inadequate information about the skills associated with in-demand jobs. Without coordination, aspiring workers cycle through agencies, frequently dropping out due to the apparent unavailability of support services or clarity that a step will really result in a better job.

Recognizing the Need for Collaboration

In 2018, the Bold Goals Coalition of Central Alabama's Workforce Action Network, a group of over 200 organizations committed to a common agenda and shared measurements, released "Building (it) Together: A Framework for Aligning Education and Jobs in Greater

Birmingham."[1] Developed by Burning Glass Technologies, a labor market analytics firm, and the Council for Adult and Experiential Learning (CAEL), an adult learning nonprofit, the report came out after Birmingham saw losses of hundreds of jobs the year before. Key organizations in the coalition included the University of Alabama at Birmingham, the United Way, the Alabama Power Company, and the Birmingham Business Alliance.

Building (it) Together highlighted the region's relatively low level of educational attainment and high dependence on low-skilled jobs. It held out the promise that the area could produce 19,000 additional bachelor's degree-level positions a year. The report focused also on the mismatch between supply and demand for labor, concluding that "local colleges and universities do not consistently graduate students in the degree areas that are required by local employers. Some industries, such as IT and engineering, are undersupplied by local universities. In other areas, the credentials awarded do not align with the skills that employers need."[2]

The report's release marked the launch of a public engagement campaign designed to spark a realignment of education and workforce training. The then new mayor of Birmingham, Randall Woodfin, a Birmingham native with degrees from Morehouse College and Samford's Cumberland School of Law, used the report as a launching pad for community action.

Woodfin followed the release with opinion pieces in the newspaper and presentations emphasizing that Birmingham presented a tale of two cities (or, variously, a tale of two opportunities). A growing tech sector represented one city and the other city featured a 30 percent poverty rate, with three times as many unemployed Black residents as white. The mayor announced the launch of Birmingham Promise, which was designed to connect struggling young workers to quality jobs, and appointed Josh Carpenter as the city's director of innovation and economic opportunity, as well as liaison to Promise. Carpenter, an Oxford University Ph.D., retained his faculty position at UAB while also supporting the city.

The cross-sector collaboration that emerged incorporated many of our design principles. First, the community came together to examine, with clarity and transparency, its current labor situation. A high-profile and broadly supported report helped the mayor rally public opinion. These steps sparked the formation of Birmingham Promise, a respected intermediary, which, along with the mayor's office, continues to promote collaborative action founded on shared data. Led by Carpenter, Promise, the city, its nonprofit economic development corporation, and UAB share data sets and analyses broadly to ensure adoption of common objectives.

At the start of her term, Mayor Lori Lightfoot appointed a top aide, Samir Mayekar, as deputy mayor for neighborhood and economic development. He partnered with Alberto Ortega, then director of workforce strategy and business engagement, a coordination position in city hall funded by the Pritzker Traubert Foundation. These individuals guided the mayor's development efforts in response to the pandemic. They supported a Recovery Task Force composed of an impressive roster of Chicago leaders that released a comprehensive report on needed workforce initiatives.

We asked Ortega and Mayekar how they coordinate skilling efforts in Chicago, especially given the substantial activity of the alliance. Ortega explained that he and Mayekar provide informal coordination, especially in areas where economic development and workforce overlap. For example, Mayekar uses the authority of the mayor's office from time to time to connect employers seeking to establish apprenticeships or internships with City Colleges of Chicago. Ortega, referencing Chicago's logistics sector, provides an example. In order to help warehouse workers step up the mobility ladder to forklift operators, Mayekar encouraged community colleges to promote certificate programs to prepare students for this area of growing demand. While the Chicago model lacks the formal network manager of the other examples we later profile, it illustrates how data helped city officials coordinate workforce activities across multiple nodes. The mayor's office promotes economic development within the city's growth sectors using data to project needs and anticipated workforce availability for certain skill sets. Table 10-1 shows a comparison of approaches in some of the cites we studied. Regardless of structure, the best regional response incorporates cross-sector governance and implementation of the design principles.

Table 10-1. **Comparison of Cross-Sector Skilling Collaboratives**

City	Convenor	Intermediary or Network Manager	Emphasis	Data
Houston	Business Partnership	UpSkill Houston, subsidiary of Houston Partnership	Mid-skill jobs	Emsi; LinkedIn for connections; AI to help understand skills
Atlanta	Mayor	NGO-UNCF	Men and women of color; Upskilling	Emsi
Chicago	Philanthropy	At least two (mayor's office and philanthropy alliance)	Multiple: Sectoral, apprenticeship, and skilling	Multiple
Birmingham	Mayor	NGO (Birmingham Promise)	Improve supply of skilled workers and close education gaps	Burning Glass
San Diego	Workforce Partnership	Workforce Nonprofit Subsidiary	Multiple: Including upskilling and tech jobs for challenged workers	Burning Glass, Emsi, Google, support from JFF

Recognizing the Challenges of Collaboration

Workforce coordination requires the participation of stakeholders, many of whom compete against each other for employees, student admissions, or clients. Effective collaboration requires community and political leadership and a strong network manager.

Society benefits when competition drives schools to produce the very best curricula to attract more students and when employers invest in training to become desirable places to work. A community college that creates breakthrough programming by maintaining relationships with particular employers may not want to share the story behind its successes. However, it is also the case that leading education and training providers and, particularly, aspiring workers benefit from collaboration. A higher education institution may not have the budget to respond to a regional need absent financial incentives. And large and small employers in the same industry may have different perspectives regarding how much to invest in training.

For many unemployed or underemployed workers, the disparate elements of a job training system represent a maze with an elusive finish. A region wishing to grow more fairly needs leadership that brings together critical parties and gets them to commit to a joint endeavor. But who should be that leader? Even among regional government units, no single elected official and no particular agency has an inherent convening role around workforce. The mayor of the largest city in the area will have more visibility on the issues and a better ability to secure business attention than others, but mayors have few resources to deploy specifically on workforce development itself.

County executives often control the funding necessary for wraparound services through their health and human services budgets. And states fund and manage policy for a range of other services, including public institutions of higher education and certain economic development efforts, but they do not play a natural leadership role in regional economies. Depending on the community, the local chamber of commerce, the United Way, or a specially created nonprofit or community foundation also may occupy potential leadership roles. Who should lead, who should participate, and who should manage or coordinate are each separate and important questions.

In terms of participation, Workforce Investment Boards (WIB) play an important role in regional ecosystems. However, their regional nature and quasi-federal accountability structure present challenges. In each region of the state, a WIB exists with major employment responsibilities. They vary widely in quality and reach; however, by federal law, they play critical roles in the provision of services. Set up by the Workforce Investment Act of 1998, these structures are important building blocks in terms of cooperation. But the size and scope of their role depends on the region and the WIB.

Congressional restructuring in 1998 improved the effectiveness of the hundreds of WIBs across the country. The law focused greater attention on employers and introduced a stronger performance management system. Board composition now must include more community and private-sector appointees.

These federally authorized, regionally configured, state-regulated organizations should participate in collaborations formed to address skilling, but normally should not take on the role of network manager. Different elected local officials appoint their board members, creating the potential for blurred lines of accountability. Overly prescriptive federal rules administered by the states reduce local flexibility. Much of the funding for WIBs goes to maintain one-stop centers, leaving less for actual training. WIBs, just like other stakeholders, would be more effective with better data, including transparent performance information about training providers. Even though WIBs invest a relatively small amount of the total regional training and education budget, their exclusive focus on job training makes them an indispensable part of the collaboration.

Fragmented spending argues for the importance of the network manager function. A study by McKinsey & Company revealed the relatively small percentage of regional education and training investment that flows from federal or local government funds, as well as the number of participants and their relative weight if measured by spending (figure 10-1).

Most cities task economic development organizations, whose budgets are not represented in this figure, with assisting new or existing employers interested in adding jobs and consider workforce agencies as labor supply entities. Coordination needs to improve between the

Figure 10-1. **Annual Postsecondary and Training Spending in the United States**

Annual postsecondary education and training spending in the United States, billions of dollars

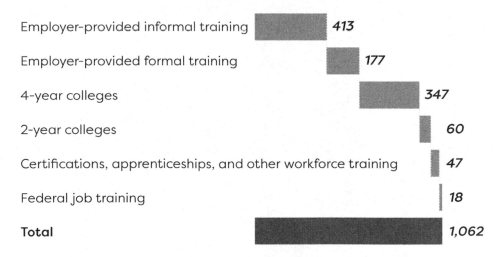

Employer-provided informal training	413
Employer-provided formal training	177
4-year colleges	347
2-year colleges	60
Certifications, apprenticeships, and other workforce training	47
Federal job training	18
Total	1,062

Source: McKinsey & Company, www.mckinsey.com/industries/public-and-social-sector/our-insights/creating-an-effective-workforce-system-for-the-new-economy.

two. Sometimes workforce and economic development entities carefully share data and strategy, but in many places, they operate in parallel, not in concert.

The reasons for collaboration are many. The number of involved parties not only presents the challenge but also the opportunity. A distributed system can produce great value if it shares data and knowledge to strengthen its component parts. Each of the entities in figure 10-2 has levers it can deploy to improve economic mobility.

These entities have their own institutional goals, cultures, and professional backgrounds, which causes them to see issues in different ways. They will undoubtedly agree in general on the need to cooperate. Yet without meaningful management and coordination, the risk is not so much that the parties will not agree to cooperate as that they will not meaningfully modify what they are doing despite agreeing to collaborate.

In addition, markets change. So do jobs. The speed of change in

Figure 10-2. Entities Frequently Involved in Workforce Development Systems

Mayors/county executives

Economic development corporations

Representatives of umbrella NGOs

Workforce investment boards

Community colleges

Employers

Chambers of commerce

Union apprentice programs

Secondary schools, vocational education, counseling

Universities

Philanthropists

Workers/ learners

the nature of work makes recruiting and training future employees challenging, especially when it includes the goal of equipping non-traditional employees with the tools and skills they need to succeed. For example, job training programs that rely on government appropriations typically have longer planning cycles or are too dependent on labor data that lags real-time changes in the market. A coordinating entity that uses data to anticipate and prepare for these changes will add value.

Given the multiple stakeholders and their broad range of interests, a cross-sector collaboration that brings with it a highly prescriptive approach seems neither possible nor advisable. But a totally fragmented response comes at a cost, too, especially to workers of color and those from densely populated, low-income communities. We argue here for a middle ground in terms of cohesiveness that includes not only shared data but also some shared processes and structures. When advocating for cross-sector collaboration, we are talking about more than ad hoc meetings. Each region needs a network, managed by a trusted entity that brings together private, public, nonprofit, and citizen groups; insists on transparency of performance; and ensures its workers can achieve basic skilling and upskilling goals.

In the Birmingham and Atlanta examples and that of Houston that follows, successful coordination includes a set of steps: a call to action by a leader, formation of the collaborative, and identification of the core functions of the network manager and their application to the operation of the collaboration.

The Burning Platform: A Call to Action

Success begins with a call to action. A community leader who wants to address workforce issues needs to actively involve both key stakeholders and the community at large. The leader who calls the community together could be a mayor whose authority comes from his or her position as the senior elected official in the region. Or the leader could be a respected institutional CEO, Chamber of Commerce principal, or university or philanthropic executive. Regardless of the source of authority, a leader's summons to collaborate should be powered by a call to action. We have seen different leaders involved in the call to action.

In Atlanta, the mayor and her workforce, education, and operations teams brought organizations together around the issue of workforce equity and opportunity, especially for people of color. The group that responded to her call included the Atlanta Committee for Progress, the Federal Reserve Bank of Atlanta, InvestAtlanta (the city's economic development arm), KIPP Charter and Atlanta Public Schools, the Chamber of Commerce, the United Way, WorkSource Georgia (the workforce board), the Atlanta Regional Commission, nonprofit college-advising service provider AchieveAtlanta, and a range of colleges and universities, including the city's HBCUs, and training institutes.

As detailed in the next chapter, Houston's preeminent business organization, the Greater Houston Partnership, created a subsidiary called UpSkill Houston and similarly convened partners. The partnership took on the role of convener due, in part, to the fact that the regional workforce board covers thirteen counties, diluting the influence of any one city.

In San Diego, the region's leading employment organization, the Workforce Partnership, acted as convenor, generating the necessary authority and support. Unlike many of its peer workforce boards across the country, the fact that the San Diego partnership raises over half its budget from private sources and operates through a separate nonprofit allows it to be free of strict regulatory restrictions, and this produces wider participation.

The leaders who call stakeholders together can hold any of a variety of positions. However, to be successful they must have the respect of the key participants and a separate source of authority, power, or budget. They must also be adroit at capturing the attention of the community around the importance of tackling societal inequities that impact job and economic mobility. A critical component of leadership is the ability to paint a picture or create a narrative compelling enough to galvanize the community, change public opinion, and make the case for collaboration.

The broader narrative, as in Birmingham's tale of two cities, should be designed to produce community support for efforts to help those not succeeding financially. Reframing the narrative has consequences that extend beyond making the case for collaboration.

Too often, the subtext around economic success blames the victim. Changing the public narrative from a criticism of those who might be poor to a criticism of the socioeconomic environment that holds them back is important on multiple levels. The leader must be able to appeal both to those who struggle and need hope as well as to those already benefitting from the local economy even if living in areas segregated by wealth and, often, race.

The leader, through narrative and visualization, must generate support for a broad and urgent response. A well-painted, fact-based description of the challenges faced by those associated with the shortage of equity and hope of those who feel trapped in low-income neighborhoods should help better-off residents understand the moral imperative. A convincing narrative should also appeal to enlightened self-interest about how lack of opportunity reduces productivity and inhibits the local economy, impacting everyone.

When the Indianapolis Chamber of Commerce, a few years ago, presented the key themes of its economic mobility initiative, it referred to the importance of personal fulfillment and positive neighborhood impacts. The chamber also featured the results of a Brookings Institution study that showed that greater economic mobility among those currently left behind would increase regional GDP by $5 billion to $16 billion dollars. In many of the cities we visited, leaders supplemented their call to action with a benchmarking study of the workforce funded by local businesses and philanthropies.

Calls to action can take different forms. For example, in New York City, then Mayor Mike Bloomberg, responding to an economic downturn early in his tenure as mayor, brought nonprofit, business, philanthropic, and academic leaders together and formed the Commission for Economic Opportunity, which conducted a comprehensive examination of poverty. The data collected by the commission built a case for the establishment of a new center by the same name, which eventually bolstered the reach of hundreds of city organizations by creating better coordination among them.

Forming the Collaborative

Once a leader makes the case for collaboration, demonstrates to potential partners their stake in addressing the issue, and convenes stakeholders, the next step is to work toward consensus (at least preliminarily) on desired outcomes and how to achieve them. A new or existing organization should be designated to serve as the intermediary that manages the network. We use the terms "intermediary" and "network manager" interchangeably to refer to the coordinating entity. The leader who calls the group together can host the collaboration, or the intermediary function can be assigned to another entity. In Atlanta, Mayor Keisha Lance Bottoms, who coauthored the foreword to this book, asked the United Negro College Fund, a locally respected group with expertise both in opportunities for youth of color and in project management, to provide day-to-day coordination. The roles and responsibilities of the coordinating organization may vary, but every city needs an entity to assume this role.

Committed sponsors, well-defined initial agreements, a clear agenda, and concrete accountability systems for tracking outcomes are critical components of effective collaboration. Both formal and informal processes and structures advance cross-sector partnerships. Formal processes that guide the actions of the participants enhance transparency and open communication, which, in turn, creates trust and furthers collective agency.

The intermediary that manages the hub needs sufficient resources to ensure that it can produce the data needed to monitor results and guide services. In Chicago, local philanthropies generated those resources. In Houston, businesses provided the funding. And in Atlanta, the project received start-up funding from a national grant.

Responsibilities of the Intermediary

Intermediaries provide a range of services, depending on their charter, the needs of the region, and the willingness of partners to share information and engage in comprehensive joint planning. Five of the core responsibilities are described here.

Ensure Availability

The manager of a collaborative must ensure that all critical components of a workforce development system that improve economic mobility are present in the region; that is, that the area's response incorporates the design principles discussed in this book. An initial review starts with people and looks at the varying needs of diverse populations to ensure that a variety of offerings are available (Principle 7). Second, mindful of the barriers that impede participation, like transportation or childcare, these systems also must include access to services that mitigate the effects of these daily challenges (Principle 9).

Ensuring the availability of services that meet the varied experiences and issues of myriad populations is no simple feat. In a system that depends on the interest of nonprofit entrepreneurs and socially minded philanthropists, and that is dominated by government funding for specific services demanding adherence to a relatively narrow set of rules, how does a coordinating group ensure the availability of necessary services?

We are reminded of our good friend Judge James Payne, a national child welfare expert from Indianapolis. While serving as the judge responsible for ordering placement of children in need of services, he took the responsibility for making sure the service mix offered by nonprofit organizations matched children's needs. This led him to call out the fact that too many local organizations were providing inadequate respite care for parents needing assistance while too few offered services for the more severe acute care needs. Judge Payne suggested that one of the larger organizations providing respite help to families with less dire problems alter its mission and provide care for children with more serious issues. But the organization had its own board, funders, and interests, which made change slow and politically unpleasant for the judge.

Starting with people, not programs, requires an organized effort by the collaborative to evaluate access and quality and, where necessary, to push back against existing practices. Nontraditional workers present themselves with a broad variety of needs that require a spectrum of responses (Principle 2). The regional collaboration needs to shine a bright light on where the region has too few or too many services, in a manner that causes philanthropists, the United Way, and government officials to understand both gaps and redundancies. Geospatial visualization is increasingly being deployed at the neighborhood level to identify gaps in services relative to need, and to identify where coordination among overlapping service providers would yield greater efficiencies.

The intermediary, through the use of evidence, needs to constantly challenge the status quo. Is the region moving to incorporate skills as a currency in its hiring and training (Principle 7)? Does the community offer apprentice and sectoral opportunities (Principle 6)? Cross-sector leadership is needed to bring together schools and employers to produce more apprentice and intern programs and to vet programs to ensure that the skills that are taught match the skills necessary for different jobs.

Promote Effectiveness, Outcomes, and Transparency

In most cities today, no one owns the excellence portfolio. The design principle "Commit to Transparency" requires agreement on what should be measured, how it should be reported, and who can see it (Principle 8). For example, in the case of training outcomes, a commitment to shared transparency on critical issues would reveal what percentage of students who start a training course get jobs, and the range of salaries associated with the jobs they secure as a result. Outcome transparency helps those who counsel students avoid guessing about whether they should refer someone to a particular course. And if a school is recruiting students into a training class, referring agencies will know whether their marketing pitch is accurate.

Not every intervention will work, nor will every nonprofit be equally successful. Our research suggests that effective programs share several common attributes. These attributes are reflected in the program-level design principles summarized in chapters 3 through 6. To achieve success, leaders and network managers must be willing to use their political capital to evaluate outcomes and shift resources into better performing organizations and more critical tasks. An important role of the cross-sector collaborative is to leverage its profile and the financial resources of its members to highlight what works and what shortfalls need to be addressed, while maintaining a community-wide spotlight on the economic and moral importance of the effort.

Provide a Data Infrastructure

Technology continuously alters the workforce, destroying some jobs and creating others. These changes alter the regional mix of in-demand skills. New digital breakthroughs, however, allow communities to deftly respond to such changes.

The managing entity must ensure robust use of data and evidence. The power of new technologies to help organize upskilling opportunities often exceeds the ability of local organizations to effectively make use of them. Artificial intelligence and machine reading of millions of job postings and résumés can identify needed and available skills. AI tools can evaluate syllabi to identify the skills taught in classes. Digital tools can help learners calculate return on investment in terms of how much the skills taught in a given course produce economic opportunity.

Geographic information systems can identify trends by city or neighborhood. When well visualized in maps, data create a common reference point for potential partners to translate their points of view into shared understanding, allowing, for example, insight into transportation or training availability relative to unemployment by neighborhood. Spatial visualizations shared in the formative stages of a collaboration enhance understanding and prove to be an important factor driving ongoing success.

If the network manager provides a process for aggregating data from multiple parties, this new information will create knowledge that allows partners to adapt their interventions in something approaching real time. Ideally, network managers should offer data services and a platform that not only provides useful insights to its partners but does it in a way that those receiving the data can add to and configure it for their own use. The information produced should be openly and widely disseminated to support learners and produce a community narrative of economic mobility. Regional data platforms coordinated by network managers will further adoption of common nomenclature, help direct resources, and create trust through transparency.

Figure 10-3 displays one simplified approach of how a shared data platform might connect partners.

The exchange of data broadly improves effectiveness, from job seekers determining where they can secure specific skills and how to calculate return on investment from a course to a WIB or state funder deciding where government funding should flow. Open outcome data help educators configure course offerings and aid counselors in the career advice they provide to students.

The work of Peter Callstrom and his team in San Diego demonstrates some of the applications of shared data. The San Diego Workforce Partnership (SDWP) combines data with in-person employer meetings to understand and support a talent pipeline, in a process Callstrom likens to supply chain management. SDWP as an intermediary articulates employers' needed skill sets by job type and then identifies training institutions that can deliver matching programs. "And that helps to connect the dots because the training institutions want to make sure that what they're delivering is going to get people jobs at the end of the day," Callstrom says. "We want to make sure that employers' talent requirements will be met with people equipped with the skills they need. Having a robust and person-centered process in place is crucial – and why it works."

Callstrom explains the Workforce Partnership market-making role that helps arrange services and advance employability:

> We talk to a wide range of employers regularly and dig deep, "What is your need for specialized programs and/or skills?" Not just, "Let me help you find a resource for one opening." But to larger companies that repeatedly need the same kind of employees, where they know they're going to need 25 developers the next time. For sectors that continually need employees with specific skills or credentials, we would say, "Let's design a specific program where we equip learners that meet your needs and are rewarded with a family sustaining-wage job."

Figure 10-3. **Collaboration Founded on Data**

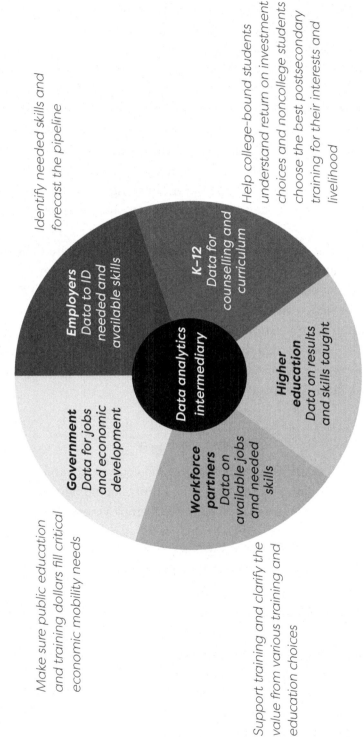

Identify needed skills and forecast the pipeline

Help college-bound students understand return on investment choices and noncollege students choose the best postsecondary training for their interests and livelihood

Provide degrees and certifications that both educate and produce career readiness skills

Support training and clarify the value from various training and education choices

Make sure public education and training dollars fill critical economic mobility needs

Employers
Data to ID needed and available skills

K-12
Data for counselling and curriculum

Data analytics intermediary

Government
Data for jobs and economic development

Higher education
Data on results and skills taught

Workforce partners
Data on available jobs and needed skills

Practically speaking, when stakeholders in a system have an interest in contributing their data, aggregate information tends to produce better decisionmaking. At first, perhaps only a few of the larger institutions will possess internal analytic capability, which means the cross-sector intermediary, with government and philanthropic support, should provide analytics as a service to the other partners. For example, Maria Flynn, CEO of JFF, hopes that her Outcomes for Opportunity Initiative pilot project with Google in San Diego will "increase the availability, accessibility, aggregation, and analysis of data and information." Data-informed programming will help workforce professionals provide better advice to those who come to them for assistance.

In addition, the network manager needs to make sure data support individuals trying to make decisions about their lives. Apps help consumers of education and training know whether a certain course or path furthers their journey to the right destination. The role of the intermediary on behalf of the cross-sector collaborative is not necessarily to build an application but, rather, to examine how useable, transparent data will produce better outcomes, and then to advocate, organize, fund, or manage the solution.

Advocate for Equity

The network manager also should help the community and partners advance important public policy goals. Equity should be at the top of that list. The Atlanta team examined Black employment, determining where Blacks were underrepresented in top career or higher-paying areas, where they were overrepresented in the lowest-paying areas, and which low-paying jobs amounted to dead ends. UNCF partnered with data provider Emsi to analyze millions of data points from government sources, job postings, job titles and skills, pay levels, and much more using a system that scraped data from applicable websites daily. The resulting analysis pertaining to equity in upskilling prompted changes in approaches by the organizational partners and the broader community. As discussed in chapter 7, skill-based hiring and promotion helps advance equity and is a critical component of an effective workforce development system.

Many of the right offerings may be present in a region. And community leaders may share the best of intentions. But true collaboration requires a process, common goals, leadership, and, most of all, ongoing management. Only with coordination across sectors, organizations, and agencies will it be possible to make the gains so critical to America's cities. Inequity and lack of upward mobility are serious issues that threaten not only prosperity but civic cohesion. We know what works. Now, cities and their residents need to organize in ways to make it happen.

11

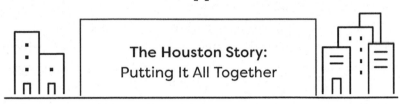

The Houston Story:
Putting It All Together

We first visited UpSkill Houston in October 2019 at the invitation of Peter Beard, a former colleague at the Fannie Mae Foundation from many years earlier.

Beard, executive director of UpSkill, knew of our search for a high-performing regional organization that coordinates economic mobility strategies—our last design principle in action (Principle 10). We attended UpSkill's October meeting to better understand the scope of its activities. The Greater Houston Partnership launched the organization in 2014, and by 2019, it included more than 200 employers, educational institutions, and community-based organizations, and the regional Workforce Investment Board.

Beard previously had worked at other social purpose national organizations, including United Way Worldwide and Habitat for Humanity International. On the day of our first visit, he chaired a meeting of fifty area business leaders and a broad array of involved local organizations. Over the next eighteen months, we visited and interviewed people associated with the entities in attendance that day who best illustrated UpSkill Houston's approach. Their words—officials of the organization, field workers, and participants—illustrate the design principles outlined in this book.

Fittingly, that October meeting started with data. Harvard Business School professor Joe Fuller, an expert in the future of work, led off with his analysis of critical trends. His presentation depicted the disproportionate growth of lower-wage jobs, even as the demand for educated workers increased concurrently. The growth that Fuller referenced that day featured nonroutine cognitive jobs. Without question, UpSkill Houston needed to double down on upskilling.

Houston's experience illustrates this book's last design principle of how a managed collaboration can ensure that the principles come together at the individual program and systems level for an effective response—in this case, to the challenge presented by Fuller at that meeting. The only principle not directly addressed by UpSkill is the one concerning "making places work," the responsibility for which appropriately resides with government.

Organize for Collaboration

The Houston effort demonstrates how an intermediary can make the sum greater than the parts by convening a broad set of community stakeholders, focusing their efforts through the use of data, and ensuring the availability of critical services. UpSkill sets out as its goals bringing key business, education, and community leaders together; facilitating industry collaboratives; inspiring collective action by aligning efforts; and increasing awareness of mid-skill careers while addressing the skills gap. It accomplishes these goals by orchestrating the direct services necessary to create a pipeline of skilled workers.

The Greater Houston Partnership, an organization of more than 1,000 member companies, played the role of convener when it formed UpSkill to act as intermediary. Beard tells us that by starting with a partnership where employers already meet and discuss challenges provided a head start. Even though the effort puts employers at the center, and those same companies sponsor much of the activity, the community views UpSkill as a neutral place to exchange ideas and concerns.

The organization manages the collaboration while also promoting awareness and encouraging community support. Its goal of inspiring collective action fulfills a fundamental responsibility of the entity leading cooperative work. UpSkill successfully fits the profile of a high-performing regional intermediary. Its convenor, the Greater Houston Partnership, created and, in part, funds UpSkill to provide ongoing management of the initiative. The actions of the UpSkill partners and the people they assist illustrate how Houston puts our design principles into action.

Start with People, Not Programs; Offer Meaningful Choices (Principles 1 and 2)

UpSkill started with a mission: increase upward mobility through middle-skill employment. The organization then brought together 130 employers, fifteen community organizations, twenty school districts, and seven community colleges to launch a major effort aimed at mid-skill jobs. The initiative focused on the needs of those wanting better jobs; that is, the people, not the existing programs.

UpSkill set a three-year goal of helping 130,000 people improve their lives. A goal at that scale requires accommodating disparities in the lives of struggling Houstonians and understanding the needs of regional employers arrayed across several different industry clusters.

The collaboration included not simply the plug-and-play of existing offerings by schools and social service agencies but, rather, an exploration of better pathways. "We have the ability to actually get the superintendent in the room with the plant manager, the chancellor of the community college, leading social service agencies, and secondary school executives so that they can actually have a leadership conversation, and not just a tactical conversation," Beard emphasizes.

In addition, UpSkill promotes outreach so that interested learners and workers can find a path or program tailored to their needs. These cross-sector efforts involve career guidance and hands-on exploration fairs as well as work-based training to help connect the learner to what makes the most sense for him or her. Beard adds that UpSkill "helps workers understand what skills they have, and what are adjacent skills that would allow them to easily jump into a new, higher-paying industry."

Accommodating disparities here applies to both employer and employee needs. "If an employer has a very specific need on the spot-market, there's a way to meet that need; but if they need employees with soft skills or more workers with middle skills, those aren't going to happen on the spot market," Beard said. UpSkill as an intermediary demonstrates the need to constantly evaluate options in response to the changing economic and social needs of the region.

Use Skills as Currency (Principle 7)

UpSkill by name and focus embodies the design principle we call "using skills as a currency." Joe Fuller's presentation in that October meeting centered on attracting, training, and placing individuals in middle-skill jobs.

The language of skills dominates the collaboration given that the demand for middle-skill jobs in Houston is projected to grow by approximately 1 million jobs in the next decade. Today, 75 percent of the workforce lacks those skills. The establishment of skills as a currency shows through UpSkill's focus on connecting individuals to employers with skills-based education and hiring.

Middle-skill employment, as Houston applies the term, covers a broad scope of jobs that require more education and experience than a high school diploma but less than a four-year college degree. The Houston effort concentrates on middle skills in the city's competitive clusters. The Greater Houston Partnership enlisted consultants TEConomy Partners to examine high-demand jobs in the region and match projected jobs against annual job openings over the next five years. This effort examined results by industry: construction, energy, manufacturing, petrochemicals, transportation, corporate headquarters administration, and biomedical, which included healthcare and industrial life sciences.

"Early on, we thought there were more technical jobs that required one- or two-year degrees, but in reality, there were a good amount of options for on-the-job training or CTE [Career and Technical Education] training," Beard said. "Most of these employers care more about competency and skills than about a particular degree or certificate."

Nevertheless, we noticed, and many of the Houston partners confirmed, that the term "middle-skill" does not create excitement for either students or incumbent workers, who admittedly might not be aware of the breadth of occupations in that category. Simply put, the terms "low," "middle" and "high" do not capture the valuable technical and soft skills required in any occupation.

A system that uses the skills as a currency requires the participation of those who do the hiring and those who do the training and education. But it also needs translators, often career counselors or providers of wraparound services, to express the language of skills in a manner that drives action.

Create Bridges to Employment (Principle 6)

UpSkill creates connections among learners, colleges, secondary schools, and employers. Bridges such as internships and relationships with employers incorporated into training make the difference. The partnership provides a forum for its members to learn from one another and to customize the bridges among them to provide learners with highly tailored pathways. Beard notes that both the school districts and community colleges pivoted "when an employer sat down and said, 'I've got this problem. Can you help me solve it?'"

HD Chambers spent thirty-five years teaching and serving as an administrator in Texas public education before becoming superintendent for Alief Independent School District (AISD). He does not mince words. He does not speak in academic jargon or abstract principles when he says his goal is to fight "so that students who are not on a college trajectory will not be labeled failures." He argues that they can do good work and have a good quality of life derived from jobs requiring technical skills but not four-year degrees. His path to this mission started when he first read Harvard's Robert Schwartz's influential report on career and technical education, "Pathways to Prosperity: Meeting the Challenge of Preparing Young Americans for the 21st Century."

For Chambers, UpSkill's most valuable contribution comes from making it possible "for employers to work with us, in our buildings and with the students. That was the catalyst for us to actually sit with the right people and talk about the right things. Because up until then, we were not talking the right language. We were not talking about the areas where they truly needed the help. So, it's allowed us to forge relationships with the industry sector." Students, employers, and the school district all benefit from these interlocking relationships.

Listen, Respond, Get Personal (Principle 3)

The Houston organizations profiled in this chapter know they cannot approach each individual in the same way. From recruiting at the high school by TRIO to the applied industry experiences at San Jacinto College (SanJac), we see a never-ending effort to personalize outreach and paths to success.

We can observe these personalized approaches in the words and actions of apprentices we met, such as Guadalupe, who is profiled in chapter 6, and her eventual employer, TRIO's Beau Pollock, who attended the October meeting. From a private discussion that day and in multiple conversations that followed, we better understood how he used his place at the table to solve his pipeline challenge and to attract and train learners.

When Pollock explains his success, he starts with the importance of designing a system personalized around the learner. He customizes his outreach and training to appeal to more students. He engages directly with students to describe the jobs in meaningful and personal terms. He notes that "not a lot of young people look at construction as a career. They look at it as something they end up in—although they may stick there once they realize they can make money and they're good at it."

Students react based on their backgrounds but also based on their peers. The young adults Pollock approaches come from lower-income neighborhoods, use English as a second language, and rarely have parents who have gone to college. Pollock knows that reaching students in school with a more focused message and more tangible opportunities is the key to convincing them to take the first step into a pre-apprentice program:

> They may not view the job of an electrician as a skilled job, or they may not want to take a step that looks like an admission they won't be going to college. Usually, we make presentations to students who are identified by the counselors as students that would benefit from this program. But for many years, young men and women who would have been great employees have been led to believe if they can't make it to college, they have failed. And even if college

is not for them, they don't take the steps to prepare for a good job early enough. It's not until their senior year, second semester. They think, "If not college, then what is next?"

We asked Pollock about recruiting at schools and how he responds to what he hears. He describes how he personalizes his outreach with encouragement and the promise of a better tomorrow:

One is what gives them confidence, persistence, thinking that they could take this step and be successful when they have seen a lot of folks around them not be successful. The second is, "I got to take care of my younger brother, how do I get there and do the job training and get back and help Mom?" There's just such a set of support services that may affect them. So, they need to factor in what the opportunity means and how realistic it is they can get to the finish line. That's usually the hook, when they see the trajectory of how much they can make, either as an intern or once they graduate. That's usually when their eyes light up, and they become super-focused and fill out the interest cards.

Of course, it is not just a personalized, appealing message but also who delivers it that counts. Depending on corporate CEOs is not a reasonable path to scaling up the delivery of such messages. Most high school students do not receive enough tailored counseling to help them with difficult career-related decisions. Chambers, pushing back against the established way of doing things, claims one does not need to be a licensed counselor to be valuable to students. In fact, he believes it is better to use someone who knows the world of work to help students move forward.

"If you're going to put as much money and effort and importance on this as we do preparing students for a meaningful postsecondary opportunity, you need to invest in the adults who can help them do that," Chambers said. Recognizing the large caseloads and the need for advisers who know the workforce world better, AISD created a new approach and new positions that allow Chambers to hire more individuals with practical experience to work with students on their futures.

The Houston story suggests another, more subtle form of personalization that involves context and proximity. We universally heard from the leaders we met—social service, high school, business, and community college—empathetic and positive comments about those they serve. They see potential in their students/employees and believe deeply that they deserve a chance. It is refreshing to hear Chambers fight for them or for Pollock to say, "First and foremost, I realize most of these students already have a pretty good work ethic, because they come from working families, and they're already doing something outside of the house, in addition to school to support their families."

Chambers continues to offer large doses of realism to our conversations:

> Almost 90 percent of our students come from low, low, low economic conditions. And not all want to go to college. But we don't think of them as inferior. I grew up with my dad working at DuPont in Orange, Texas. He never stepped foot on a college campus as a student, but he's the smartest man I've ever known. Ask anyone that worked with him. I just kept noticing that society seemed to discriminate against students who weren't going to college. I had a relative who did not want to attend college, but he was concerned about being deemed a failure in high school because he couldn't pass some standardized test!

The efforts of Chambers and Pollock combine three design principles: contextualization, personalization, and bridging to employment. "We needed to grow and diversify our business," Pollock said. "After years of going to the traditional outlets and resources that were supposed to be producing that supply of skilled labor . . . we realized there was just a big disparity in what was being taught versus what we needed as employers."

The personalization built into the outreach makes the bridge to employment more appealing, and contextualization makes the successful passage over the bridge more likely. These efforts work best when configured by those who, because of their own personal experiences or proximity, understand the context and anxieties of the students.

Contextualize Learning (Principle 5)

We traveled across town to learn about contextualized learning at San Jacinto College's LyondellBasell Center for Petrochemical, Energy, and Technology. SanJac, under Chancellor Brenda Hellyer, plays a critical role in UpSkill's efforts. The college has been named one of ten finalists for the 2021 Aspen Prize for Community College Excellence, for high achievement and performance among community colleges.

LyondellBasell, one of the largest plastics, chemicals, and refining companies in the world, fits squarely in the bailiwick of UpSkill Houston. It needed workers with the middle skills necessary to handle sophisticated equipment. It also fits in the vision of Hellyer, an accountant by background who, before her doctorate in community college leadership, worked in large and small businesses. Having a seat on the UpSkill board facilitated relationships with corporate CEOs and helped Hellyer contextualize the learnings she offered, both with respect to pedagogy and classroom design. SanJac's state-of-the-art facilities were designed to emulate the workplace. The new $65 million center we visited was funded as part of a $425 million general obligation bond endorsed by the East Harris County Manufacturers Association, which represents 130 plants in the region. The bond was approved by almost 70 percent of the voters. In addition, industry partners contributed significant time, equipment, and cash donations to supplement the facility design. Basically, the Petrochemical and Energy Center was designed by industry for industry.

Hellyer describes a visit to the businesses, where they talked about the gaps that, at the time, held back even graduating students:

> What they talked about was how we were teaching some of those skills in the courses, but they needed these skills to be laddered on top of each other. And our laddering was out of sync. What industry said is, "You've got to require chemistry in that first semester, because it's the whole basis of everything else they need." And so, we restructured how courses were being offered so that there was that laddering throughout the curriculum. LyondellBasell actually went even deeper discussing skillsets and courses.

SanJac combines contextualized learning with internship bridges because students often need more than just skills. Some students receive internships that not only provide hands-on training but also help launch them toward employment. These internships persuade students to stay enrolled until they complete the necessary certifications. Contextualization crafts a message that students need to hear, and it crafts a curriculum that blends academic and technical curricula in a manner that employers know will work, in part because they have had input into it.

Chambers reinforces the importance of contextualization when describing his interaction with the oil and gas industry, which came to him wanting to upgrade the skills of process technicians. That job title doesn't describe much, but Chambers's explanation does: "It is, basically someone who works with instruments in a chemical plant as they manufacture plastic. We discovered in our conversations with those in the petrochem industry that the math and science courses that we were teaching in our K–12 system, based on what the state required, produced absolutely no alignment with the actual on-the-job, math and science type skills that these potential employees needed."

UpSkill's partners, and the activities they provide, highlight multiple examples of contextualized learning. Chambers and Pollock use language similar to Hellyer when describing the need for more curricular relevance. For the cross-sector collaboration to be real, they believe the very nature of the classroom needs to change.

Now, when a student walks into the TRIO "classroom," he sees what looks like a job site—metal studs, ladders, tools, students wearing personal protective equipment. It replicates a real work site and produces an environment that facilitates learning. Contextualization does not stop with the physical setup of the room; it also includes a joint project between school and company officials to design a relevant curriculum that combines math and reading with learning-by-doing.

Our end goal is not to do an in-depth review of curriculum. Rather, we have highlighted the benefits of a collaborative where all parties are willing to change a bit to design a system that works better for students. Those involved in SanJac and AISD reject off-the-shelf curricula in favor of a more customized and contextualized effort to prepare students so that, when they are sent "out to the workforce, we know they are prepared. They need more than theory."

Support Learners and Remove Barriers (Principle 4)

Pollock understands and accommodates, to the extent possible, the family responsibilities of his apprentices' first step. However, many hopeful workers require more than understanding to overcome the barriers that stand in their way, which takes us to the design principle of "support learners and remove barriers." Here UpSkill nonprofit community organizations play a critical role. We look, in particular, at the Wesley Community Center, which helps clients overcome obstacles both in providing traditional wraparound services such as childcare and in nurturing confidence and self-actualization for job seekers.

We met Iris at Wesley Community Center. Wesley is tucked away in a lower-middle-class neighborhood in north-central Houston. The center embraces a neighborhood-based identity, fitting in well among the single-family units stretching down the road on either side. With a gym and an upstairs classroom, the center provides an array of supports for struggling families and a place to obtain the tools necessary to change their lives. Learning about Iris and her journey tells us much about Wesley—and why having such an organization in the mix makes a huge difference—but it also tells us a great deal about the importance of personalization and confidence.

Iris was homeless and living in a shelter. She found her way to Wesley because "one of the ladies who came to help people at the shelter with GED programs told me about a place where there were programs that could actually help me land a job, and it was so true for me." Iris expected to experience something like the more impersonal, somewhat more degrading group approach of the homeless shelter, but Wesley focused much more on the participant and her goals.

"What made me latch onto Wesley was that they didn't have a way of making you feel like they're more than you," Iris said.

She followed up:

And that's very important. To feel like "Hey, when I come in this door, I'm not looked down upon." Wesley really worked on inspiring participants to set goals. It was not a false sense of hope. It was like, "OK, this is going to require some work. This is what you do, and we're here for you. Not only are we offering you an opportunity to better yourself, we're gonna help you bridge the gap." Things like transportation, having something to eat, childcare, studying.

Iris's declaration underscores the feelings of many people who need help and have trouble taking the right steps. "If I will allow them to help me, I can go all the way to the end," she says. With pride, she explains her newfound confidence: "I may be here right now, but through a few steps I can end up in a better state. It's not a success overnight type of thing. But I can feel myself becoming someone else as I go through the program." She previously experienced many false starts, and even a community college course. But for her, Wesley "built confidence."

We see aspects of CUNY ASAP's peer connectedness approach and of Capital IDEA's realistic onboarding almost immediately after being ushered into one of Wesley's classes. The students were in their final class of the program and engaging in an activity called vision boarding, which included digging through magazines to find pictures that embodied their goals for the future, cutting them out, and gluing them to a poster board. The classroom facilitator, a woman in her late thirties named Schirell, showed an example of a vision board from the year before, and talked briefly about the person who had created it and how she has progressed along her career path. Schirell encouraged students to create their vision boards with an eye toward the future. Each student was given the option of sharing it in front of the class.

Schirell engaged with the students both jokingly and pointedly, encouraging them to believe in themselves and set attainable goals. Schirell assigned another activity that included an exercise the students had just finished on playspent.org, a website designed to put players in the "position of balancing on the edge of homelessness." The activity walks students through a "month of decisions," the kind many people in poverty face as they wrestle with how to use their money. It challenges users to reach the end of the month with money left in the bank. We made it to the end of the exercise, but not without selling our dog, driving away from the scene of a car accident, opting out of health insurance, ignoring heart pain, and eating primarily beans and ramen noodles for the month. The students who participated in the exercise discussed their decisions with the class. Schirell talked to us about the daily tradeoffs that people face and the complexity of making it to the end of the month with limited resources.

We returned to watch the graduation. Schirell emphasized the ongoing career coaching and support services that Wesley offers, telling students that, to succeed, they will continue to need a network of people around them. At one point, she went up to and linked arms with a graduate and talked about the importance of mutual support as one navigates the shoals of life and career. Relations with a spouse, children, or neighbors played a central part in most conversations.

Iris's explanation of how Wesley helps participants pursue a better job shows how the community center removes barriers in a way that gives learners the confidence to take additional steps such as those offered by others in UpSkill:

> You start with introductory classes that talk about professionalism, prep for actually being in a CNA [certified nurse assistant] class and [get an] introduction to the CNA-related material. We received uniforms that made me feel really connected to my class. The process of finding out how you are going to get from point A to point B in terms of transportation helped a lot. Connecting with the other ladies made a difference. Classmates would pitch in to help out with gas. They would hold one another accountable for getting the assignments done on time. The employment specialist prepared us for the company before they came in. The mock interviews felt like real ones. All leading up to us being taken together on a bus to a real interview with our notes, resumes, and professional-looking clothes.

Wesley illustrates the many ways an exceptional organization can support learners. The organization offers counseling on how to overcome barriers while also providing critical services, including: Early Head Start, childcare, after-school and summer care for youth, food for struggling families, and a training center for GED, ESL, financial literacy, and workforce development.

Wesley leadership uses the same positive, asset-oriented language we heard from Pollock and Chambers—and not a language of pathologies. Wesley does not make the case that employers should hire "these people because it's a good thing to do." Rather, they prepare their clients well and present them to employers with a simple declaration: "Here are people with the skills and attitudes that are going to be helpful to you."

Commit to Transparency; Use Data to Drive Performance (Principle 8)

In advancing its principle of being "data- and action-driven," UpSkill uses data to examine market and skilling opportunities and to advocate for more data access. UpSkill supported changes in the state unemployment compensation system that would make anonymized information available to allow researchers to track the route from higher education graduation to post-graduation placements and wages.

Beard hopes to build UpSkill's analytics so that his team can examine local data in real time. He plans to create a data analytics function that would: (1) enhance public policy analysis and development; (2) improve the general public's ability to access and use education and workforce information, (3) strengthen continuous improvement by the agencies and their primary stakeholders; and (4) support expanded cost-benefit analyses of workforce efforts across sectors. This important list should be a fundamental part of the strategic plan of every network manager.

However impressive the trajectories of Iris or Guadalupe might be, both benefited from a journey that began almost accidentally, through a fortuitous meeting. The random nature of these solutions demonstrates the need for a more systematic approach accompanied by resources flowing where they will do the most good.

Conclusion

We close our book with the story of UpSkill Houston because it combines an effective intermediary with an inspiring goal, strong partners, and a community call to action. We learn from UpSkill how the cross-sector fusion of various points of view into a set of coordinated, data-driven responses can create opportunity. The benefits of coordination, resting on a skill-based foundation, are manifest in many ways, from the design of curriculum and classrooms to the creation of intern or apprentice programs to arranging support services like transportation.

In this book, we examine the components of a successful skilling system—at the individual, program, and system levels. Successful cross-sector collaborations bring together parties from different sectors, with different points of view, around the goal of economic mobility as part of a network dedicated to a coordinated vision of economic opportunity. However, even this impressive step, though necessary, is not sufficient.

Intolerance of Mediocrity

Houston's model is worth emulating. But it is only a start. The urgency with which we must address flaws in the current system requires intolerance of mediocrity. We cannot accept what does not work or become complacent when an earnest idea does not produce results. Lifting the incomes of Americans requires more than coordination. It requires cross-sector leaders willing to use their platforms to challenge the status quo and drive resources to what works.

Levers

We started this book by calling for a shared goal and a new narrative concerning the urgent need to improve economic mobility so we can grow together fairly. This goal requires more than new programs, new structures, and new funds tethered to an imperfect status quo. Government, business, and philanthropic leadership must advocate for change, challenge what does not work, and drive resources to what does, using all available levers, including the following:

1. **Rhetoric:** *Elected leaders have an outsized voice that they should use to call the community together on behalf of fairness and human potential.* A shared narrative of a better economy with more fairness needs to be clear. This includes acknowledging the grievous systemic flaws that have produced the inequities we see today.

2. **Authority:** *Government exercises real authority. It designates preferred community groups in ways that empower them, enhancing their funding and representation.* Officials appoint board members to governmental, quasi-governmental, and nonprofit boards. A condition of appointment should be that board members rigorously insist on results for every dollar spent. We cannot afford good intentions disconnected from excellent performance.

3. **Resources:** *Governments, foundations, and businesses fund and invest in organizations, workers, and prospective workers.* Performance funding and an insistence on reasonably demonstrated results should be part of every contract and expenditure of public dollars.

4. **Information and transparency:** *Leaders must insist on collecting and publishing real-time information.* This will enhance consumer choice and ensure resources go where they are likely to make the most positive impact.

Activation

At the end of our research, we gathered together in a few small groups the leaders of the high-performing organizations we had studied and come to know. We asked them about reach, about what they thought would accelerate conversion to a more effective and equitable workforce development system like the one proposed here. Not unexpectedly, these high-performing organizations started and ended our conversations with performance, although they got there in different ways. They argued that investment should follow performance, a point that should be obvious but is not, in practice, widely applied. Paying for results drives resources to programs that work through mechanisms such as pay for success contracting and income sharing agreements, much needed accelerants for change.

They cautioned, however, that paying for results makes sense only if we pay for the right results. They allude to the sometimes perverse consequences of current metrics that measure activity rather than outcomes. Two leaders cited, for instance, payments contingent upon whether a person was in a classroom or had completed a training session rather than whether he or she actually got and kept the intended job. The butts in seats phenomena, as they so elegantly put it.

The group shared a variety of recommendations for structural changes to free up resources for effective programing. Workforce investment boards should, they argued, use a higher percentage of their funds for training individuals and less maintaining so many "one-stop" intake centers. They suggested investing in career and employment navigation systems rather than physical infrastructure. Fragmented federal and state funding streams mean that all too frequently too low a percentage of the monies allocated actually make it into training. Some noted, as recipients of government and philanthropic grants are wont to do, that grant requirements create high overhead costs and can be so onerous as to make their receipt unworthy of the time. Some have opted to forgo Work Innovation and Opportunity Act (WIOA) funding altogether.

They took up the subject of certifications where substantial resources are currently invested. Of course, certifications can ensure quality, but they also can create costs and processes unrelated to results. If a person can pass the licensing test because she is unusually smart and in an unusually good program, does she need to endure the hardship of finishing every week of training? They proposed taking a hard look at occupational certification requirements to determine which are and are not truly necessary. They also suggested looking at who provides those certifications, observing that, for instance, monopoly power situates training for certain health care certifications with hospitals rather than skilling intermediaries with lower operating costs.

Looking to the future, the group argued for a more expansive, less tradition-bound way of thinking about the roles of different players in the system. Private employers, they said, should more frequently partner with knowledgeable and successful training organizations—furnishing capital and then paying for successful training and preparation of the nontraditional student. This, they argue, would force education and training entities to focus on growing occupations and skilling gaps and reward those that produce qualified employees. They see a role for philanthropy to provide risk and innovation capital to prove out interventions.

Of course, the high performers challenge their own models constantly. Thus, they encourage funders to reward risk! To this insistence, we add an aside of our own. The best programs use analytics to evaluate their own interventions, to calibrate them to the needs of specific individuals, and to constantly understand which actions create the most good. For many small organizations, sophisticated use of data is an elusive dream. Funders should consider funding third-party services that assist organizations in their pursuit of operational excellence.

Inexpensive, quick fixes for many nontraditional workers do not last. There are, they say, no silver bullets. Pay attention to the science, expect relapse, and move quickly when a person needs something additional or a program needs something new. These leaders are willing to take chances. We must, too.

Leadership can and should elevate a shared understanding about the unevenness of opportunity. Collaboration will more fairly unlock growth. Individuals like Iris will flourish when not held back at the starting line. Iris's job as a nursing assistant produces more than just income; it makes her proud. And it makes her daughter proud—now mom has a car and an apartment and can make that sandwich and drive her to school. Iris's path from boarding a bus in front of a homeless shelter to taking her daughter to school in her own car is quite the journey.

Iris's words echo what we heard over and over: "When I walked into that new apartment right after graduation, I saw a refrigerator, a stove, a bed. Having a place where I'm actually going and turning the key. Those things built confidence in my daughter, not just me, because these were things that we didn't have before." Mobility is possible. We can grow more fairly. The right local action will create millions of success stories, producing hope for families and communities and economic progress for regions.

Notes

Chapter 1

1. Jessica Kursman and Nick Zettel, "Who Can Live in Chicago? Part I," Voorhees Center, June 6, 2018.

2. Unless otherwise noted, the interviews in the book were conducted by us and our researchers between June 2020 and May 2021. Those interviewed were conducted in the home city of the interviewee. We were either there in person or present during COVID-19 by Zoom.

3. "Pursuing the American Dream: Economic Mobility Across Generations," Pew Charitable Trusts, July 2012, pp. 20–21.

4. David Ellwood and Nisha G. Patel, "Restoring the American Dream: What Would It Take to Dramatically Increase Mobility from Poverty?" Harvard Kennedy School, January 2018.

5. Robert Doar and others, "Work, Skills, Community: Restoring Opportunity for the Working Class," AEI, May 1, 2018, p. 14.

6. Catholic Church, Pope (1978–2005: John Paul II), "On Human Work: Encyclical Laborem Exercens" (Washington, D.C.: Office of Publishing Services, United States Catholic Conference, 1981).

7. Jon Hilsenrath, "Five Cities Account for Vast Majority of Growth in Tech Jobs, Study Finds," *Wall Street Journal*, December 9, 2019.

8. Richard Florida, "Mapping America's Stark Wage Inequality," Bloomberg CityLab, December 3, 2019, www.bloomberg.com/news/articles/2019-12-03/mapping-america-s-stark-wage-inequality.

9. Megan McArdle, "Cities Will Make a Comeback after the Coronavirus. They Almost Always Do," *Washington Post,* June 3, 2020.

10. Edward L. Glaeser, *Agglomeration Economics* (University of Chicago Press, 2010), pp. 1–14.

11. Ibid.

12. See Urban Institute, "Nine Charts about Wealth Inequality in America," 2017, https://apps.urban.org/features/wealth-inequality-charts/.

13. Jonathan Rabinovitz, "Stanford/Cornell Study Shows Increasing Segregation by Income: Mixed-Income Neighborhoods become Less Common as Gap Grows between Rich and Poor," Stanford Graduate School of Education, March 6, 2016.

14. Raj Chetty and others, "Where is the Land of Opportunity? The Geography of Intergenerational Mobility in the United States," Working Paper 19843 (National Bureau of Economic Research, January 2014).

15. The Editorial Board, "The Cities We Need," *New York Times,* May 11, 2020.

16. Jennifer L. Eberhardt, *Biased: Uncovering the Hidden Prejudice that Shapes What We See, Think, and Do* (New York: Penguin Books, 2020).

17. Chetty and others, "Where Is the Land of Opportunity?"

18. David H. Autor, "Work of the Past, Work of the Future," AEA Papers and Proceedings 109 (2019), pp. 1–32. DOI: 10.1257/pandp.20191110.

19. Peter Q. Blair and David J. Deming, "Structural Increases in Demand for Skill after the Great Recession," *AEA Papers and Proceedings,* 110 (2020), pp. 362–65.

20. Ibid.

21. Autor, "Work of the Past, Work of the Future."

22. Stephen Rose, "Squeezing the Middle Class: Income Trajectories from 1967 to 2016," Brookings Institution, August 10, 2020.

23. Angela Simms, "The 'Veil' of Racial Segregation in the 21st Century: The Suburban Black Middle Class, Public Schools, and Pursuit of Racial Equity," *Phylon (1960–),* 56, no. 1 (2019), pp. 81–110.

24. Richard Fry, "The Pace of Boomer Retirements Has Accelerated in the Past Year," Pew Research Center, 2020.

25. Rob Sentz and others, *The Demographic Drought: How the Approaching Sansdemic Will Transform the Labor Market for the Rest of Our Lives* (ebook), Emsi, 2021, https://economicmodeling.com/2021/05/04/demographic-drought/.

26. Alicia Sasser Modestino, "The Importance of Middle-Skill Jobs," *Issues in Science and Technology,* 33, no. 1 (Fall 2016), pp. 41–46.

27. Mark Muro, Jacob Whiton, and Patrick McKenna, "Could 'Mid-Tech' Jobs Elevate More People and Non-Coastal Places?" *The Avenue* (blog), June 20, 2018.

28. Modestino, "The Importance of Middle-Skill Jobs."

29. See Joint Center for Housing Studies of Harvard University, "The State of the Nation's Housing 2020," 2020, www.jchs.harvard.edu/state -nations-housing-2020.

30. Vincent A. Fusaro and H. Luke Shaefer, "How Should We Define 'Low-Wage' Work? An Analysis using the Current Population Survey," U.S. Bureau of Labor Statistics, October 2016, www.bls.gov/opub/mlr/2016/ article/how-should-we-define-low-wage-work.htm.

31. Martha Ross and Nicole Bateman, "Meet the Low-Wage Workforce," Brookings Institution, November 2019.

32. Lawrence Aber and others, "Opportunity, Responsibility, and Security," Brookings Institution, 2015.

33. Ibid.

Chapter 2

1. U.S. Bureau of Labor Statistics, "Number of unemployed persons per job opening, seasonally adjusted," Graphics for Economic News Releases, www.bls.gov/charts/job-openings-and-labor-turnover/unemp-per-job -opening.htm.

2. U.S. Bureau of Labor Statistics, "Glossary of terms," June 7, 2016, www.bls.gov/bls/glossary.htm.

3. Ibid.

4. Terry-Ann Craigie and others, "Conviction, Imprisonment, and Lost Earnings: How Involvement with the Criminal Justice System Deepens Inequality," Brennan Center for Justice, September 15, 2020.

5. Molly Baldwin and others, "Cognitive Behavioral Theory, Young Adults, and Community Corrections: Pathways for Innovation," Harvard Kennedy School, April 24, 2018.

6. Martha Laboissiere and Mona Mourshed, "Closing the Skills Gap: Creating Workforce-Development Programs that Work for Everyone," McKinsey & Company, Public & Social Sector, February 2017.

7. Melanie A. Zaber, Lynn A. Karoly, and Katie Whipkey, *Reimagining the Workforce Development and Employment System for the 21st Century and Beyond* (RAND Corporation, 2019).

8. Beth Akers and Ellie Klein, "Serving the Underserved in Workforce Development: A Q&A with Beth Weigensberg," *Social Mobility Memos* (blog), September 1, 2015, www.brookings.edu/blog/social-mobility-memos/2015 /09/01/serving-the-underserved-in-workforce-development-a-qa-with-beth -weigensberg/.

9. Michele R. Weise, "Future of Work," Rise & Design LLC, www.riseand design.io/long-life-learning-preparing-for-jo.

10. Raj Chetty and Nathaniel Hendren, "The Impacts of Neighborhoods

on Intergenerational Mobility I: Childhood Exposure Effects," *Quarterly Journal of Economics*, 133, no. 3 (August 2018), pp. 1107–62.

11. Elisabeth Babcock, "Using Brain Science to Transform Human Services and Increase Personal Mobility from Poverty," Mobility Partnership Organization, March 2018.

12. LaDonna Pavetti, "Using Executive Function and Related Principles to Improve the Design and Delivery of Assistance Programs for Disadvantaged Families," Paper Prepared for Innovating to End Urban Poverty, Sol Price Center for Social Innovation, Washington, D.C., March 27–28, 2014.

13. Nina Castells and James Riccio, "Executive Skills Coaching Plus Incentives in a Workforce Program: Introducing the MyGoals Demonstration," MDRC, May 2020.

14. A. Hamoudi and others, "Self-Regulation and Toxic Stress: A Review of Ecological, Biological, and Developmental Studies of Self-Regulation and Stress," OPRE Report 2015-30, Washington, D.C.: Office of Planning, Research and Evaluation, Administration for Children and Families, U.S. Department of Health and Human Services; and Pavetti, "Using Executive Function and Related Principles to Improve the Design and Delivery of Assistance Programs for Disadvantaged Families."

15. Nicki Ruiz de Luzuriaga, "Coaching for Economic Mobility," EMPath, October 2015.

16. Daniel C. Marston, "Neurobehavorial Effects of Poverty," *American Psychological Association*, January 2013, www.apa.org/pi/ses/resources/indicator/2013/01/poverty-behaviors.

17. Nicki Ruiz de Luzuriaga, "Coaching for Economic Mobility," EMPath, October 2015.

18. Elisabeth D. Babcock, "New Strategies for Fishing: Coaching for Economic Mobility in the 21st Century," American Enterprise Institute, September 17, 2020.

19. Pavetti, "Using Executive Function and Related Principles to Improve the Design and Delivery of Assistance Programs for Disadvantaged Families."

20. See Roca, Inc., "Annual Report," 2019, https://rocainc.org/wp-content/uploads/2020/02/Roca_2.12.2019_AR.pdf.

21. Nadine Dechausay, "The Future of Executive-Skills Coaching and Behavioral Science in Programs that Serve Teens and Young Adults: Lessons from the Annie E. Casey Foundation's Pilot Project," MDRC, January 2018.

22. Gabrielle Caverl-McNeal and Dana Emanuel, "New Moms: An Executive Skills Approach to Job Training PowerPoint," Chicago Jobs Council, March 11, 2020, https://cjc.net/frontline-focus/workforce-360/.

23. de Luzuriaga, "Coaching for Economic Mobility."

24. Castells and Riccio, "Executive Skills Coaching Plus Incentives in a Workforce Program."

25. Ibid.

Chapter 3

1. See Strada's on-going surveys: "Public Viewpoint (2020 to 2021); Weekly surveys, March 25–May 28, 2020; Biweekly surveys, June–October 2020 and 2021; and Strada-Gallup Education Consumer Survey (2020) and Values of Education: Likely to Enroll (2019)," https://cci.stradaeducation.org /public-viewpoint/.

2. See Strada, "Strada Public Viewpoint: Covid-19 Work and Education Survey, Results from March 25–26, 2020," August 2020, http:// stradaeducation.org/wp-content/uploads/2020/04/Public-Viewpoint-Charts -Week-1.pdf.

3. Whitney Engstrom, David Fein, and Karen Gardiner, "Pathways for Advancing Careers and Education Career Pathways Program Profile: Year Up," OPRE Report 2014-51, July 2014, Washington, D.C.: Office of Planning, Research and Evaluation, Administration for Children and Families, U.S. Department of Health and Human Service, https://career-pathways.org /career-pathways-year-up-pdf-24-pp-7-9-mb-august-2014/.

4. Michael Friedrich, "Proving that Skills Training Programs Can Help Working Families," Arnold Ventures, February 8, 2021.

5. Susan Patrick, "Trends Powering Personalized Learning," *Educational Technology*, 55, no. 2 (March–April 2015), pp. 56–69.

6. See Strada, "Strada Public Viewpoint: COVID-19 Work and Education Survey, Interested but Not Enrolled: Understanding and Serving Aspiring Adult Learner," September 19, 2020, https://cci.stradaeducation.org/wp-con tent/uploads/sites/2/2020/12/Public-Viewpoint-Charts-September-16-2020 .pdf.

Chapter 4

1. Elizabeth Mann Levesque, "Improving Community College Completion Rates by Addressing Structural and Motivational Barriers," Brookings Institution, October 8, 2018, www.brookings.edu/research/community -college-completion-rates-structural-and-motivational-barriers/.

2. CUNY ASAP, "Innovations in American Government Award Application," CUNY's Office of Institutional Research and Assessment, 2018.

3. Jesse Segers and others, "Structuring and Understanding the Coaching Industry: The Coaching Cube," *Academy of Management Learning & Education*, 10, no. 2 (June 2011), pp. 204–21.

4. Eric Bettinger and Rachel Baker, "The Effects of Student Coaching:

An Evaluation of a Randomized Experiment in Student Advising," *Educational Evaluation and Policy Analysis*, 36, no. 1 (2014), pp. 3–19.

Chapter 5

1. Theresa Anderson and others, "Implementation of Accelerating Opportunity, Research Report, Urban Institute, Aspen Institute," May 2016, www.aspeninstitute.org/publications/implementation-accelerating-opportunity-final-implementation-findings-lessons-field-may-2016/.

2. See Jobs for the Future Organization, "Contextualizing Adult Education Instruction to Career Pathways," September 2013, https://tcall.tamu.edu/docs/ContextualizatingAdultEdInstructionCareerPathways.pdf.

3. Anderson, "Implementation of Accelerating Opportunity Research Report."

4. Dolores Perin, "Facilitating Student Learning through Contextualization: A Review of Evidence," *Community College Review*, 39 (July 2011), pp. 268–95.

5. See Jobs for the Future Organization, "Contextualizing Adult Education Instruction to Career Pathways."

6. Ibid.

7. See Jobs for the Future Organization, "Contextualizing Adult Education Instruction to Career Pathways.

8. Karen Gardiner, "Year Up Impact Brief (PACE)," WorkforceGPS, 2019, https://strategies.workforcegps.org/resources/2020/07/29/19/50/Year-Up-Impact-Brief-PACE.

9. David Fein and Jill Hamadyk, "Bridging the Opportunity Divide for Low-Income Youth: Implementation and Early Impacts of the Year Up Program Pathways for Advancing Careers and Education (PACE)," OPRE Report 2018-65, May 2018.

10. David Fein, "Scaling Up to Close the Opportunity Divide for Low-Income Youth: A Case Study of the Year Up Program," OPRE Report 2016-55, May 2016.

11. Fein and Hamadyk, "Bridging the Opportunity Divide for Low-Income Youth."

12. Ibid.

13. Whitney Engstrom, David Fein, and Karen Gardiner, "Pathways for Advancing Careers and Education Career Pathways Program Profile: Year Up," OPRE Report 2014-51, July 2014.

14. Fein and Hamadyk, "Bridging the Opportunity Divide for Low-Income Youth."

15. John Wachen and others, "How I-BEST Works: Findings from a Field Study of Washington State's Integrated Basic Education and Skills Training Program," Community College Research Center Teachers College, Colum-

bia University, September 2010, http://ccrc.tc.columbia.edu/media/k2/at tachments/how-i-best-works-findings.pdf.

16. Ibid.

17. Asaph Glosser and others, "Washington State's Integrated Basic Education and Skills Training (I-BEST) Program in Three Colleges: Implementation and Early Impact Report," OPRE Report 2018-87, September 2018.

18. Rachel Pleasants McDonnell and Lisa Soricone, "Integrated Career Pathways: Lessons from Accelerating Opportunity," in *COABE Journal, The Resource for Adult Education, Special Edition Featuring Career Pathways* (New York: Coalition on Adult Basic Education, 2019), pp. 52–62, https://coabe.org /wp-content/uploads/2019/09/TheResourceforAdultEducationCareerPath waysSpecialEdition.pdf.

Chapter 6

1. Whitney Engstrom, David Fein, and Karen Gardiner, "Pathways for Advancing Careers and Education Career Pathways Program Profile: Year Up," OPRE Report 2014-51, July 2014, Washington, D.C.: Office of Planning, Research and Evaluation, Administration for Children and Families, U.S. Department of Health and Human Service, https://career-pathways.org /career-pathways-year-up-pdf-24-pp-7-9-mb-august-2014/.

2. David Fein and Jill Hamadyk, "Bridging the Opportunity Divide for Low-Income Youth: Implementation and Early Impacts of the Year Up Program Pathways for Advancing Careers and Education (PACE)," OPRE Report 2018-65, May 2018.

3. See U.S. Department of Labor, "Apprenticeship Fact Sheet," 2021, www.apprenticeship.gov/sites/default/files/Apprenticeship_Fact_Sheet.pdf.

4. Jessica Shakesprere, "Five Common Misconceptions about Apprenticeships," *Urban Institute*, April 22, 2019.

5. Tamar Jacoby and Ron Haskins, "Kentucky Fame Fulfilling the Promise of Apprenticeship," Opportunity America, October 2020, https:// opportunityamericaonline.org/kyfame/.

6. William C. Symonds, Robert Schwartz, and Ronald F. Ferguson, "Pathways to Prosperity: Meeting the Challenge of Preparing Young Americans for the 21st Century," Harvard University Graduate School of Education, 2011, www.gse.harvard.edu/sites/default/files/documents/Pathways _to_Prosperity_Feb2011-1.pdf.

7. Stephen Goldsmith, "Government Employment for Those Who Need a Leg Up: An Innovative Apprenticeship Program is Working to Bring Some of Los Angeles' Neediest Residents into the City's Workforce," Governing, May 21, 2019, www.governing.com/archive/col-los-angeles-targeted-local -hire-program-city-employment.html.

8. Ibid.

9. Edwin L. Armistead, Robert Guess, and Shannon R. Blevins, "Cyber Apprenticeship: A Traditional Solution to a Vexing New Problem," *Journal of Information Warfare*, 17, no. 1 (Winter 2018), pp. 87–98.

10. Naomi Sharp and Eli Dvorkin, "The Promise of Apprenticeships in New York," Center for an Urban Future, September 2018, https://nycfuture .org/pdf/CUF_Apprenticeships_9_18.pdf.

11. Sheila Maguire and others, "Tuning into Local Labor Markets: Findings from the Sectoral Employment Impact Study" Issue Lab (Philadelphia: Public Private Ventures, 2010).

12. Debra D. Bragg and others, "What Works for Adult Learners: Lessons from Career Pathway Evaluations," JFF, July 10, 2019, https://jfforg-prod-new .s3.amazonaws.com/media/documents/SPUB-Adult-Learners-070219.pdf.

Chapter 7

1. Marc Muro, Jacob Whiton, and Patrick McKenna, "Could 'Mid-Tech' Jobs Elevate More People and Non-Coastal Places?" *The Avenue* (blog), June 20, 2018.

2. Peter Q. Blair and others, "Searching for STARs: Work Experience as a Job Market Signal for Workers without Bachelor's Degrees," NBER Working Paper 26844 (March 2020).

3. Ibid.

4. Matthew Sigelman and others, "The Hybrid Job Economy: How New Skills Are Rewriting the DNA of the Job Market," Burning Glass Technologies, January 2019.

5. Barton J. Hirsch and Deans Alliance, "Wanted: Soft Skills for Today's Jobs," *The Phi Delta Kappan*, 98, no. 5 (February 2017), pp. 12–17.

6. Peter Q. Blair and Shad Ahmed, "The Disparate Racial Impact of Requiring a College Degree," *Wall Street Journal*, June 28, 2020.

7. Brent Orrell, Mason M. Bishop, and John Hawkins, "A Roadmap to Re-Employment in the COVID-19 Economy: Empowering States and Workers," American Enterprise Institute (AEI), July 24, 2020.

8. Sanjay E. Sarma and William B. Bonvillian, "Fixing an Imperfect Labor Market Information System," *Issues in Science and Technology*, 35, no. 1 (Fall 2018), pp. 56–61.

9. From a description of the UNCF Atlanta project proposal.

10. Joshua Bolten, "Multiple Pathways Initiative Emphasize Skills in Hiring and Promotion Decisions to Open More Career Pathway," Federal Reserve Bank of Minneapolis (2020), www.minneapolisfed.org/~/media/ assets/events/2020/racism-and-the-economy-focus-on-employment/racism -and-the-economy-employment-proposal-bolten.pdf?la=en.

11. See Accenture, "The Future of HR: Five Technology Imperatives," 2014, www.accenture.com/_acnmedia/accenture/conversion-assets/dotcom

/documents/global/pdf/digital_1/accenture-oracle-hcm-ebook-future-of-hr
-five-technology-imperatives.pdf.

12. Alicia Sasser Modestino, "The Importance of Middle-Skill Jobs," *Issues in Science and Technology*, 33, no. 1 (Fall 2016), pp. 41–46.

13. See Credential Engine, "Counting U.S. Postsecondary and Secondary Credentials," 2021, https://credentialengine.org/counting-credentials-2021/.

14. See Business Roundtable, "Racial Equity and Justice: Business Round-table Launches Initiative to Place Greater Emphasis on Skills in Hiring and Advancement, Improve Equity and Diversity in Employment," December 4, 2020, www.businessroundtable.org/business-roundtable-launches-initiative
-to-place-greater-emphasis-on-skills-in-hiring-and-advancement-improve
-equity-and-diversity-in-employment.

15. Elizabeth Zachry Rutschow, Betsy L. Tessler, and Erika B. Lewy, "Advising for Opportunity: Perspectives and Considerations for Supporting Movement Across Workforce and Academic Programs in Community Colleges," MDRC, February 2021, p. 1, www.mdrc.org/sites/default/files/iPASS
_CTE_Advising.pdf.

16. Blair and others, "Searching for STARs."

17. See San Diego Workforce Partnership, "Essential Skills Rubrics," 2020, https://workforce.org/wp-content/uploads/2020/10/EssentialSkills
_Rubics_2020.pdf.

18. Source: Strada and Gallup Polling, Georgetown Center on Education and the Workforce, Harvard Business School.

Chapter 8

1. Philip Oreopoulos and Uros Petronijevic, "Making College Worth It: A Review of the Returns to Higher Education," *The Future of Children*, 23, no. 1 (Spring 2013), pp. 41–65.

2. See Credential Engine, "Counting U.S. Postsecondary and Secondary Credentials," 2021, https://credentialengine.org/wp-content/uploads/2021/
02/Counting-Credentials-2021.pdf.

3. Sanjay E. Sarma and William B. Bonvillian, "Fixing an Imperfect Labor Market Information System," *Issues in Science and Technology*, 35, no. 1 (Fall 2018), pp. 56–61.

4. See Federal Reserve Bank of New York, "The Labor Market for Recent College Graduates," 2020, Q4, www.newyorkfed.org/research/college-labor
-market/college-labor-market_underemployment_rates.html.

5. Steve Lohr, "Job Training That's Free until You're Hired Is a Blueprint for Biden," *New York Times*, April 7, 2021.

6. Stephen Goldsmith, *The Twenty-First Century City: Resurrecting Urban America* (Lanham, MD: Rowman & Littlefield Publishers, 1999).

Chapter 9

1. Jennifer L. Eberhardt, *Biased: Uncovering the Hidden Prejudice that Shapes What We See, Think, and Do* (New York: Penguin Books, 2020).

2. Robert Manduca and Robert J. Sampson, "Punishing and Toxic Neighborhood Environments Independently Predict the Intergenerational Social Mobility of Black and White Children," *PNAS*, 116, no. 16 (April 16, 2019), pp. 7772–77.

3. Ryan Streeter, "Social Capital and Public Policy," *National Affairs*, 46 (Winter 2021).

4. George C. Galster, "The Mechanism(s) of Neighbourhood Effects: Theory, Evidence, and Policy Implications," in *Neighbourhood Effects Research: New Perspectives*, edited by Martin van Ham, David Manley, Nick Bailey, Ludi Simpson, and Duncan Maclennan (London: Springer Dordrecht Heidelberg, 2012).

5. Caroline M. Hoxby and Christopher Avery, "The Missing 'One-Offs': The Hidden Supply of High-Achieving, Low-Income Students," Working Paper 18586 (National Bureau of Economic Research, December 2012).

6. Dolores Acevedo-Garcia and others, "The Geography of Child Opportunity: Why Neighborhoods Matter for Equity: First Findings from the Child Opportunity Index 2.0," Diversity Data Kids, January 21, 2020, www .diversitydatakids.org/research-library/research-report/geography-child -opportunity-why-neighborhoods-matter-equity.

7. Shigehiro Oishi, Minkyung Koo, and Nicholas R. Buttrick, "The Socioecological Psychology of Upward Social Mobility," *American Psychologist*, 74, no. 7 (October 2019), pp. 751–63.

8. Richard Florida, "Kids Raised in Walkable Cities Earn More Money as Adults," Bloomberg CityLab, October 24, 2019; and Shigehiro Oishi, Minkyung Koo, and Nicholas R. Buttrick, "The Socioecological Psychology of Upward Social Mobility," *American Psychologist*, 74, no. 7 (October 2019), pp. 751–63.

9. See Joint Center for Housing Studies of Harvard University, "The State Of The Nation's Housing 2020," 2020, www.jchs.harvard.edu/state -nations-housing-2020.

10. See PEW Charitable Trusts, "American Families Face a Growing Rent Burden: High Housing Costs Threaten Financial Security and Put Homeownership Out of Reach for Many," April 19, 2018, www.pewtrusts.org/en /research-and-analysis/reports/2018/04/american-families-face-a-growing -rent-burden.

11. Chang-Tai Hsieh and Enrico Moretti, "Housing Constraints and Spatial Misallocation," *American Economic Journal: Macroeconomics*, 11, no. 2 (April 2019), pp. 1–39.

12. Solomon Greene and Jorge Gonzales, "How Communities are Re-

thinking Zoning to Improve Housing Affordability and Access to Opportunity," Urban Institute, June 12, 2019, www.urban.org/urban-wire/how-communities-are-rethinking-zoning-improve-housing-affordability-and-access-opportunity.

13. George C. Galster, Jackie Cutsinger, and Ron Malega, "The Costs of Concentrated Poverty: Neighborhood Property Markets and the Dynamics of Decline" in *Revisiting Rental Housing: Policies, Programs, and Priorities,* edited by Nicolas P. Retsinas and Eric S. Belsky (Brookings Institution, 2008), pp. 93–113.

14. Dylan Matthews, "America has a Housing Segregation Problem. Seattle May Just Have the Solution," Vox, August 4, 2019.

15. Raj Chetty and Nathaniel Hendren, "The Impacts of Neighborhoods on Intergenerational Mobility I: Childhood Exposure Effects," *Quarterly Journal of Economics,* 133, no. 3 (August 2018), pp. 1107–62.

16. David Philips, "Research: Hiring Managers are Biased against People with Longer Commutes," *Harvard Business Review,* December 10, 2018.

17. Adie Tomer and others, "Missed Opportunity: Transit and Jobs in Metropolitan America," Brookings Institution, May 12, 2011, www.brookings.edu/research/missed-opportunity-transit-and-jobs-in-metropolitan-america/.

18. Christina Stacy and others , "Access to Opportunity through Equitable Transportation," Urban Institute, October 21, 2020.

19. Betsy Gardner, "Supporting Economic Mobility by Innovating Transit Mobility," DataSmart, March 3, 2020, https://datasmart.ash.harvard.edu/news/article/supporting-economic-mobility-innovating-transit-mobility.

20. Commuters' Trust, "Report: 2020 Program," City of South Bend, 2021, www.commuterstrust.com/s/Commuters-Trust-2020-Phase-2-Report.pdf.

21. See Care.com, "Childcare Costs More in 2020, and the Pandemic Has Parents Scrambling for Solutions," 2020, www.care.com/c/stories/2423/how-much-does-child-care-cost/.

22. See U.S. Department Of Health & Human Services, "The Effects of Child Care Subsidies on Maternal Labor Force Participation in the United States," 2016, https://aspe.hhs.gov/effects-child-care-subsidies-maternal-labor-force-participation-united-states.

23. Aparna Mathur and others, "Paid Family and Medical Leave: An Issue Whose Time has Come," American Enterprise Institute, May 2017, www.aei.org/research-products/report/paid-family-and-medical-leave-an-issue-whose-time-has-come.

24. Diana Furchtgott-Roth and Jared Meyer, "How Occupational Licensing Harms The Young," Manhattan Institute, May 22, 2015, www.manhattan-institute.org/html/how-occupational-licensing-harms-young-6209.html.

25. See Department of the Treasury Office of Economic Policy, the Council

of Economic Advisers, and the Department of Labor, "Occupational Licensing: A Framework for Policymakers," July 2015, https://obamawhitehouse.archives.gov/sites/default/files/docs/licensing_report_final_nonembargo.pdf.

26. Dick M. Carpenter II and others, "License to Work: A National Study of Burdens from Occupational Licensing," Institute for Justice, May 2012, http://ij.org/wp-content/uploads/2015/04/licensetowork1.pdf.

27. Thomas J. Snyder, "The Effects of Arkansas' Occupational Licensure Regulations," University of Arkansas, Spring 2016, https://uca.edu/acre/files/2016/06/The-Effects-of-Arkansas-Occupational-Licensure-Regulations-by-Dr.-Thomas-Snyder.pdf.

28. Regulatory Reform Team, "Regulatory Reform Framework," DataSmart, February 17, 2015, https://datasmart.ash.harvard.edu/news/article/regulatory-reform-framework-597.

29. Sandra Susan Smith and Jonathan Simon, "Exclusion and Extraction: Criminal Justice Contact and the Reallocation of Labor," *Russell Sage Foundation Journal of the Social Sciences*, 6, no. 1 (March 2020), pp. 1–27.

30. Robert Apel and Gary Sweeten, "The Impact of Incarceration on Employment during the Transition to Adulthood," *Social Problems*, 57, no. 3 (August 2010), pp. 448–79.

31. See Pew Charitable Trusts, "Collateral Costs: Incarceration's Effect on Economic Mobility," 2010, www.pewtrusts.org/~/media/legacy/uploaded files/pcs_assets/2010/collateralcosts1pdf.pdf.

32. See What Works Cities, "What Works Cities: Ensuring Opportunity through Driver's License Restoration & Reform," 2019, https://whatworks cities.medium.com/a-call-to-action-cities-and-drivers-license-restoration-18edb5b7b358.

33. See Durham System of Care, "Durham Expunction and Restoration (DEAR) Program," 2020, https://durham.nc.networkofcare.org/mh/services /agency.aspx?pid=DurhamExpunctionandRestorationDEARProgram_371 _2_0; and What Works Cities, "What Works Cities."

34. Sandra Susan Smith and Jonathan Simon, "Exclusion and Extraction: Criminal Justice Contact and the Reallocation of Labor," *Russell Sage Foundation Journal of the Social Sciences*, 6, no. 1 (March 2020), p. 12.

Chapter 10

1. See Building (it) Together, "Building (it) Together Report: A Framework for Aligning Education and Jobs in Greater Birmingham," 2018, http:/ /buildingittogether.com/wp-content/uploads/2018/06/Building-it-Together -Report.pdf.

2. Ibid.

Index

Boxes, figures, and tables are indicated by b, f, and t following the page number.